Xmas 2016

To Jay

I hope you
reading about
Edmonton's latest
hockey hero.
Go Oilers + Flyers!

Love, Mum

THE
McDAVID
EFFECT

CONNOR McDAVID
AND THE NEW HOPE FOR HOCKEY

MARTY KLINKENBERG

PUBLISHED BY SIMON & SCHUSTER

NEW YORK   LONDON   TORONTO   SYDNEY   NEW DELHI

SIMON &
SCHUSTER
CANADA

Simon & Schuster Canada
A Division of Simon & Schuster, Inc.
166 King Street East, Suite 300
Toronto, Ontario M5A 1J3

This Simon & Schuster Canada edition October 2016

SIMON & SCHUSTER CANADA and colophon are registered trademarks of Simon & Schuster, Inc.

For information about special discounts for bulk purchases, please contact Simon & Schuster Special Sales at 1-800-268-3216 or CustomerService@simonandschuster.ca.

Library and Archives Canada Cataloguing in Publication

Klinkenberg, Marty, author
The McDavid effect : Connor McDavid and the new hope for hockey / Marty Klinkenberg.
Issued in print and electronic formats. ISBN 978-1-5011-4603-9
(hardback).—ISBN 978-1-5011-4605-3 (html)
1. McDavid, Connor, 1997–. 2. Edmonton Oilers (Hockey team). 3. Hockey players—Alberta—Edmonton—Biography. 4. Hockey—Social aspects—Alberta—Edmonton. I. Title.
GV848.5.M38K65 2016 796.962092 C2016-903174-8
C2016-903175-6

Manufactured in the United States of America

10   9   8   7   6   5   4   3   2   1

ISBN 978-1-5011-4603-9
ISBN 978-1-5011-4605-3 (ebook)

*This book is dedicated to my son, Matthew, who has taught me
my love for hockey and given me a great appreciation
for persistence and hard work, on and off the ice.
I love you, Matt. This is for you.*

THE McDAVID EFFECT

PROLOGUE

BRIMMING WITH OPTIMISM BUT CURSED BY BAD LUCK, VERN HUNTER ASSUMED THE hole he was digging would be bone dry, as so many others he had dug had been. Instead of prospecting for crude deep beneath the soil on the outskirts of Edmonton in the 1940s, he might as well have been Ponce de Leon searching for the Fountain of Youth, or one of those crackpots trying to lasso the Loch Ness monster.

Being on an expedition with the Spanish explorer would hardly have been any less comfortable. It was the middle of winter in Alberta, and so bitterly cold that a roughneck could freeze his ass off in those britches with a trap door in the rear.

It had been nearly a century since North America's first oil field was discovered by a fellow digging a water well near Sarnia in present-day Ontario. It was the first of many finds, the most significant of which had been in 1914 at Turner Valley, just southwest of Calgary in the foothills of the Rocky Mountains. For thirty years, Turner Valley had been the main source of oil for the British Empire, but now it was running dry. Companies were scrambling to find a new supply.

It would be charitable to say that Vern had a spotty record at wildcatting. In the past several years, crews under his direction had drilled fifteen barren holes while looking for oil, earning him the nickname "Dry Hole."

During such a slump, even if black gold were trapped beneath the wheat fields, it was not a sure thing that Vern would find it. The team of sixteen men he was managing was one of five such crews that Imperial Oil had engaged in a high-stakes treasure hunt across the prairies. The company had spent $23 million—the equivalent of about $280 million today—bankrolling the wildcatters' exploration efforts, and together they had drilled 133 holes without finding anything but dirt.

After starting in the 1920s as a junior clerk with one of the first petroleum companies operating in Alberta, Vern worked as a truck driver and roughneck before being hired by Imperial in 1940 to oversee an Arctic drilling project. He later became the foreman of one of those wildcat teams and, after drilling in Saskatchewan proved fruitless, was directed in November 1946 to go to Leduc, a small town about twenty miles southwest of Edmonton. Seismic studies had identified two areas of interest there, but Vern was skeptical for a number of reasons—chief among them that few oil discoveries are made in a place so remarkably convenient to a major city. He was so certain the venture would prove a waste of time that he hauled his team's heavy equipment through the landowner's dooryard rather than construct a road for it. Vern figured that after a few unproductive days, the team would be instructed to pull up stakes and continue elsewhere.

The hole that they drilled uncovered traces of oil and natural gas, however, so for two months they persevered, probing deeper and deeper into a formation geologists thought promising. They were ready to give up when, on February 3, 1947, Hunter persuaded his crew to drill a little longer, perhaps just another metre more. A short while later, the rig poked a hole in an ancient subtropical reef, similar to the Bahamas today, nearly one mile beneath the earth. A geyser of oil shot to the surface and blew halfway up the 145-foot-tall derrick, drenching one worker.

Ten days later, on a chilly Thursday afternoon, a crowd of five hundred people, including company executives and Alberta government officials, were invited to the site for an unveiling ceremony. Shortly before four o'clock, after a delay of a few hours caused by an equipment malfunction, Nathan Eldon Tanner, the mines minister for Premier Ernest Manning's Social Credit Party, opened a valve on the wellhead. At first, mud and water was coughed up, and then, after a sound similar to a train approaching, a mixture of crude and gas roared out of the pipe and burst into a streak of flames in the air. That night, Imperial held a party in Edmonton, which would soon be transformed into the oil capital of Canada.

Given the name Leduc #1, the well produced 318,000 barrels of oil and 324 million cubic feet of natural gas before it was decommissioned by Imperial in 1974. More important, it held the geological key to Alberta's petroleum reserves and changed its economy forever. Oil and gas supplanted farming as the primary industry and resulted in the province becoming one of the richest in the country. Nationally, the discovery allowed Canada to become self-sufficient within a decade and become a major exporter of oil.

Today, pumpjacks dot Alberta's landscape, bobbing like rocking horses each time they plumb the depths for oil and gas. A heritage site, museum and campground have been established near the spot where Vern Hunter's crew made the province's first significant find of oil. That oilfield itself remains active, with more than 300 million barrels extracted thus far. Leduc's neighbouring communities of Devon and Nisku have flourished, and Edmonton's population has grown from a little more than 118,000 in 1947 to nearly 900,000 today.

For mostly better and occasionally worse, Alberta's economy, and Canada's with it, ebbs and flows with the price of oil. Several hundred miles north of Edmonton, the Athabasca Oil Sands contain the third-largest proven reserves of crude in the world. The thick, tarry bitumen extracted there is transported through a complex system of pipelines from Edmonton to Montreal, the U.S. Midwest and as far south as the Gulf of Mexico. More than 130,000 people are employed in Alberta's energy industry and, as a result, the province has one of the highest standards of living in the world.

Every day, tens of thousands of vehicles pass the derrick that Vern Hunter's crew used to make the discovery that changed millions of lives and altered Alberta's environmental landscape so dramatically that it has become a geopolitical powder keg. The retired piece of machinery rises like a beacon on a strip of land at an abandoned visitor centre in the middle of the Queen Elizabeth II Highway near the Edmonton airport.

A short distance away, along the same stretch of road, a sign welcomes travellers as they enter Edmonton's city limits. Put up in the 1980s to cel-ebrate the city's thriving civic pride, the sign originally included Edmon-ton's motto, "City of Champions." When it was unveiled, the self-assigned accolade spoke to Edmonton's status as a provincial capital, a growing me-tropolis and an energy powerhouse. The title was also adopted by the city's population as a means of trumpeting their pride and joy: the Edmonton Oilers.

From 1983 to 1990, Edmonton's pro hockey franchise won five Stanley Cups, a reign recognized by the Hockey Hall of Fame as the NHL's last true dynasty. Wayne Gretzky, the skinny player upon whose back four of those five Stanley Cups were hoisted, changed the nature of the game with his otherworldly offensive skills and the team he led transformed the city of Edmonton, in turn.

From sea to sea, hockey rekindles the spirit of Canadians. But only in Alberta is its identity connected to adventurous roughnecks and wildcatters who lived in converted chicken coops and ten-by-twenty-foot shacks in the dead of winter. There would be no Edmonton Oilers if not for Vern Hunter. Without him, there would no oil derrick under which players skate onto the ice during pregame festivities. There would be no new $480 million arena in the shape of an oil drop in downtown Edmonton. There would have been no Wayne Gretzky, at least as we know him.

In early 2015, Edmonton City Council voted to remove the tagline "City of Champions" from the welcome signs in an effort to rebrand the city. In recent years, the city's image has waned. Gone are the Oilers' glory days and the years of profitable energy. Everything from global recessions to changing populations to the interminable rebuild of sports franchises has sapped many of their patience. From the outside, the City of Champions appears to be merely a memory.

And yet, if you walk the streets of the city and cast your eye over the cranes that dot the downtown skyline, if you speak with the people who live, work and play there, if you listen to sports talk radio, there is a sense that things are about to change. You get a glimpse of the first thing that any team or individual needs if they are to begin again: Hope. In this case, hope comes in the form of a six-foot-one, 190-pound teenager. And his name is Connor McDavid.

ONE

CONNOR McDAVID WAS NINE YEARS OLD IN 2006, THE LAST TIME THE EDMONTON Oilers reached the NHL playoffs. It was a season that lives on in memory for Edmonton's long-suffering fans, one in which the Oilers became the first eighth-seeded team to reach the Stanley Cup Final. They began the playoffs with a stunning defeat of the Detroit Red Wings, the league's most dominant team, in six games. The hockey gods continued to smile as the Oilers defeated San Jose and Anaheim in the next two series. They hadn't won the Stanley Cup since 1990—seven years before Connor was born—and the city was delirious at the prospect of another championship. The good fortune continued through to Game 7 of the Final but, in the end, it wasn't enough. The Carolina Hurricanes defeated the Oilers, ending an unlikely postseason run that few had foreseen.

A slight kid who was so talented he had to play against boys several years older to feel challenged, McDavid was a hockey prodigy along the lines of Sidney Crosby, the NHL superstar who perfected his shooting as a kid by taking aim at the clothes drier in his family's home in Cole Harbour, Nova Scotia.

Even at nine years old, Connor was becoming a prodigy. Twenty-three inches long and ten and one-quarter pounds at birth, he was three years old when he skated on the rink his father flooded in their backyard in Newmarket, Ontario, an upper-middle-class community less than an hour north of Toronto. It is a tidy neighbourhood with well-manicured lawns, flowers that spill out of the window boxes and kids playing street hockey in culs-de-sac. Half as tall as a hockey stick, Connor spent hours on rollerblades in his basement, slapping pucks at nets at either end. He and his brother Cameron, who was nearly four years older, waged epic battles in their underground arena. Twice during their skirmishes, Connor incurred wounds that needed stitches, but he remained undeterred. He would hound Cameron until he was exhausted, then Connor's mother, Kelly, would take over and play goal. When she grew tired, Connor's grandmother would fill in, eventually to be followed by his dad, Brian.

"It wasn't long before Connor was elevating his shots, and it got to be too scary for us," Kelly recalled. "Brian would take over, but he always put on lots of gear."

Connor's parents registered him for organized hockey for the first time at age four. Technically, he was too young to play, so Kelly and Brian fibbed about his age, saying that he was a year older. By then, Connor was clamouring to join Cameron as his father taught his oldest son drills in the garage.

"We'd all be in there together, and Connor would stare and insist he be allowed to play," Brian remembered. "It was fun, a dad playing with his boys, but Connor took it very seriously. He knew what he wanted to do. He emulated his brother and understood everything we were doing."

At five, Connor started wearing a dress shirt and tie like the older boys when he attended Cameron's hockey games, and would listen attentively to pregame speeches in the locker room. A year later, the hockey association in his hometown refused to allow Connor to play at a level above his age group, so his parents registered him in neighbouring Aurora, where he competed against nine-year-olds. After that, Connor joined the York Simcoe Express, a team that was coached by his father. They went on to win four straight Ontario Minor Hockey Association championships.

By the time he was eight, Connor was sharpening his skills on an obstacle course that Brian set up along the length of the driveway outside the family home. The youngster would be out there for so many hours that neighbours began to fear for his welfare. Some thought that Brian was overbearing and forcing Connor to train too much, but that was never the case. Connor loved it, and, by then, was already talking about playing in the NHL.

Connor was always single-minded. Once, when he was ten, his dad dragged him out of a dressing room to pose for a picture with Mario Lemieux during a peewee tournament in Quebec. Afterward, Connor complained, saying that the photo opportunity with the NHL Hall of Famer had interrupted his pregame routine.

In his many hours of rollerblading on the driveway, Connor began to develop extraordinary stick-handling ability. First, he learned to control a puck while navigating around paint cans. Then, he created an obstacle for himself by attaching the ends of discarded hockey sticks to the paint cans, and pretended they were opposing players he needed to outmanoeuvre. When it became too easy for him, he taped the cans to a skateboard and used it to teach himself how to toe drag, deke and dangle beneath and around a moving object. As Connor practised, he timed himself, recorded the information and kept track of his improvement.

"The neighbours thought we were nuts," Brian said.

When Connor was ten, he began training with Joe Quinn, a hockey skills instructor from southern Ontario who has fashioned a lucrative career out of teaching elite players to maintain possession of the puck while skating in close quarters at top speed.

"I still remember him as a skinny, freckle-faced little boy," said Quinn, who coached Connor when he attended the Premier Elite Athletes

Collegiate School, a private sports academy in North York, Ontario, where the tuition is more than $20,000 per year. "He was the youngest of fifty-two kids in the school, playing against boys three and four years older, and he was better than all of them. He was young, but right away you could recognize he was special. He could stickhandle in a telephone booth."

After playing for his father's team, Connor joined the Marlboros of the Greater Toronto Hockey League, where he excelled for three years at the bantam and minor midget levels. During the 2011–12 season, he scored seventy-nine goals and had 130 assists in eighty-eight games, receiving the award as the league's top player.

By the time Connor was thirteen, scouts were regularly showing up at his games. NHL agents, meanwhile, began predicting that he would become one of the sport's biggest stars.

Bobby Orr, a Hall of Fame defenceman and one of the greatest players of all time, remembers seeing Connor as a teenager at an invitation-only hockey camp in Toronto. Connor had not been invited, but Cameron had, and Connor tagged along and then joined his older sibling on the ice.

"I arrived a bit late, and noticed this little guy out there and said, 'Holy crap, who is that?'" Orr said. "It turned out that Connor was the one I was watching. My first thought was, 'Wow, does that kid ever have great hands.'

"Looking back at it now, I think I was a pretty good judge of talent."

Not long after that, Orr visited the McDavids at home on a Sunday morning. Beforehand, Connor was calm, but Kelly was a basket case. Eventually he told her, 'Mom, you really have to calm down.'" After meeting with Orr, the family agreed to allow his sports agency, the Orr Hockey Group, to represent the young prospect. Specifically, he would be represented by Jeff Jackson, a former NHL player who once served as assistant general manager for the Maple Leafs.

Jackson, who ran his own agency before he joined the Orr Group, first heard about Connor from one of his other clients, Sam Gagner. Then a centre for the Oilers, Gagner was training during the summer of 2011 at a rink in Oakville, Ontario, when McDavid approached and politely asked if he could join him on the ice. Gagner agreed, and was dazzled by what he saw.

"Afterward, Sam called me," Jackson recalled. "He said, 'You have to find this kid. I've been in the NHL for five years, and he can already do things I can't do. His name is David O'Connor.'"

Although he transposed the name, Gagner remembered that the youth had told him he was about to begin playing for the Midget AAA Marlies. So, Jackson, who had just established his own agency, called the club and inquired about him.

"I asked about the O'Connor kid and the guy chuckled," Jackson said. "He said, 'Oh, you must mean Connor McDavid.'"

Jackson tracked the young talent down and told Brian he would like to represent the budding star. However, the McDavids had already agreed to sign with Orr. Later, Jackson was invited to join Orr's firm, and by co-incidence was appointed to be Connor's agent. As Connor continued to develop, Jackson and Orr could only marvel at the young man's potential.

"Watching him is a joy for me," Jackson said. "Connor will make a play, and Bobby will ask me, 'What did he just do?' I tell him, 'I don't know. I don't know how he does the things he does out there.'"

At fifteen, McDavid was granted exceptional player status by Hockey Canada, which allowed him to join the Ontario Hockey League one year earlier than the official entry age. At the time, he was only the third player ever granted permission to enter the league as a fifteen-year-old, after John Tavares, now with the New York Islanders, and Aaron Ekblad, of the Florida Panthers.

The OHL teams were all desperate to land McDavid, and the Erie Otters wasted no time in choosing him as the first overall pick in the 2012 Priority Selection Draft. For the next three years, Connor would be playing in the hardscrabble city of one hundred thousand people in western Pennsylvania.

Of course, as a teenager, Connor wasn't going to live alone. He was billeted for all three years with Bob and Stephanie Catalde, living in their household alongside their daughters, Caisee and Camryn, and young son, Nico. The Cataldes had never billeted anyone, but they were good friends with Sherry Bassin, then the general manager of the Otters, and Sherry convinced them to take in their prized rookie.

"I like to think we have a good home and a nice family, and I thought it would be a good environment for him," Catalde, a lawyer and youth hockey coach, said. "It wasn't long before things started to sink in and I knew how special he is."

At their first meeting, Catalde made it clear that he expected Connor to behave properly, especially around his daughters. At the time he moved in, Caisee was fifteen and Camryn, who was named after the former Boston Bruins right wing Cam Neely, was twelve.

Connor quickly became a member of the family, an older brother to the girls and a mentor to Nico, then seven. McDavid would play knee hockey with Nico in the family room, skate with him and his teammates at practice and occasionally sit on the bench with them during their games. He even attended one game with his face swollen, a day after having his wisdom teeth removed.

"The experience we had with him turned out to be everything we hoped it would be and more," Catalde said. "Connor talks in terms of how he owes a debt of gratitude to myself and my wife, but I see it as the other way around."

On game days, Catalde cooked for Connor, always preparing the same meals. For breakfast, Connor would eat eight scrambled eggs, a large helping of organic berries and a whole-grain bagel. For dinner, he always asked for grilled chicken breast lightly brushed with olive oil, with brown rice and quinoa.

After he was done eating, Connor would rise from the table and put his dishes in the dishwasher every time.

"None of my own kids would do that," Catalde said.

McDavid kicked off his first season with the Erie Otters by putting together a fifteen-game scoring streak that began in just his second game. He won OHL Rookie of the Month honours for October and November, and eventually finished the year with twenty-five goals and forty-one assists in sixty-three games. That was good enough to earn the title of the league's top rookie.

All eyes were on McDavid from the outset that year. During the season, Wayne Gretzky called and told Connor he was rooting for him, and Lemieux invited him to watch a Penguins game with him in his suite in Pittsburgh, which is about 125 miles from Erie. The hockey world recognized the immense talent that was budding in Connor, and seemed to be opening its doors to him.

In his second season with the Otters, McDavid was named a second-team OHL All-Star and, as he began his final year in Erie, the hysteria around him continued to grow. Every rink the Otters visited over the second half of the season was sold out, and fans waited for hours to meet him. As teammates climbed aboard the bus following games, McDavid would wade into the crush of people and sign autographs. Eventually, the team hired a retired police officer as a bodyguard.

"It was beyond anything you could imagine," said Sherry Bassin, who was involved in hockey for fifty years, including a stint as assistant general manager of the Quebec Nordiques. "I've never seen anything like it. Signing autographs could have been a full-time job for him."

McDavid couldn't go to a restaurant in Erie without being mobbed. When he would arrive at the Cataldes' home late at night, the dining room table was piled with photographs for him to sign.

"There was one extremely cold night in Guelph where I suggested to Connor that he should go out a side door and hop on the bus instead of navigating through the crowd," Bassin recalled. "He looked at me and said, 'No, Bass, I was a little kid once, too,' and went out into the cold and signed autographs for forty-five minutes. How many seventeen- or eighteen-year-olds, when given an out, would say, 'No, I was a kid once, too'?

"He's an unselfish person both on and off the ice. He made a point to come to my wife and I's fiftieth wedding anniversary party, and stayed to the end."

In Connor's final year with the Otters, the team lost in the OHL finals, but McDavid shone throughout, accumulating forty-nine points in twenty playoff games. In one game in the second round, McDavid scored five goals against the London Knights: snapping in the first, tucking in the second, wrapping a third around the goalie for a natural hat trick, flipping the puck over the net minder for the fourth and tapping in a rebound from an impossible angle for the last. He was nearly unstoppable.

"I'll cherish the moments I was able to watch him and the fact that I was able to coach him," Chris Knoblauch, his coach for two and a half seasons in Erie, said. "As you watch him, you realize at times that you have become a fan. He does remarkable things, but never acts like he's different from anyone else. He's almost embarrassed when he pulls something off."

That attitude extended beyond the ice, too. While setting records and building a reputation as the player of a generation, Connor was also excelling in school. In his final year of high school, on top of a grueling hockey schedule full of workouts, games and travel, he also held down a straight A average, studying everything from algebra to creative writing to digital design. Unwilling to be the stereotypical star athlete, Connor applied himself to his schoolwork with the same combination of diligence, integrity and hard work that he brought to the rink.

Connor's peers and coaches recognized that mixture of skill, intelligence and modesty, and he was rewarded for it. At the end of Connor's final year in junior hockey, he was selected not just the Ontario Hockey League's top player, but also the top player in the Canadian Hockey League, the umbrella organization that represents the three Canadian major junior hockey leagues across the country. He also won the CHL's Student of the Year. Twice. In a row. By the time Connor was done in Erie, he had racked up ninety-seven goals and 285 points and had become the most decorated player in the history of the OHL.

"There is a difference between being liked and respected, but he is respected and loved," Bassin said. "I've been around hockey for a long time, but feel blessed to have spent three years with him. One of the ways I judge a person is by asking if I like who I am when I'm around them. I love who I am when I'm around Connor McDavid."

There was little doubt that Connor would be the first player selected in the 2015 NHL entry draft. The question was, by whom? Each year, a lottery is held to determine who gets the first overall pick, with the weakest teams having the greatest chance. Beleaguered fans in Toronto were overjoyed by the thought that Connor could land with the Maple Leafs. Some suspected that Arizona and Buffalo, the NHL's worst teams, might have tanked near the end of the 2014–15 season to improve their chances of getting him. Whether or not there was any truth to that conjecture, it spoke volumes that people were rooting for their favourite team to give up a chance at success just for better odds at having McDavid on their team.

In the analysis and speculation leading up to the draft, the Oilers were a possibility to win the lottery, but nobody was predicting that McDavid was on a collision course with the team. Once one of the most successful sports franchises in history, the Oilers hadn't made the playoffs since 2006 and the team's roster of young talent had yet to produce the results that the fans and front office expected. And, besides that, the Oilers had won the lottery in three of the last four years. Nobody thought that it could happen again.

IN 2006, AT ABOUT THE SAME TIME THAT BRIAN McDAVID BEGAN TELLING HIS WIFE that he thought their son's hockey skills were supernatural, Daryl Katz began thinking about buying the Oilers.

The shy son of a pharmacist, Katz had grown up in an upper-middle-class family in Edmonton and, like just about everyone else in the city, was a huge hockey fan. He was twenty-one in 1984 when the Oilers won their first Stanley Cup, and he came to socialize with Gretzky, Mark Messier, Kevin Lowe and other stars, which made the Oilers even more special to him.

After graduating from law school at the University of Alberta in 1985, Katz articled for a local firm and was hired by another before setting up his own practice specializing in corporate and franchise law. In 1991, in a partnership with his father, Katz paid $300,000 for the Canadian rights to the U.S.-based Medicine Shoppe chain, and in 1992, the Katz Group of Companies—now one of Canada's largest privately owned enterprises—was founded.

In 1996, Katz purchased the fading Rexall pharmacy chain, which by then had only a few dozen stores in Canada, and the following year he acquired the 134-store Pharma Plus outlet for $100 million. By 1998, the Katz Group's portfolio included eighty Rexall stores, thirty Medicine Shoppes, all of Pharma Plus's holdings and a few smaller independent retailers.

Over the next half-dozen years, Katz amassed billions through one acquisition after another and, by 2006, he began making a concerted effort to buy the Oilers. In May 2007, he made a $145 million bid that was rejected by the team's ownership group of thirty-eight investors, and he was spurned again two months later when he increased his offer to $185 million. On January 28, 2008, Katz raised the ante to $200 million, an offer that was accepted, pending approval from the league. In June, Katz received permission from the NHL, and on July 2 he was officially introduced as the team's owner during a news conference at Rexall Place.

Katz hoped, of course, that the Oilers would return to their spot among the NHL's elite, but his interest in the team was more than a heartfelt gamble and an attempt to revisit the fond memories of his youth. It was an investment in something much bigger: a vision he had for the city.

Before he acquired the Oilers, Katz had quietly begun purchasing land in Edmonton's downtown core. The city centre was suffering from the same urban blight as other major municipalities, but the demise of downtown had been exacerbated in 1981 by the opening of the West Edmonton Mall, the largest shopping complex in North America. Alberta's top tourist attraction, the mall is home to more than eight hundred stores, as well as hotels, a giant waterpark, amusement park, a casino, a skating rink and an aquarium with penguins and sea lions. It was spectacular and, when it opened, it diverted shoppers from downtown and discouraged development in the city's core.

Recognizing the need to bring the Oilers and the city into a new era, Katz talked about the necessity of building an arena to replace Rexall Place. The rink opened in 1974, and ranked as the second oldest in the NHL behind Madison Square Garden, which underwent a $1 billion renovation in 2013. Located a few miles to the south of downtown, Rexall Place was once the jewel at the centre of a bustling shopping district. Over the years, however, the neighbourhood had faded, and Katz believed that a new team needed a new home if it were to rejuvenate the city.

At the time that he bought the Oilers, Katz said he was prepared to spend $100 million exploring the possibility of building a modern arena, a process he had already begun by seeking property downtown that was suitable for development.

"I didn't have to be in the hockey business, but I saw it as the opportunity of a lifetime to do something for the city," Katz said. "I would never have considered buying the team without the challenge and opportunity of building an arena and using it as the centrepiece for revitalization that would make us proud of our downtown again."

Upon taking over, Katz left the Oilers in the hands of managers he admired, including Kevin Lowe and Craig MacTavish, key members of those teams that had formed a dynasty. Leaving the business of hockey to his trusted lieutenants, Katz began pursuing in earnest his dream of building an arena. It was a protracted process that played out in public, requiring years of negotiations with the city and often heated debate. At one point, when talks were at a standstill, Katz even visited Seattle to meet with officials there who were anxious to acquire an NHL team. That move infuriated detractors who opposed using taxpayers' dollars to help bankroll the billionaire's building project.

Slowly—and, at times, agonizingly so—snags were resolved. Finally, on May 15, 2013, Edmonton's city council approved the final piece of funding for the arena, and construction on Rogers Place began the following March.

As part of the deal that was brokered, the Katz Group agreed to provide $161 million in financing for the arena, with the city contributing $279 million. The rest of the money came from a variety of sources, including ticket surcharges and a community revitalization levy. The city also required Katz to spend $100 million to help stimulate development around the arena. Katz agreed, and didn't stop there; in short order, he committed to spending more than $2 billion.

As Katz had envisioned it, the arena would be only a small part of a much bigger project. As plans emerged and development spread, the arena became the anchor of a sports, entertainment, retail and residential corridor. Called the Ice District, the area would cover twelve million square feet—roughly the size of twenty football fields—and include Canada's tallest office towers outside Toronto. The construction would take years and, at its height in 2015, it was the largest private real estate development in Canada and the second-largest in North America, behind only Hudson Yards, a commercial and residential district on the Lower West Side of Manhattan.

"We did exactly what we said, and more," Katz said. "It's a public–private partnership, and because we have been so successful, I think it's a model that other people will follow."

The centrepiece.of the Ice District would be the new Rogers Place. Katz laboured over plans for the arena, which was complicated by his insistence that it be built in the shape of an oil drop in deference to the energy industry.

"That's Alberta, and that's Edmonton," Katz said. "I wanted it to be iconic. This city deserves that."

By summer 2015, Katz's plans for rebuilding Edmonton were well under way. Cranes dotted the skyline and construction in the downtown core was incessant. It seemed like Katz's vision of a new heart of his city was coming together. His hockey team, meanwhile, remained a work in progress. From 2008 to 2014, the Oilers had finished twenty-eighth, twenty-eighth, twenty-fourth, twenty-ninth and last (twice) in the thirty-team league. Katz knew that something had to change; the product he put on the ice at the new Rogers Place had to match the quality of the facility they were building.

"My biggest wish was that the hockey team would be beginning to make a turnaround when we moved into the building," Katz said.

And so, in June 2014, the team owner brought in Bob Nicholson, previously the president of Hockey Canada for sixteen years, as Vice-Chairman of the Oilers Entertainment Group. Nicholson's first assignment was to examine operations on and off the ice and determine what was needed to take the team from a basement dweller to a playoff contender.

It was clear that major changes had to be made, but at the time there seemed to be no reason to rush. The Oilers had rebuilt their roster with a handful of number-one draft picks during their tenure at the bottom of the league: Taylor Hall, Ryan Nugent-Hopkins and Nail Yakupov had each shown that they were highly skilled players, even if the team as a whole had been slow to improve around them.

The Oilers finished the 2014–15 season with a disappointing 24–44–14 record; at one point, they only recorded two victories in a span of forty-nine days. They ended the year as the third-worst team in the league, leaving them with a slight chance of winning the NHL lottery and the right to pick McDavid. Few believed the Oilers could get that lucky.

"I thought for sure that Toronto's name would be called," Katz said. "I thought it seemed like destiny."

TWO

A MAN WITH A PAST AS COLOURFUL AS THE EDMONTON OILERS, CONSTANTINE Stavropoulos was only eleven years old when he set out by himself for Athens from his home in Kaltazia, a tiny village in Greece. After arriving in the Greek capital, Constantine was hired as a shoeshine boy, and spent the next few years working diligently until he saved enough money to buy a ticket on a passenger ship to Halifax when he was fifteen. His trip across the Atlantic Ocean aboard the New Halla in 1953 took two weeks, but his journey didn't end there. After arriving on the east coast of Canada, he immediately continued westward, heading straight to Toronto. Drawing on his experience in Athens, Con opened a shoeshine stand on the bottom floor of an office tower on Bloor Street, charging fifteen cents to polish a pair. Customers loved how quickly Con worked, often giving a quarter for his efforts, which was big money for a teenager in the fifties.

"I could shine as many as eighty in a day," Con said. "I made enough money to live."

After a day of working on executives' shoes, Con's hands were a dirty mess. Desperate to clean them, Con went to the restaurant next door and offered to wash drinking glasses in exchange for a meal and access to soapy water. He got much more than that. Con landed a paying job at the restaurant and was quickly promoted to the position of soda jerk, making sundaes and milk shakes. He started waiting on customers at the counter shortly after that, learning skills that he then called upon when he went to work at a restaurant in Banff that summer.

Con arrived in Banff at an opportune moment. Not long after that, Marilyn Monroe came into town to film a cowboy flick, *River of No Return*. The former Norma Jean Baker played a dance-hall singer, with Robert Mitchum starring as her love interest. The filming was an added bonus for Con, who earned a part in one scene as an Indian sitting on horseback at the top of a hill. It might not have been the most glamorous role, but Con cared more that the work as an extra paid the grand sum of ten dollars per day.

"They asked me if I could ride a horse and I told them yes," he said. "To be honest, I wasn't a very good rider."

In the early 1960s, Stavropoulos settled in Edmonton, and became a server in a downtown steakhouse, earning sixty-five cents an hour. Eventually, he made enough working there to allow him and two partners to open a series of restaurants, Fireside Steak and Pizza among them. Part of the eatery's success was thanks to its menu: Their deal of a steak and a baked potato for $4.95 led to lineups out the door. But what really mattered was that old real estate rule: location, location, location.

Hearing that an arena was being built, Con bought the property across the street in 1973 from a pair of local hockey players, Doug MacAuley of the Edmonton Mercurys and Hugh Coflin, a defenceman who toiled briefly with the Chicago Blackhawks and spent eight seasons with the Edmonton Flyers, a Western Hockey League affiliate of the Detroit Red Wings. Building on the site where the hockey players had operated an old-fashioned drive-in restaurant, Con opened the Fireside in January 1974, just months before the Northlands Coliseum opened its doors.

A founding member of the World Hockey Association, the Oilers had played their 1972 and 1973 seasons in Edmonton Gardens, a 5,200-seat rink that was built along 118th Avenue on the city's fairground. The Gardens was famous, but for all the wrong things. It was known for its bad sight lines and girders that dripped water onto spectators and the playing surface. As a result, the team moved into the new $16 million Northlands Coliseum in the fall of 1974, with a league record 15,326 fans turning out for the home opener against the Cleveland Crusaders. The Crusaders started Gerry Cheevers, a former Stanley Cup hero with the Boston Bruins, in net. The Oilers were backstopped by Jacques Plante; it was the opening game of the final professional season for the forty-five-year-old former Montreal Canadien. The Oilers won, 4–1, and thus began their long tenure at Northlands Coliseum.

The facility took on several different names over the years, from the Edmonton Coliseum to the Skyreach Centre to Rexall Place, the title it retained from 2003 through the end of the 2015–16 NHL season. Just like the Gardens, the Coliseum wasn't without problems. There were few luxury boxes, the concourses were crammed, the lines to get into the bathrooms were so lengthy that the wait to get in often took longer than the intermissions and the press box was only accessible by stairs and a considerable jaunt over a rickety catwalk. But its presence generated an enthusiasm and reverence that spread into the surrounding community. Figures of hockey players and other athletes were erected on top of the lampposts along 118th Avenue near the arena, like statues of gods lining the route to the city temple, and murals of the Oilers and Canadian Football League Eskimos were painted on exterior walls of nearby businesses. One of the oldest streets in Edmonton, 118th Avenue was renamed the Avenue of Champions in 2001 as a deferential nod to the handful of Stanley Cups the Oilers won between 1983 and 1990.

There were many businesses along 118th Avenue that benefitted from being in the backyard of the Oilers' long-standing home rink. Some were so reliant on the old institution that they tied their names to it, like Coliseum Steak and Pizza, owned by Peter Varvis. Peter arrived in Edmonton in 1949 as a seventeen-year-old. Growing up in Greece, he had heard stories about Edmonton from his uncle, a fellow immigrant who had preceded him, and he wanted to experience it for himself. "It was a whole new world when I arrived," Peter said. "I wore newspapers under my coat as insulation; it was so cold; I had put them there to keep the wind off my chest."

The frigid weather didn't discourage him, and Peter built a life in his adopted country. He opened a diner in Jasper, where he, too, counted Marilyn Monroe among his customers. In 1957, he and his late brother, Chris, established a restaurant on 118th Avenue called the Nite-N-Day Café. It was open around the clock, but became locally famous for its luncheon special: a bowl of soup, veal cutlets and an enormous slab of pie for ninety-five cents.

In the early seventies, when the Varvis brothers learned that a hockey rink would be built in their neighbourhood, they registered the name Coliseum Steak and Pizza and set up shop about a half-mile from the Northlands. The restaurant opened in 1976, and it was a family joint from day one: Chris's wife, Barbara, cleaned stalls in the bathroom while Chris worked the dining room. The restaurant quickly became popular with Oilers' fans and players, the latter of whom would sneak in through the back door and party late into the night following games.

The first team allowed to take the Stanley Cup anywhere for visits, the Oilers brought it to Coliseum Steak and Pizza in the days after they won in 1984.

"The first time the Oilers brought the Cup there, I was more excited than when Chris and I got married," Barbara Varvis said.

In the drawer behind the cash register there is a picture of the Cup, with

Christopher Varvis being hoisted into it by his mother and aunt Helen. He was a baby then; now he helps run the family business.

In the days after winning the first Stanley Cup, the Oilers also held a dinner party in the restaurant, where photos of each of Edmonton's five winning teams hang in the lobby.

"The Oilers loved this place," Helen Varvis, whose late husband helped found the business, said. "They treated it as a second home."

In that era, the Oilers were often out in the neighbourhood. One time, Lord Stanley's mug accompanied the team's young stars to a topless bar in the Forum Inn, a hotel across the street from the coliseum.

"We used to go there to see girls dance," said Dave Lumley, a forward who was a member of the team that won the Stanley Cup in 1984. "One time, I think the Stanley Cup went with us. One of the girls might have danced with it."

The neighbourhood around 118th Avenue was given new life during the Coliseum's tenure, but places like Coliseum Steak and Pizza owed part of their success to what had come before them, places like Tony Mazzotta's Pizza Palace. Tony emigrated from Italy to Edmonton in 1959, and when he arrived, he worked in the kitchen at the sprawling Hotel MacDonald, built in the early 1900s by a Titanic survivor. He earned fifty-five dollars every two weeks and by the early 1960s, he had enough saved enough to open a pizza parlour on 118th Avenue. Tony's success allowed him to later move to New York City, where he opened restaurants in the Bronx and neighbouring Westchester.

But even from the Big Apple, Tony heard Edmonton calling. Seeing it as a better place to raise his kids, he and his family returned in 1980 and set up a small grocery and deli in a building on 111th Avenue, a little more than a mile from the Northlands Coliseum. Five years later, he turned the joint into Tony's Pizza Palace. In the restaurant's heyday, memorabilia covered every wall; sadly, much of it was stolen in a robbery in 1996. Signed hockey sticks and an autographed photo of Wayne Gretzky and Janet Jones walking out of the St. Joseph's Basilica on their wedding day in 1988 were among the pieces taken. "To Tony, the pizza king," read the Great One's autograph on the picture.

Both Tony Mazzotta and Con Stavropoulos were early Oilers season-ticket holders. Con bought his in 1979, the year that the Oilers, along with the WHA's New England Whalers, Quebec Nordiques and Winnipeg Jets, all joined the NHL. The previous season, Glen Sather, now a Hall of Famer in the builders' category, had taken over as head coach of the Oilers, and Wayne Gretzky, then only seventeen, had been purloined from the cash-starved Indianapolis Racers. That was the move that changed everything in Edmonton.

As skinny as a whip, Gretzky had been identified in his youth as the next great player. Born and raised in Brantford, Ontario, Gretzky started skating before he was three years old, and was taught to play hockey by his father, Walter, on a rink behind the family's home. Drills included skating around jugs of bleach and tin cans, and picking up pucks at top speed after flipping them over sticks scattered on the ice.

As a seventy-pound ten-year-old, Gretzky scored 370 goals for the novice Brantford Nadrofsky Steelers and, by age thirteen, he had already scored more than one thousand. Three years later he was drafted in the third round by the Sault Ste. Marie Greyhounds, and played one season in the Ontario Hockey League before signing a contract with Indianapolis of the upstart WHA on June 12, 1978. It was only a matter of months before Gretzky was dealt to the Oilers and joined new teammates in Edmonton, who were bemused by his slight stature and age.

"I remember my first practice there," Gretzky said. "I was a baby. One of my teammates, Jim Neilson, had a daughter the same age. I used to take her to school." With Gretzky leading the team in scoring and winning rookie-of-the-year honours, the Oilers reached the WHA finals for the only time in

1979. They lost to the Winnipeg Jets in six games, then jumped to the NHL. There, their fortunes would suddenly change.

In short order, Edmonton put together one of the greatest teams in history, and won four Stanley Cups in five years, beginning in only their fifth season. It was during that run that Gretzky, who won eight consecutive Hart Memorial Trophies (most valuable player awards) and seven straight scoring titles, became known as the Great One.

"I tell people that I don't know if we were the best team ever, but I would match us against any team anybody says was the most exciting," Gretzky said. "I remember showing up for training camp one year, and there were sixty-five guys in the locker room at the Northlands Coliseum. Glen (Sather) addressed everyone and said, 'I'd like to tell you every job is available, but that's not true. To be honest, one position is open. We'll see who gets it.'

"All of the new guys who hoped to make the team sat there in silence, completely stunned."

It was easy to love the Oilers in the 1980s, and Tony Mazzotta was no different from anyone else in Edmonton in the pride he took as they dominated the league. Tony kneaded dough and tossed pizzas while watching his beloved team on a television in a corner of the restaurant. As soon as the dinner rush was over, he would hurry to the Coliseum, watch the game for two periods, then head back to work for the late-night crowd. His hundred-year-old mother accompanied him to games, climbing slowly up the arena stairs and cursing at the referees in Italian. Mama Mazzotta died at 105, and she watched the Oilers on television in her nursing home until the end.

Over the years, Tony's Pizza Palace became wildly popular. Part of its success came thanks to an advertisement for the restaurant that was played at the Northlands with ten minutes remaining in the third period. The commercial featured lively Italian music and reminded spectators to visit the restaurant. It also served as Tony's cue that it was time to go back to work.

After the game, players came to the restaurant as well. When the Oilers were really rolling, the pizzeria was open until the wee hours, with players sometimes staying until three or four in the morning. Eventually, it became too difficult for Tony to handle, and he cut the hours back. Business continued to boom.

It wasn't just restaurants that felt the halo effect of the nearby Coliseum. Many businesses had a connection to the rink that was at the literal and figurative centre of their community. Originally from Ontario, Mike McCleary was among those who found its pull irresistible. He first visited Edmonton in 1977, stopping to see an uncle on the way out to Vancouver, but he never made it past the Rockies. He found work in an automotive machine shop on 118th Avenue a few miles from the Northlands, eventually marrying the boss's daughter and running the business with her when his father-in-law became ill.

Although he was a Maple Leafs fan growing up, McCleary began following the Oilers just as they were entering their dynasty era. The tone that people used to speak about Wayne Gretzky, the way the neighbourhood revered the Coliseum and the players within it, the atmosphere along 118th on game nights; McCleary soaked it all up. "The era was so innocent, that was the part that got me," he said. "The Oilers were a bunch of ragtag innocents that put everything together, and people fell in love with them from the get-go. I remember looking at Gretzky, a skinny, pimply faced kid with long hair, and thinking he was the same size as me. How could he possibly do the things that he was doing? It changed the face of the city."

Although the Coliseum brought good fortune to businesses in the area, Fireside Steak and Pizza still had the best real estate of the bunch. People would call to ask how far the restaurant was from the arena, to which Con would respond, "If I was any closer, I'd be inside." On game nights, fans crowded the place, and the occasional celebrity in town for an event at the Coliseum would sometimes stop by. Muhammad Ali walked over to the restaurant after making his final appearance in a boxing ring at the Northlands on June 12, 1983. That night, the great fighter, then forty-one, tangled with Dave Semenko, the Oilers' tough guy, in a three-round charity fund-raising bout. Many players became patrons. "Before he was famous, Wayne Gretzky would come in and have a sandwich and tea," Con said. "When he played for the Winnipeg Jets, Bobby Hull would come after a game and say, 'Con, I need a cold one.' He could drink five or six beers without ever taking a breath."

At times, the crush of people could be overwhelming for the staff. Late one evening, Con received a call from his night manager, who was terrified by the looks of one customer.

"Boss, you better come down here right away," she told him. "There's a monster of a man in here, and I'm scared something's going to happen."

Con rushed to the Fireside, only to discover that the gargantuan diner was Andre the Giant on a food run after a wrestling show at the Northlands.

"He was the nicest guy you could ever meet," Con said. "He was a monster of a man, but no monster."

At the height of the Oilers' success, things couldn't look brighter. The team was unstoppable. The Coliseum was the epicentre of a swelling optimism and success that rippled across Edmonton. Fans gathered in restaurants, bars and shops to celebrate their team and their city. Life along 118th Avenue was great for a time, but nothing can last forever. On August 9, 1988, the unthinkable happened, as it was announced that Gretzky would be traded to the Los Angeles Kings. Tony Mazzotta was so upset that he drove, seething, to Molson House, a former brewery where the news conference was staged.

Slumped before of a bank of microphones, Gretzky cried as the deal was announced, three months after the Oilers had closed out a four-game sweep of the Boston Bruins to win their fourth Stanley Cup in five years.

Tony stood in a crowd outside, still covered in flour from his kitchen, shouting and crying as he watched an era of record success come to an end. Hockey fans across Edmonton cried with him, Rachel Notley included.

Alberta's premier was articling as a law student for a local firm at the time. The year before, her father, Grant Notley, Alberta's New Democratic Party leader, came home after a celebration with Mark Messier's autograph on a napkin for her. "Everyone stopped working and there was a collective mental breakdown," Notley said. "There was a lot of wailing and airing of grievances."

The Oilers won only one Stanley Cup—in 1990—after Gretzky was traded. The organization wore that badge of dishonour like the Red Sox, who went eighty-six years between World Series victories after the team's owner, Harry Frazee, sold Babe Ruth to the New York Yankees in 1920 for $125,000. In the case of Edmonton, despite all the goodwill that Oilers owner Peter Pocklington created with the team's unparalleled run, most people despised him for trading Gretzky. It would be a quarter of a century before fans would put the deal behind them.

Mike McCleary was sitting at a traffic light once when Pocklington, still the Oilers' brash owner, pulled up beside him in his Rolls-Royce convertible. Although Pocklington had been the one who broke the Oilers' spell of success, McCleary couldn't help but hold him in high regard. "Pocklington did a lot for this city," McCleary said. "It was an ugly little sister and, with his help, Edmonton became a piece of history."

CALLED AN IMPOSSIBLE DREAM WHEN IT OPENED, THE NORTHLANDS COLISEUM became a faded debutante over time, if not completely antiquated in its final years. No doubt the arena is loaded with history but, by the end, it looked as if it had been frozen in time. All but a few of the banners hanging from the rafters dated back to the Gretzky years, and replicas of the team's five Stanley Cups were displayed in a case at the end of the runway that led from the Oilers' bench to their dressing room. Outside that room, photos of Gretzky, Mark Messier, Grant Fuhr, Paul Coffey and Glenn Anderson decorated the wall.

After Gretzky's departure, the team's fortunes suffered and, as it skidded, so too did 118th Avenue. Carved out of the bush in the late 1800s, it became a bustling business district with its own streetcar line in the early 1900s, and flourished during the Oilers' triumphant reign. Loyal customers had always flocked to places like the Fireside, but the Gretzky era brought in a whole new wave. After those golden years, however, fans had little to celebrate, and the area began a gradual decline. Family-owned businesses and mom-and-pop restaurants were outnumbered by cheque-cashing stores, pawn shops, payday loan companies, furniture rental outlets and a handful of merchants selling wigs.

Since 2001, more than twenty-five million dollars were spent as part of an initiative to make 118th Avenue an attractive place to work, shop and dine again. As part of the project, the facades of buildings were improved, the sidewalks were widened, benches were painted and police presence was increased to reduce drug activity and prostitution. All of the measures were well-intentioned, but failed to generate much enthusiasm beyond the immediate area.

It would be unfair to say that the Oilers moving from Rexall Place to the new Rogers Place was a crushing defeat for merchants along the avenue that leads to the old arena, but it certainly wasn't helpful. Drawing sellout crowds, the Oilers generate more traffic than any art show or community festival could ever bring. Local activists argued that the neighbourhood could change for the better, but it was little solace for old-timers who had sailed along in the Oilers' wake. Business owners in the area—people like Con Stavropoulos, Peter Varvis and Tony Mazzotta—were left with more fond memories than hope for the future.

The Fireside's business mirrored that of 118th Avenue, as did so many others. Over the years, fewer players came in. Con added to his coffers by charging for parking at Oilers games—twelve dollars with the purchase of a meal, twenty dollars without—and lamented the fact that he probably bypassed tens of thousands of dollars by not seizing on the idea sooner. Some things never changed. Oilers memorabilia was always featured around the restaurant, including a large, signed photo of Gretzky above a corner booth, a hockey sweater autographed by longtime fan favourite Ryan Smyth and a signed picture of Craig Simpson scoring his fiftieth goal of the season against the Buffalo Sabres on March 15, 1988. Loyal clients still came through the door, showing that those who remained in the neighbourhood still cared for it. However, in the spring of 2016, Con decided to put the restaurant on the market for $1.7 million, more because of his age than the fact that the Oilers were moving. "After having been here from the start, I find it hard to believe," he said. "But I wish them well in their new surroundings. I'm a proud Edmontonian. The city is always much better off when they're winning."

More than forty years since the Oilers played their first game across the street, and a quarter of a century since he last watched them hoist the Stanley Cup, Con held out hope.

HOPE WAS RENEWED ON APRIL 18, 2015, THE NIGHT OF THE 53RD NHL ENTRY DRAFT.
After being brought in by Daryl Katz in 2014 to diagnose the problems with the Oilers organization, Bob Nicholson had been promoted to president and chief executive officer on April 15, placing him in charge of the team's hockey operations in the final few days before the NHL lottery. In three of the preceding five years, the Oilers had won the lottery and with it the number-one draft spot, and they had used those first overall picks to add Hall, Nugent-Hopkins and Yakupov. However, 2015 was unlike any other year. This was the year that Connor McDavid—touted as the best player in a generation, the next Gretzky, and the presumed first overall pick—was eligible to be drafted. Nobody had talked about a player in such breathless terms in a decade. The last was Sidney Crosby.

Statistically speaking, the Oilers had an 11.5 percent chance of landing the first pick in 2015, so they weren't banking on it. The Arizona Coyotes edged them with a 13.5 percent chance of taking the pick, and the Buffalo Sabres, the last-place team the year before, had a 20 percent chance. The Oilers' hopes were so slim, in fact, that team officials expressed little enthusiasm when a post-mortem conference call was arranged for an hour after the lottery.

Nicholson sent Bill Scott, the team's assistant general manager, to the proceedings, tucking a one-dollar coin in his pocket and giving him a pair of twelve-dollar socks in a maple-leaf pattern to take with him for good luck.

The ceremony itself was held on April 18 inside a studio at CBC headquarters in downtown Toronto. After the numbered ping-pong balls had been propelled out of a machine, the order of the draft was unveiled by Bill Daly, the deputy commissioner of the NHL. An official of one desperate team snapped a pencil in half as the results became known and his hopes were dashed.

"There is far more emotion in the room than you see on TV," Guy Laurence, the Rogers CEO, said. "The tension is unbelievable."

Across the country, 1.6 million viewers were tuned in to the proceedings, four times as many as normal, all because of the anticipation surrounding McDavid. The dining room at Tony's Pizza Palace in Edmonton was packed. "I was working in the kitchen as the lottery occurred and it was so quiet you could hear a pin drop," Sal Mazzotta, Tony's nephew, recalled.

As Daryl Katz watched from the couch in his winter residence in California, one team after another fell out of the race to get the first pick. As each subsequent team was announced, Katz realized that the Oilers actually stood a chance of securing it. Finally, there were only three teams left: Arizona, Buffalo and Edmonton. A hush fell over the room as Daly picked up the card that would reveal the winning team. As Daly turned the card to the camera, the Oilers logo beamed out to the millions of eyes watching around the world. The first overall selection would be theirs and, almost assuredly, Connor McDavid was coming to Edmonton.

At home in Palm Springs, Katz and his fourteen-year-old son, Harrison, jumped up and ran around screaming. The commotion frightened the family's pooch, a shih tzu–miniature poodle mix named Rex. Katz's phone lit up as emails and text messages began to pour in, some congratulatory, others quite nasty. "I didn't know so many people hated us," Katz said. "If they didn't hate us before, they did then."

In the moment after the Oilers won the lottery, Connor McDavid, on camera in the studio wearing a navy blazer and a gingham check shirt, looked shocked, apparently overwhelmed by the moment. The reaction in Tony's Pizza Palace was decidedly more enthusiastic as fans applauded and congratulated each other.

At home in his condo, Nicholson nearly dropped the bottle of water he was drinking when Daly turned over the card bearing the Oilers' logo. His phone began buzzing. Within an hour, Nicholson presided over the conference call that almost nobody had wanted to take part in only a day earlier. It was a giddy call with people shouting to be heard over one another. Almost immediately, the men who were running the once-great franchise began looking for ways to return to the golden days.

Overnight, optimism swept over Edmonton like nothing in a generation. A new favourite son was headed to the Oilers; Connor McDavid was the player who would lead fans out of their misery, as Gretzky had done decades before. "As soon as we got the first pick, everything changed. We wanted to have that déjà vu all over again," Sal Mazzotta said.

A FEW MILES AWAY FROM THE OLD GUARD ON 118TH STREET—AND A SLAPSHOT'S distance across from the construction pit that was Rogers Place—Devin Pope, the young proprietor of a tavern opposite the newly christened rink, experienced the city's newfound energy. Born and raised in Edmonton, Devin grew up attending Oilers' games with his dad. A half-dozen years earlier he and his father had purchased a landmark property: a big, brick building that cigar merchant John B. Mercer had constructed in 1911. The building housed the most prized space, fronting on 104th Avenue, one of Edmonton's busiest downtown thoroughfares, so the father and son planned on refurbishing the place, then leasing it out to entrepreneurs. But there were few takers, and the Popes decided to do it themselves. Digging into their own pockets, they opened the Mercer Tavern in July 2012.

When they opened the bar, there was chatter about an arena going up nearby, but no location was mentioned. When city officials signed off on an agreement a little less than a year later that would see an arena built for the Oilers directly across the street, the Popes couldn't believe their good fortune. Their restaurant was going to be so close that they could toss a hamburger from the kitchen onto the ice.

The elder Pope had been a proponent of revitalization in Edmonton's urban centre for more than twenty years and, when it finally happened, a gold mine fell into his lap. The arena, Rogers Place, would be the centrepiece of a multibillion-dollar downtown renewal project, and the 18,641-seat facility would boast all of the most spectacular accoutrements. It would take two years to construct the arena, but the Popes were going to watch their neighbourhood, and their lives, transform. Before the introduction of Rogers Place, the neighbourhood around the bar was an island in the middle of the city, a place that people might pass through, but not a destination in and of itself. Soon, it would be flooded with hockey fans, bringing hundreds of thousands of thirsty and hungry spectators trotting past the Mercer Tavern. More than that, it signalled a cultural shift. Gone would be the quiet nights when Rexall Place drew the crowds and businesses in its shadow fed and watered fans after the final horn. On game nights, the Mercer Tavern would be packed. The Popes even added a McDavid burger: a patty, topped with shaved brisket and smoked cheddar sauce, with the number 97 branded on the bun, to their menu. Patrons joked that the name of the place should change to McDavid's Tavern.

"It has been a long journey," Devin said as he thought back on the years leading up to his change in fortune.

THREE

GROWING UP IN TORONTO, CHERYL LUNDY WAS AN AVID HOCKEY FAN. WHEN SHE played street hockey with the kids in her neighbourhood, the lack of goalie pads didn't stop her; she wrapped newspaper around her shins instead. "The *Star Weekly* was the perfect size for it," Cheryl said.

As a teenager, she got a job as an usherette at Maple Leaf Gardens and started a fan club and newsletter for her favourite player, the Leafs' Hall of Fame left winger Frank Mahovlich. On her seventeenth birthday, in 1966, the *Toronto Telegram* published an article about her; by then, the Mahovlich fan club had grown to five hundred members.

A dozen years later, Cheryl accepted a job with the City of Edmonton and moved across the country with her boyfriend. They broke up a short while later, but Cheryl stayed, went back to school and became a child-protection worker. "I had too much pride to go back and admit defeat," she said. Living in Edmonton, she became a fan of the Oilers, an affection she shares with her husband, Brian Stuart, an insurance underwriter who has had season tickets since he moved west from Toronto in 1977. They met in 1988, and have attended games together ever since.

Nearly thirty years later, there are Oilers blankets draped over chairs in their house in the suburbs, Oilers gnomes in their yard and a room covered with Oilers memorabilia. Among a dozen and a half hockey sticks sit two autographed wooden Titans that belonged to Wayne Gretzky, including the one he used to score five goals for the first time on February 18, 1981. Gretzky gave it to Cheryl's son, Trevor, then seven, when he visited the dressing room with Peter Pocklington after the game. Cheryl and Trevor had bumped into Pocklington, then the Oilers' owner, at a mall a few weeks earlier. The little boy walked over to Pocklington, shook his hand and thanked him for signing Gretzky to a twenty-one-year personal-services contract two years earlier. Pocklington was smitten with the youngster, and when he learned that Cheryl was a single mom who could not afford hockey tickets, he invited them to join him and his wife, Eva, at a game. That game turned out to be the contest where Gretzky scorched the St. Louis Blues, and the stick became one of Cheryl's most treasured possessions. But it was more than a mere memento: It was a piece of history, and the story behind it helped explain her unwavering affection for the Oilers. "When they're successful, the whole community benefits," she said.

Over the years, the Stuarts have amassed a collection of souvenirs so impressive that CBC wanted to feature it once during a broadcast of *Hockey Night in Canada*. Brian declined, in fear that somebody would track him down and break in. Along with the sticks, the couple has acquired pencil drawings, gift plates, autographed pictures and game-worn jerseys. One of Brian's favourites is the blood-stained sweater Ryan Smyth was wearing when he was struck in the face by a puck shot by one of his teammates, Chris Pronger, during those 2006 playoffs. Maintenance crews scraped three of Smyth's teeth and blood off the ice as he was rushed to the dressing room to have his lips stitched back together. Making a heroic return to the game, Smyth then set up the winning goal in triple overtime, and the Oilers went on to win the second-round series over the San Jose Sharks.

Cheryl, who dresses her dogs in Oilers kerchiefs, was at a genealogy conference in Edmonton on the night of the 2015 NHL Draft Lottery. The battery in her phone died seconds after she received a text from Brian saying Edmonton had just won for the fourth time in six years. Excited, she ran out to her car, plugged the phone into a charger and listened to radio reports to make certain her husband wasn't playing a cruel practical joke on her. By the time she got home that evening, her phone was full of grouchy emails from family back east who were infuriated that the Oilers and not their beloved Maple Leafs would get first crack at Connor McDavid. That night, Brian watched the draft unfold at home with their son, Doug, who attended his first Oilers game at six weeks old. When the Oilers won the golden ticket, they could barely talk. "We just sat there looking at each other in shock," Brian said. "I remember thinking, 'My God, what just happened?'"

The jealousy of friends in the centre of the country couldn't dim the anticipation that Cheryl and Brian were feeling as they, not to mention the rest of the city, waited to officially welcome Connor to Edmonton. On June 26, that moment arrived. Cheryl and Brian were so excited that they went to a draft party that night for the first time, gathering to watch the telecast at a downtown bar with hundreds of other fans. In the sixty-nine days since they had won the lottery, the Oilers had prepared for McDavid's arrival by taking a broom to their scouting staff, hiring a new president and general manager in Peter Chiarelli and bringing in Todd McLellan as head coach.

The draft was held at the BB&T Center, the rink in the Fort Lauderdale suburbs. Outside, before the doors opened, several hundred Oilers fans, many wearing number ninety-seven McDavid jerseys, waited in long lines. The atmosphere was celebratory, but cautious. "I swear to God, if Peter Chiarelli walks on stage and announces a trade, we are going to burn the place down," Sean Piper, an engineer back in Alberta, said.

The arena was packed that night, as thousands of fans, players, families and executives crowded the facility. Possibilities were weighed, decisions were made and futures were changed. As the proceedings got under way, all eyes were on Connor and his family.

Just moments before he was selected, as he sat between his parents, the teenager was overcome. The draft was the culmination of everything he had worked for throughout his short life. Even putting aside the years of development, training and living away from home, the draft marked the end of a frantic few weeks during which Connor had aced his final high-school exams, attended the NHL scouting combine in Buffalo and taken batting practice and thrown out the first pitch before a game at Marlins Park in Miami. The night before the draft, he had dinner and talked shop with Bobby Orr; in the hours immediately before it, he had gone jet skiing to get his mind off the enormity of the occasion. Now, all he could do was wait to hear his name called, alongside a rink full of people and hockey fans everywhere. "I'm going to throw up, I think," the teenager told his parents.

Three thousand miles away, Cheryl Lundy Stuart held her breath as Chiarelli approached the microphone on the stage at one end of the floor. "I know it sounds crazy, because we all knew what was going to happen, but I was afraid he would suddenly blurt out the wrong name or get laryngitis or something," she said.

In the annals of pro sports, stranger things have happened. In the 1982 NFL draft, a name misheard over a faulty speakerphone caused the Tampa Bay Buccaneers to use their first-round pick to take a player they didn't want. In 1988, the Calgary Flames chose the wrong one of two Stefan Nilssons available in that year's draft. And, in 1996, the Montreal Alouettes selected a player in the Canadian Football League draft that was dead. Somehow or other, they were unaware that James Eggink had died months earlier from cancer, and they picked the defensive end from Northern Illinois in the fifth round.

Hired after a successful tour running the Boston Bruins, Chiarelli would not make an egregious error. He later said the Oilers had never considered drafting any player other than McDavid, not even the consensus second choice, Jack Eichel, a broad-shouldered centre from Boston University. In fact, everyone in the NHL was so certain Edmonton would take McDavid that not a single team approached Chiarelli to ask if he was interested in trading away the first overall pick. "It was a no-brainer," he said.

Unruffled, Chiarelli did what everyone expected, pronouncing, "The Edmonton Oilers would like to select, with their first pick, from the Erie Otters, Connor McDavid." As the crowd erupted, the young man stood, accepted a soft kiss on the cheek from his father, a long hug and smooch from his mother and a warm embrace from Cameron, the brother he had scrapped with so often while playing roller hockey.

In Edmonton, Cheryl and Brian toasted McDavid with other Oilers devotees as they watched their newest hope accept congratulations from NHL commissioner Gary Bettman. On stage with them stood Daryl Katz and a contingent of Oilers' executives, Chiarelli, McLellan and senior vice-president of hockey operations Craig MacTavish included. After accepting a handshake and compliments from each, McDavid yanked a number ninety-seven jersey, the number he has always worn as a reminder of the year he was born, over his head. Connor and the team and league executives then gathered for a celebratory portrait. Minutes later, the team announced that each of its fourteen thousand season-ticket holders would receive a commemorative sweater identical to the one McDavid was wearing.

Backstage, Upper Deck, a trading card company, snapped photographs of McDavid and within minutes distributed a news release saying it had already signed him to an exclusive deal. Via Twitter, Oilers players celebrated. "Welcome to Edmonton, Connor," Taylor Hall, the Oilers' star forward, said, tongue in cheek. "Don't mess up everything we've built these last five years."

McDavid was immediately taken to a room where dozens of journalists were waiting to talk to him. In his inaugural interview as an Oiler, McDavid was unfailingly polite, if also seeming that he was not entirely comfortable with the process, either.

Asked to recount what it was like hearing his name called, Connor said that he didn't really know what to expect, but that the moment was still more exciting than he ever could have imagined. Then he was asked whether he had set goals for his rookie season. "I think my expectations exceed any of those that anyone else puts on me," he said. "It's something I can't really worry about. If I meet my expectations, chances are I'll meet everyone else's."

For the first time in many years, Oilers fans, who had endured the pain of failure and repeated expectations dashed, had reason to rejoice. The team's prospects for the future looked decidedly better with McDavid on board.

"I was holding my breath until his name was announced," Cheryl said. "Over the years, we've been through the good, the bad and the ugly and we've prayed for small miracles. At the end of last season, I didn't think there was anything that could possibly make this next year exciting."

Sitting beside Cheryl at the draft party, Brian breathed a sigh of relief. He was no fair-weather fan and would root for the Oilers no matter what, but suddenly, cheering for them had just gotten a heck of a lot easier.

"I made a prediction two years ago—I think I was sober at the time— where I said I thought the Oilers would be the next Canadian team to win the Stanley Cup," he said. "I had no idea anything like this was going to happen. This McDavid thing has changed everything. I'm enthusiastic and guardedly optimistic."

ON THE SUNDAY MORNING FOLLOWING THE DRAFT, CONNOR McDAVID STOOD TALKING to his family about the weekend's developments in the lobby of the Westin Fort Lauderdale Beach Resort, a hotel along the strip that has played host to spring breakers for decades. Although it was nearly twenty miles from the rink on the edge of the Everglades where the draft was held, the resort served as one the NHL's host venues and the grounds were swarming with fans. Hockey players were pestered by autograph seekers as they walked to their rooms or lounged by the pool. For Connor, it was impossible to be inconspicuous; at one point, fans even pursued him as he was getting into a car.

For a few quiet moments, though, the teenager was finally able to gather with his family and exchange good-byes with friends and relatives who had come to Florida to experience the thrill of watching him realize his dream. His billet parents in Erie, Bob and Stephanie Cataldo, were there, at the invitation of McDavid. "It was one of the best nights of my life," Bob said. "We were still celebrating at six the next morning. I've gotten a little bit old for that."

A die-hard Sabres fan, Bob had hoped Connor would end up playing in Buffalo, or at least Toronto, a four-hour drive north of Erie. He was disappointed that he would only get to watch him on television. "I'm jealous of people in Edmonton," Cataldo said. "It's going to be so exciting for them. With the speed Connor generates, every time his stick touches the ice anticipation there is going to rise. I don't think they know what they're in for."

Later that day, McDavid flew back to Toronto with his parents. The next morning, he spent a few hours packing, then headed to the airport for a four-hour flight to Edmonton. The send-off was bittersweet for his mom and dad. They were only hours removed from the hockey spotlight, yet Kelly McDavid was reminiscing and worrying about her little boy. It seemed as though just the other day Connor was setting up stuffed animals around the basement and pretending they were spectators as he imagined playing in the Stanley Cup Finals.

"It's exciting and we are very lucky to go through something like this, but as a mom, I know he's going to be far away," Kelly said. "To me, he's still the same normal kid with the messy room he has always been. My stomach hurts a little bit."

Brian McDavid drove Connor to Pearson Airport and sent him off to embark on his NHL career. He thought about the many times he woke up before dawn to take Connor to those early practices every hockey parent comes to dread. He remembered those countless hours Connor had spent perfecting his skills in the driveway when he was a kid. "It's something he has been preparing for a long time," Brian said. "It has been his single-minded goal since he was a little boy. This is his dream. Whether we want it to happen or not, it's happening. We need to let him go and do what he needs to do."

AT TIMES, THE LOVE THAT FANS HAVE FOR THE OILERS AND HOCKEY TRANSCENDS OTHER daily or material concerns. As Connor spent the last days of his summer training, the people of Edmonton waited anxiously for their new star to arrive. But, while each passing day allowed Connor to get a little stronger and more prepared, the same period had been difficult for both the city and Alberta at large.

With the price of crude cratering, Alberta's oil-driven economy suffered terribly in 2015. At the end of the year, seventy-one thousand people were unemployed, an increase of sixty thousand from the previous January. In all, fifty-one thousand full-time jobs were lost, a large percentage of which were in the oil-sands region just a short distance north of Fort McMurray.

Although the origin of the oil sands is open to debate, most geologists believe they were formed millions of years ago at a time that Alberta was covered by a tropical ocean. When the tiny marine inhabitants of that sea died, they fell to the ocean floor and through pressure, heat and time, their bodies were condensed into the ooze that we know today as petroleum. Rivers flowed away from the sea into northern Alberta, carrying with them sand and sediment that they deposited across the landscape. The formation of the Rocky Mountains then placed immense pressure on the land, and the liquid oil that rested at the bottom of the seabed was squeezed northward, seeping into the sand.

According to industry data, 95 percent of the supply of recoverable oil in North America is buried beneath the soil in northern Alberta. Its rich geological formations contain an estimated two trillion barrels, which, at current production rates, could supply Canada's energy needs for more than five hundred years. In some places, oil seeps out of the ground naturally, leaving long greasy ribbons floating atop rivers. While it is remarkably convenient for the crude to be so close to the surface, there is a catch. The tarry bitumen Aboriginals used for thousands of years to waterproof birch bark canoes is mixed with quartz and sand, and separating those materials is very costly. That means that when the price of oil on global markets dips too low, the cost of producing it becomes excessive. At twenty-six dollars per barrel in early 2016, the price had fallen well below the break-even point for most producers.

"We had a stiff headwind in 2015, which, in 2016, has grown to hurricane force," Brian Ferguson, the chief executive officer of Cenovus Energy, told shareholders during a conference call in February. In its most recent quarter, the giant oil-sands producer had reported losses of $641 million. The previous year, the firm's payroll had been trimmed by fifteen hundred people, or 15 percent, and Ferguson warned that more job cuts were coming.

As Alberta's financial state worsened in late 2015, Canada's federal government began to consider offering financial aid to the former energy powerhouse. The flagging oil industry was wreaking havoc on the Canadian dollar and that, in turn, was impacting everyone from Ontario manufacturers to West Coast legislators to pipeline developers in the Maritimes.

The news wasn't any brighter on the provincial level. A labour force survey predicted that thirty-one thousand construction jobs would be lost in Alberta over the next four years, and the local economy was already feeling those effects. Commercial airlines shut down flights to cities that served as energy hubs and, in Fort McMurray, homeowners were drowning beneath colossal mortgages. On a Facebook page called Fort McMurray Buy and Sell, sad stories played out every day. Laid-off workers who had once earned six-figure salaries had exhausted their savings and were peddling anything they could: An excavator was being sold by an idle heavy-equipment operator, diapers were being hawked for twenty-five cents a pair and, in one particularly wrenching case, a young woman expecting her first child was pawning her 1.5 carat princess-cut wedding ring. One post after another spoke to people's despair.

At the same time, food banks across Alberta were struggling. The number of people in the province calling upon them had increased 23 percent year over year. Nationwide, the same rate had increased just 1.3 percent over the same period. In Fort McMurray, a city of about 70,000 in a sprawling regional municipality, Wood Buffalo, the food bank was struggling to keep up with a 72 percent surge in demand. Fifty-five percent of those clients were families with children; the agency was so short on resources that it had to decrease the size of the food hampers it distributed to accommodate the number of people seeking aid. The need for help became so extreme that the executive director of the food bank, Arianna Johnson, began to carefully watch volunteers and staff for signs of compassion fatigue, which is a secondary form of traumatic stress.

"I never thought the number of people we serve could go up by so much," Johnson said. "The idea that we could even go up fifty percent was startling to me. The effects are devastating."

By January 2016, the unemployment rate in Fort McMurray had climbed to 9 percent, four points higher than the previous year and two points higher than the national average. And Fort McMurray was not alone in its challenges: The province-wide unemployment figure in the same period hit 7.4 percent, marking the first time since 1988 that it eclipsed the national average.

To make matters worse, Alberta was struck by the biggest natural disaster in Canadian history on May 3, 2016. A forest fire burning out of control barrelled like a rampaging dragon through Fort McMurray and threatened other northern communities. More than eighty thousand people had to be evacuated, some escaping with nothing more than their lives, as the inferno licked at their heels. At least 2,400 people lost their homes, work in the oil patch was interrupted and the damages soared into the billions of dollars.

It would be nearly a month before some displaced residents were able to return to the fire-ravaged city—and those were the lucky ones. There were many who had nothing left at all. Anthony Hoffman, a firefighter, lost the condo he lived in and the childhood home where he grew up. He was so consumed by trying to save other people's houses that his own burned. A few days later, when he stood in front of the charred remains, the chimney was the only part that was left.

"A house is four walls, but it is so much more than that," Hoffman said, describing the pain he felt. "Everything that shapes your life happens there. Everything you experienced as a family within the four walls, it watched. It sounds stupid, but a home is a member of your family. It's every chat I ever had with my parents. It's every fight I ever had with my brothers. It's every girl I ever brought home. It's a big piece of you, and you can't help but feel a sense of loss."

A firefighter and emergency medical technician for five and a half years, Hoffman had just finished an overnight shift when the fire ploughed through the south end of the city, consuming almost everything in its path. Knowing he would be needed, he packed a change of clothes and drove from his condo to the fire hall.

As soon as he was deployed, he started battling fires. He didn't think much about his own property, and neither did any of his co-workers. A union official has since estimated that fifteen or more homes that were lost belonged to firefighters.

"The first night was insane," Hoffman said. "We had every piece of equipment rolling, and I ended up on five crews at ten or twelve different fire scenes. We jumped frantically from place to place. There were more structure fires that night than most firefighters see in a career."

There were brief moments of euphoria, followed by depths of despair.

"We would stop a fire in one place, and then we would find out another had started somewhere else," he said. "Any progress we made was gone. We've all been to fires, but this was the first time a lot of us were looking at one another like, 'What do we do?' The fire was just too big."

Susan McCue was back in New Brunswick, nearly five thousand kilometres from Fort McMurray, when the fire burned down the home her late brother had bequeathed to her only months earlier. Randy McCue died of cancer in January, and then willed his house to his baby sister, asking her to be the executor of his estate. She had just returned from Fort McMurray, where she was beginning to pack up his belongings, when the blaze hit.

"It's like I lost my brother all over again," she said days later at her home in St. Martins, a picturesque fishing village on the Bay of Fundy. "He is ashes, and now his house is ashes, too. I went from being his companion to his caregiver and then executor in a matter of minutes. I still have to settle his estate, but everything is burned."

A big guy with a big personality and an even bigger heart, Randy had left many of his most treasured possessions behind: the trophies from the baseball teams he'd coached, two guitars, an amplifier, the big brown cowboy hat he loved and an oil painting of St. Martins. The garage was full of tools he used while working in the oil sands.

"He wanted me to give those things away to people," Susan said. "He wanted them to have a piece of him. I'm just glad he wasn't here to see everything he worked so hard for lost."

Buffeted by strong winds and fuelled by tinder-dry conditions and unusually high temperatures, the fire blazed through the city and then raced to the east, getting within a few miles of the border with Saskatchewan before expanding northwards. Homes that had initially been spared caught fire, and work camps that housed oil sands employees burst into flames. Fire-fighters came from all over Canada to help contain the blaze; at one point, Russia even offered to send its biggest air tankers and a team of rescue specialists to lend a hand.

At the time, the financial toll that the disaster would take was incalculable, but it added to the misery and emotional distress that was being felt across the province. The economic losses heightened the tension within Alberta's demographic mosaic. Many people see oil as a valuable resource begging to be harvested, but others question the environmental ramifications of extracting it. Within some First Nations communities in the far north, families are divided by the debate: some rely on the energy industry to survive, while others blame it for unexplained cancer clusters and a wide range of other illnesses. In Fort Chipewyan, a former fur-trading centre upstream from energy plants, residents complain that the water is tainted, the whitefish and pickerel are deformed, and the bison, caribou and moose they eat are growing scarce. For a time, it seemed that there was always another struggle, another challenge, another setback.

In such times, the relief that hockey brings to so many Albertans is incalculable. Their love for the game is something that seems inbred in all Canadians, whether in the small community rink in Fort Chipewyan or the giant facilities with multiple ice surfaces in Calgary, Edmonton, Halifax, Toronto and Winnipeg.

A health and safety officer for an oil and gas company, Scott Myers grew up in Fort McMurray. His parents moved west in the 1970s from Toronto, where his dad, Shawn, had been an aspiring goalkeeper for the Marlboros of the Ontario Hockey League. Shawn was recruited to play net for Suncor's puck team, the Blades, and, along with the roster spot, he received a well-paying job as a labourer in the company's construction branch.

When Shawn and his wife arrived in Fort McMurray, the Oilers were just beginning their ascent to greatness, and it was enough to make Shawn repledge his hockey allegiance. "My father was a die-hard Leafs fan, and almost played for them, but you've never seen someone throw a Toronto jersey into a garbage can faster than he did," Scott, who still lives and works in the northern energy gateway, said.

Shawn's newfound affinity for the Oilers was passed on to his son. One of Scott's most enduring memories is watching them win the 1987 Stanley Cup as he sat on his dad's lap. He was three years old, and has been smitten with the Oilers ever since. Even living four hours north of Edmonton doesn't keep him from attending home games. He is a season-ticket holder, and tries to make it to Rexall Place ten to fifteen times each year. On game days, he goes into the office at four in the morning, works an eight-hour shift, then drives to Edmonton. After the game, he turns around and drives back to Fort McMurray, often on an icy highway, and is back for work the next day.

"I don't really have many memories as a kid, and what I have involves the Oilers," he said. Along with watching the Stanley Cup on television, he recalls his father once picking him up at school early and telling him that he was taking him to a monster-truck show in Edmonton. When they got to the Coliseum, there weren't any trucks, but there was a game being played between the Oilers and Calgary Flames.

For Scott and thousands of others like him working in Alberta's energy sector, hockey is more than entertainment. It is a rallying point in good times and a tonic in periods of hardship. Thirty-five thousand jobs were lost within the industry in 2015; if ever there were a time for a desperately needed diversion, Connor's arrival was it.

"Rooting for the Oilers allows me to come home from work and shut my mind off at the end of the day," Myers said. "For two and a half hours, I can turn on the TV and other things don't weigh on me. My dad was affected in an economic downturn in the 1980s, and the one thing he used to distract himself was hockey. I have been affected now, and I use hockey the same way. Win or lose, the Oilers are always there for me."

On the night of the NHL lottery in April, Scott Myers was at home in Fort McMurray watching on television.

"When they flipped the card over and I realized the Oilers had won, I sat there staring and shaking my head," he said. "For a second, I was like, 'Wait, what did they just say?'"

As the realization sunk in, Myers screamed, startling his wife as he dashed into the living room. Unable to contain his excitement, he ran into the backyard and continued yelling there. A group of guys attending a lottery party next door were outside screaming, too, and Myers invited them over to quaff beers in his garage.

"We had our own welcome party for Connor McDavid," Myers said.

On January 13, 2016, Myers's wife gave birth to their first son. It was McDavid's nineteenth birthday, but try as he might, Myers couldn't convince her to name their little boy Connor. From a list that she had compiled, Nicole Denney, who cares little for hockey, chose the name Eberly. Scott agreed, his partner none the wiser that the Oilers had a high-scoring forward on their roster named Eberle.

To some, Scott Myers's enthusiasm might have seemed over the top. But Edmonton has a history of devoted fans showing their love for the team in all manner of ways, whether they were born in Alberta or have adopted the Oilers as their own. Shawn Chaulk moved west with his family from Newfoundland in 1980, arriving in a small town in central Alberta on his thirteenth birthday. He moved to Fort McMurray sixteen months later when his dad got a job with Syncrude, the largest petroleum producer in the oil sands. The oldest of four boys, Shawn had a soft spot for the Bruins, whom he occasionally watched on *Hockey Night in Canada* while growing up. But upon moving to Alberta, he abandoned the Bruins in favour of the Oilers. Throughout his teens, he watched their games on a twelve-inch black-and-white television as he worked behind the counter at a mom-and-pop grocery.

A general contractor, Shawn entered the housing market just as things were beginning to pick up. In the 1990s, he could buy a sixty-foot-wide-by-one-hundred-foot-deep plot for sixty thousand dollars, and the first houses he built sold for four hundred thousand. Over the years, the housing prices increased, and within a couple of decades, those same houses were going for nearly a million. Of course, the price of the lots had also been rising: The same sixty-by-one-hundred plots that Shawn bought for sixty thousand dollars in the '90s were now costing him six or seven times as much. Then, suddenly, the bottom went out from the market—housing prices plummeted and housing construction all but stopped as companies operating in the oil sands laid off workers by the thousands. Shawn recognized that the market was gone, so he mothballed his Fort McMurray home-construction firm in 2012.

There were many others who found themselves in similar situations, suddenly out of work and wondering who had turned off the tap. Unlike most, however, Shawn had a backup plan. In his early twenties, he had started collecting hockey memorabilia, first dabbling in sticks and pucks, then focusing on pieces that belonged to Wayne Gretzky. When he was young, Chaulk had realized that, "If you were an Oilers fan, you had to be a Gretzky fan."

Shawn steadily amassed memorabilia of every shape and size and, by the time he shut down his construction company in 2012 had assembled the world's largest collection of Gretzky souvenirs. As the provincial economy wilted around him, Chaulk sold pieces of his collection in fits and starts. In 2013, he earned $550,000 by selling twenty-three items in an online auction. One of the articles—the sweater the Great One wore in 1986–87 when he scored his five-hundredth goal and won the Stanley Cup—went for $356,000. It was the second-highest amount ever spent for a hockey jersey, after the $1.2 million a collector paid in 2012 for the jersey that Paul Henderson wore when he scored the winning goal in the 1972 Summit Series.

In 2014, Chaulk appeared on a CBC TV show, Four Rooms, on which guests were invited to sell valuables to art, antique and memorabilia buyers.

Shawn presented the sweater that Gretzky was wearing in 1982 when he scored his record ninety-second goal and two hundredth point that year, a tally that broke Phil Esposito's single-season scoring record. The piece immediately caught the panelists' attention.

"It's not even a jersey, it's a Canadian trophy," one of the buyers, Scott Landon, said.

"I smelled the armpit," said Jessica Lindsay Phillips, a tribal art and oddities expert who offered $70,000. "It reeks of authenticity."

In the end, buyers were unable to meet the minimum bid of a quarter of a million dollars, and Chaulk kept the jersey, leaving $110,000 on the table. Some viewers at the time wondered what he was thinking, walking away from so much money. But in January 2016, Shawn's patience was rewarded when he found a buyer. The final price? $275,000.

Chaulk's collection attracted attention from memorabilia buyers and sellers around the world. The real validation of his work came when the Great One came to visit Shawn at home and view his collection. They had met previously when Chaulk was asked to set up a display at a charity event Gretzky was headlining in Edmonton. Before the doors opened, Shawn gave Gretzky a private tour.

"When you collect items from someone like that, you dream small, about getting that next stick or glove or another item," Chaulk said. "Never did I fathom that I would be giving a tour of my collection to him one day. He was taken aback that one person could have amassed that amount of stuff. He had some genuine questions about how and where I had gotten some of the things. It was like walking into a Hall of Fame, but with more items."

The last piece in his exhibit was Gretzky's black 1986 Mercedes-Benz 560SL convertible. Chaulk purchased it from one of Gretzky's former business partners, and had it restored to factory condition. Gretzky knew that someone owned the car, as he had signed an authentication form verifying it was his, but he was overwhelmed when he saw it.

"For a few years, he asked if he could buy it back and I turned him down," Chaulk said. "Eventually, I decided I couldn't say no anymore, and sold it back to him."

Gretzky sent Shawn a cheque overnight and, the next day, someone arrived to pick up the vehicle and begin driving it to California.

"He paid me way more than it was worth," Chaulk said. "I don't know. Maybe he had driven it once in a Stanley Cup parade."

Although he specializes in memorabilia, Shawn continues to follow the Oilers of today, and the team continues to bring Chaulk enjoyment—and irritate the hell out of him. He has retained a few select pieces from his collection, too, including the jersey number ninety-nine wore in 1984 during the Canada Cup gold medal game against Sweden at the Northlands Coliseum. Team Canada swept the final series in two games, and Gretzky was the leading scorer with twelve points in eight games. "If I got an offer for a hundred and fifty thousand dollars, I probably wouldn't take it," he said. Some things are worth more than money. "People's love for their team and passion for the game isn't tied to the economy," he said. "There are some things the price of oil doesn't drive. The list may be small, but sports is one of them."

JULY 1 MARKED THE FIRST DAY OF THE OILERS' SIX-DAY ROOKIE ORIENTATION CAMP. AS most of Edmonton's residents were preparing for a Canada Day barbecue, Connor McDavid traded the sunny warmth outside for the lights of Rexall Place, as he joined thirty other prospects in power-skating drills. All the Oilers' top prospects were there, including previous first-round draft picks Darnell Nurse and Leon Draisaitl. But the outstanding young centre was the main attraction. At the end of his first practice session, teammates awarded McDavid the day's first star; more of a good-natured initiation than an honour. As his reward, Connor had to skate a lap around the rink as the other players watched and slapped their sticks against the ice. "It was all in good fun," McDavid said.

More than anything else, the teenager wanted to fit in, and not be extended special courtesies or draw attention. Connor had always sought to offset his otherworldly skills with humility. In Erie, he was not only the Otters' best player, but also their most unselfish, often passing up goals so someone else could score. In each of his last two junior seasons, it was one of Connor's teammates who won the OHL scoring title: Maple Leafs farmhand Connor Brown in 2013–14, and Arizona draftee Dylan Strome the year after.

Upon arriving in Edmonton, McDavid refused to speculate about his future in the NHL. He deferred questions by saying there was no certainty that he would even make the Oilers. The idea was absurd. Anybody could see that. Todd McLellan, who was just beginning his reign as head coach, was more direct about it. "He talks about 'making the team' because he is very respectful, and he understands that he has to earn it," McLellan said. "But I expect him to push forward and play for our hockey club this year and I think, in his heart, he does, too. His skills are remarkable, and he is a very focused young man who does things right. That's tough for an eighteen-year-old to do."

Earlier that summer, when he was coaching Team Canada at the International Ice Hockey Federation world championships, McLellan sought out Sidney Crosby to talk to him about McDavid. The career paths of the two were eerily similar: Each had played against older kids in their youth and dominated at the major-junior level before being drafted into the NHL and anointed the saviour of a struggling franchise. And, just like the Oilers, the Penguins were lousy when Crosby joined them as an eighteen-year-old at the start of the 2005–06 season.

"I knew I was coming to Edmonton, so it was natural for me to ask Sid about his rookie year," McLellan explained. "He spent a fair amount of time revealing what he had gone through coming into the NHL, and really about being the Next One, if you will. It's exciting, but there are hardships. I wanted to know everything I could so that we would be better able to help Connor as an organization."

McLellan and the rest of the coaching staff designed the orientation week as a way of bringing players into the fold and building relationships. For the weeklong camp, the rookies would work, eat and play together almost nonstop. Most mornings, they started by riding bicycles nearly five miles to Rexall Place, after which they trained and practised. The hours that followed were a blur of drills and lessons, some relating to hockey and some aimed at rounding out the rookies' life skills. As part of their training, the Oilers organization wanted to teach recruits about hockey, but they also sought to give them real-life lessons.

One evening, arrangements were made for the rookies to take cooking classes at the Northern Alberta Institute of Technology. The class was instructed by Paul Shufelt, a chef for a hospitality group that operated eight restaurants in Edmonton. "In a sense, they have had everything handed to them, and now they are going to go out on their own," Shufelt said. "The intention is to help them make better choices."

As part of the exercise, the players were split into groups and sent grocery shopping for twenty minutes. When they returned, they had to prepare a full meal, with Shufelt grading each dish for its creativity, taste and appearance. The chef deemed all of their efforts palatable—"there was nothing I couldn't choke down"—but he scared the wits out of some students.

"It was kind of like *Hell's Kitchen*," said John McCarron, a 230-pound forward who had played at Cornell. In an attempt to help with the assignment, McCarron's girlfriend had provided him the recipe for a cranberry walnut apple salad and glazed salmon with wild rice.

McDavid cooked as part of a team with Darnell Nurse, a strapping defenceman the other players call "Doc," Leon Draisaitl and Greg Chase, a centre who had toiled in the minors in Victoria, Calgary and Oklahoma City the previous season. The group got high marks for its menu: an appetizer of shrimp tacos, an entrée of breaded fried chicken served with asparagus and a dessert consisting of angel food cake with whipped cream. "I haven't cooked a whole lot, so I enjoyed it," McDavid said. "We had a lot of fun."

Off-ice antics like the cooking class were entertaining, but they also helped the young men work better together. The lessons from the kitchen or the classroom could be carried over to the rink, making the whole team stronger than the sum of its parts. Still, from the minute he stepped on the ice with the rest of the rookies, it was clear that McDavid was a spectacularly skilled player whose gifts set him apart. Each day, Oilers executives sat in a cluster at one end of Rexall Place, intently watching him. "It's hard for your eyes not to find number ninety-seven," Peter Chiarelli said.

The rookies' practice sessions were conducted in private the first two days and then opened to the public. To say that the fans were eager to see Connor in person would be a gross understatement. For months, they had been only reading about McDavid and watching snippets of video online. Now they were going to be treated to the real deal.

On the morning of July 3, a line snaked three hundred yards from the front doors of Rexall Place through the parking lot, two and a half hours before McDavid was scheduled to take the ice. Children played tag around a bronze statue of Wayne Gretzky, while their parents, many dressed in newly acquired number ninety-seven hockey sweaters, stood baking in the summer heat. In the days leading up to the draft, CoolHockey.com, a Toronto-based company selling licensed NHL merchandise, had stocked its fifteen-thousand-square-foot warehouse with McDavid jerseys. "My guess is that however many we have in the building, we'll sell," Brody Constantine, the website's online marketing manager, said. "He is going to be as big, if not bigger, than Sidney Crosby."

The Oilers usually held their orientation camp in a small rink on the outskirts of Edmonton, but they moved the training sessions to Rexall Place to accommodate fan interest. So many spectators showed up so early that Friday that coliseum employees were sent out into the throng to pass out free bottles of water and bags of popcorn. "This is the first time I ever had popcorn for breakfast," one little boy squealed.

Approximately 3,500 people turned out to watch McDavid and other prospects participate in drills for a little more than an hour. The lower bowl of Rexall Place was nearly half full when McDavid, showing a flare for the dramatic, skated onto the ice last in a long line of players. The crowd roared at the sight of him and within seconds was chanting, "Con-nor, Con-nor, Con-nor!" They cheered wildly when one of his first shots sailed past the net, then again as another clanked off the crossbar. McDavid, skating in circles, was the butt of a little teasing from other rookies as they laughed at the raucous response.

McDavid was wide-eyed afterward, and admitted to being surprised when he came down the tunnel and realized a mob had turned out to greet him. For Connor, it was just a normal practice like any other. But for the playoff-starved fans in Edmonton, it was a look into the future. "This is the second coming; there was Gretzky, and then there is Connor," Angel David, a long-time Oilers fan and season-ticket holder, said.

A few nights later, 7,300 fans showed up to watch McDavid play against the Oilers' other rookies in an intrasquad scrimmage. McDavid scored five goals and his team won. Over the course of the evening, he scored on a wrap around, a breakaway, a pass in front of the crease that a panicked defence-man accidentally poked into his own net and a puck that was lifted over the goalie's head. His final goal, on another breakaway, was a thing of beauty. In a matter of seconds, he broke in on the net, faked a forehand, then a back-hand and then flipped the puck over the goalie. The crowd cheered every time Connor put the puck in the net, and a flurry of hats rained down after the third goal. Even though it was only a scrimmage, fans hoped it would be Connor's first of many hat tricks in an Oilers uniform, and they wanted to let him know that they already appreciated his effort.

As he left the ice following the game, McDavid pointed to a young fan on the opposite side of the glass and tossed a white ballcap in his direction. A woman in the crowd snagged it, but as she turned to celebrate, she saw Connor scrutinizing her. He gestured to the young boy to whom he had tossed the hat. The woman hesitated as Connor continued to stare her down, pointed at the child and stood watching until she handed it over.

Fans were buzzing over McDavid's performance, but in the dressing room he shrugged it off. "It was no big deal, really," he said. "I'm not in the NHL. I'm at a rookie development camp."

Fans didn't care. It had been an excellent week for Connor, and a show of what they and he could expect in the future. And that future was starting to become more certain. In the middle of the rookie camp, McDavid signed a three-year, entry-level contract that would pay him the maximum for a first-year player of $925,000 per season, with another $2.85 million in performance bonuses possible each year. The signing caused one of his future teammates, an unassuming forward named Rob Klinkhammer, to send him a tweet: "Don't worry, we won't be on the same line. I'll keep the bench from floating away."

At the end of orientation camp, McDavid still refused to publicly comment about the likelihood that he was good enough to make the team. "This week was awesome, and I learned a lot," he said. "You're just a sponge the whole time, and that's the way you have to be."

McDavid planned to take time off in summer, enough to get set for whatever the next season would bring. There was little time to waste, and so much he needed to do to get ready to play in the NHL. Connor had been working out with Gary Roberts, a former NHL player and fitness guru, since the summer before he joined the Erie Otters. Those training sessions significantly improved his strength, but now he would be stepping up to the big leagues.

"I'm going to work this summer and see where I am come September," McDavid said. "I'll take a little time off, but not much. There's only a short window between now and the start of the year.

"I need to get as big and strong as I can."

FOUR

ON MOST MORNINGS, MEGAN CLASSENS ARRIVES FOR WORK BY SIX-THIRTY. A FIELD engineer for PCL Construction, the firm engaged to build the Edmonton Oilers' new hockey arena, Megan usually doesn't return home until early evening. Sometimes, it is much later.

One Thursday in February 2016, she climbed out of bed and headed out the door to meet the construction superintendents and foremen before sunrise. As morning broke over the city, Megan huddled with trade workers at the construction site. Their breath hung in clouds of condensation above their heads as Megan outlined some of the problems that might pop up during the day. The next few hours were spent with architects and other engineers as they reviewed and inspected the work on the 18,641-seat rink that was going to serve as the home of the Edmonton Oilers. Megan's work days were long and grueling, both mentally and physically, and the cold of the Alberta winter didn't make it any easier. When temperatures drop to minus-thirty degrees, no amount of woolies can make the workday comfortable. But, like the other one thousand labourers assigned to the project, she was thrilled to be working on Rogers Place.

Growing up in Lethbridge, two hours south of Calgary, Megan rooted for the Oilers over the more regionally popular Flames. When she moved to Edmonton in 2011 to attend the University of Alberta, she became even more enamoured.

"If anything, working on the arena has made me a bigger fan," she said, sitting in a construction trailer wearing an Oilers jersey, her hardhat and safety glasses beside her. "I'm not just working on a building or office space. This is the place the Oilers will likely play for the next thirty years or more. It's in the heart of the city, and is the centre of the city's redevelopment plans. It's a unique project."

The biggest general contractor in Canada and one of the largest in North America, PCL was founded in 1913 and has been based in Edmonton since 1932. Rogers Place is just the latest in a long line of sporting venues it has created, among them the Staples Center in Los Angeles, Canadian Tire Centre in Ottawa, MTS Centre in Winnipeg, and Air Canada Centre, BMO Field and Ricoh Coliseum, all in Toronto.

Construction on Rogers Place began in March 2014, and was completed in the months leading up to the 2016 NHL season. At 1.1 million square feet, the arena is nearly twice the size of Air Canada Centre and boasts a host of amenities, including the largest high-definition arena scoreboard in the world, a grand entrance that spans over one of the city's busiest streets, five cantilevered levels of seating and a one-thousand seat community rink used for practice by the Oilers and visiting teams, as well as serving as home ice for the MacEwan University Griffins.

"I think people are going to love it," Megan said. "I'm not necessarily going to go there to watch games but to see all the details come together and to see people take it all in. Their reaction is going to be crazy."

The arena itself is the centrepiece of a bold development project, the

Ice District, that was undertaken to transform the skyline. As construction on Rogers Place continued around the clock through the winter and spring of 2016, a twenty-seven-storey office tower for city employees was going up beside it. In addition, a casino was being built, office space for the Oilers Entertainment Group was being fabricated and the finishing touches were being placed on a new rail transit station. The variety of projects generated more excitement and energy than had been seen downtown for years. From the sidewalks below, passersby gawked at ironworkers with the steely nerves of Cirque du Soleil acrobats, at the same time that they plugged their ears to drown out the cacophony created by saws, hammers, trucks and heavy machinery. Traffic clogged adjacent streets, but motorists didn't seem to be fretting much; instead, they gazed out their windows at the activity going on around them.

At the same time, work was also beginning to clear the way for future components of the Ice District: a soaring skyscraper with 264 luxury condominiums and a four-star hotel with rooms on thirty-one floors, a plaza with a public skating rink, three hundred thousand square feet of retail and restaurant space, more than one million square feet of office space, a Cineplex and a children's day-care centre.

"I believe everyone in Edmonton will want to be here," Glen Scott, vice president of real estate for the Katz Group, said. "They will either want to live here, play here or be entertained here. There were a lot of doubters maybe even twelve months ago, but I think most of those doubts have been blown away."

The steel girders being laid and concrete poured at the construction sites around the city mirrored the transformation that Connor McDavid was undergoing, albeit on a personal level. Connor had begun training with Gary Roberts in the summer of 2012. When Roberts first met Connor, he took one look at the teenager and was concerned. The former hockey player turned fitness guru believed that, at five feet ten and 166 pounds, McDavid was too frail to endure the physical punishment he would receive in the

OHL. As soon as their meeting was over, Roberts got on the phone with the Erie Otters.

"I told them, 'You better make sure you have someone to protect this kid,'" Roberts recalled.

A three-time All-Star who retired following the 2008–09 season, Roberts amassed 910 points and 2,560 penalty minutes over the span of twenty-two seasons in the NHL. After suffering a serious neck injury at thirty years old, he sat out a full season, underwent surgery and rehab, then returned to play another eleven years. Along with two neck operations, he also endured surgery on both shoulders and had pins inserted in each of his thumbs. A scar zigzags along his left leg where a torn quadriceps muscle was repaired.

"I had to reinvent myself physically to withstand the stress of the game," Roberts said. "It was tough mentally, and in the end it taught me a lot about training players. I was a full-time, twenty-four-hours-a-day hockey player, training five to six hours a day. My passion became preparation. I had to come back that much stronger to succeed."

Connor was introduced to Roberts through his former agent, Rick Curran, a principal in the Orr Hockey Group. When they first met, McDavid was intimidated by the mere sight of Roberts. A fearsome mucker and grinder, Roberts' body bears the scars from many battles that he fought—and mostly won. Roberts was so tough that fans used to joke that he took heads off, not face-offs, during games. The muscles in his arms bulge like Popeye's, and he still looks as if he could crush an opponent against the boards, even if he is approaching fifty.

"I was fifteen, and so nervous about meeting him," McDavid said. "I was scared of what he might think and how he would judge me."

McDavid was heading into tenth grade when he began working out with Roberts on the campus of St. Andrew's, a private boarding school set on one hundred acres in Aurora, a bedroom community about forty-five minutes from Toronto. Transforming a lean adolescent into a game-ready

NHL player was a daunting and complicated mission, but there was no-body better suited to the task than Roberts. Under his direction, Steven Stamkos had gone from being a young talent to a star in the NHL.

In his first summer of working with Roberts, McDavid took one look at the NHL players around him and became overwhelmed with the work he needed to do. But, just as he had been driven to perform countless hours of drills on his rollerblades in the driveway, just as he had worked tirelessly for every other coach he played for, McDavid was motivated to turn his body into one befitting an NHL star.

"When Connor saw Stamkos and James Neal here for the first time, he said, 'I can't imagine ever being that strong and that fit,'" Roberts recalled. "I told him that if he worked hard enough he could do it.

"There is a big learning curve, but he has excelled at every level and there's no reason to think he won't in the NHL. The difference is that he is going to play against men, and we have to make sure he's ready."

AT THE NHL SCOUTING COMBINE A WEEK BEFORE THE DRAFT, McDAVID FINISHED IN the top ten in only two of the fifteen tests that measure agility, fitness and strength. Jack Eichel, the centre picked by the Buffalo Sabres immediately after McDavid, ranked among the leaders in seven categories and won two—one for aerobic capacity and the other for strength of the grip of his right hand. The lone player to win as many as three categories—eighteen-year-old winger Jesse Gabrielle—wasn't selected until the fourth round, when he was picked 105th by the Boston Bruins. He managed only three games in the AHL before returning to the WHL.

Over the years, many players that have tested well have never made it in the NHL and, to the contrary, some who have struggled at the com-bine have gone on to successful careers. At the 2014 combine, Sam Ben-nett failed to complete a single chin-up, but that didn't prevent the Calgary

Flames from choosing him in the first round. And none other than Wayne Gretzky has cast doubts on the combine process, once saying, "When I scored ninety goals, I could do ten sit-ups. When I could do ninety sit-ups, I scored ten goals."

The scouting combine was held for the first time in 1993 in the basement of a hotel in Toronto. The NHL Central Scouting Bureau oversaw and designed the event to assess how well prospects will fare in the pro game. The modern process includes twenty-minute interviews with each team, as well as a battery of strength and endurance tests that measure everything from body fat to the height of a prospect's vertical jump, agility and reaction during shuttle runs, core control and reach while balancing on one leg and fatigue after cycling.

Roberts said he failed every physical test administered before he was picked by the Flames in the first round in 1984. He believes the cycling tests, which are used to measure the prospects' endurance, should be dropped from the regimen.

"The testing on the bike is really irrelevant, and it's torture for the players," he said.

As an eighteen-year-old, Andrew Ference did not receive an invitation to the NHL scouting combine. He was so disappointed at being snubbed that he wrote a letter to Pittsburgh general manager Craig Patrick a month before the 1997 draft and enclosed the results of fitness tests he had conducted for him at the University of Alberta.

"Recently, the Central Scouting Bureau conducted physical testing for selected draft-eligible players," the letter began. "Since I was not invited, I can only assume that Central Scouting believes that their current ratings accurately reflect my position with other players eligible for the upcoming NHL draft. Central Scouting has proven very inaccurate in the past, and this is no exception. I believe, without a doubt, that I will play in the National Hockey League."

Desperate for a chance, Ference sent copies to the general managers of all the other NHL teams, and shortly after that, he was chosen by the Penguins with the 208th pick. Of the thirty-eight players taken after him, only three had lengthy careers and none persevered anywhere nearly as long as Ference.

"I had a really good junior career and a lot of success, and I was frustrated about the way the NHL's scouting system worked," Ference said. "I wrote almost out of desperation because I felt I needed some way or another to get my foot in the door. If I didn't do that, then what? Just fade off into the sunset?"

Despite being a relatively modest five-foot-eleven and 185 pounds, Ference cobbled together a noteworthy career. He won a Stanley Cup with Boston in 2011 and was named the Oilers' fourteenth captain after signing a four-year free-agent deal in 2013.

A fitness fanatic, he supplements offseason training with other activities that keep him in shape, occasionally even training with triathletes and cross-country and downhill skiers. On any given day, he can be found leading free exercise classes, running trails in Edmonton's North Saskatchewan River Valley, hopscotching across rocks in a creek bed, paddling a kayak or pedaling a mountain bike.

"I like what other sports offer me," Ference said. "I don't touch a lot of heavy weights. What I do is more about natural, powerful body movements that are more dynamic than concentrating on any one muscle.

"Running stairs is probably my go-to exercise, if I had to choose one. And in summer, I pick the steepest hill I can find to pedal because I'll never feel that tired in a hockey game. It teaches me to deal with tired legs."

Ference said players report to camp in far better condition today than they did when he entered the NHL. There used to be a huge gap between the ones who were physically fit and those that weren't. "Nowadays, good results are simply expected," he said. "It is much harder to separate yourself from the group. Everyone is performing at a higher rate."

That drive to be in top shape is relatively new to hockey. The great goalie

Gump Worsley was nearly as famous for his ample girth as he was for his heroics in backstopping the Canadiens to Stanley Cup championships in 1965, 1966, 1968 and 1969. Accused once by Rangers' coach Phil Watson of having a beer belly, Worsley responded, "That just goes to show you what he knows. I only drink Johnnie Walker."

Gretzky was a bare wisp who disliked lifting weights. Grant Fuhr had a cocaine addiction when he played in net for some of Edmonton's great teams in the 1980s. And Gretzky's on-ice bodyguard, Dave Semenko, was not terribly keen on exercise.

"It was old school in the 1970s," Barrie Stafford, who spent twenty-eight seasons as the Oilers' head equipment man, said. "Players used to come into training camp to get into shape. Today, they take very little time off, and training is a big part of what they do. They have nutritionists and strength coaches and it has pretty much become a full-time job.

"In the old days, I used to have two or three guys that would smoke a cigarette between periods. The stakes have changed."

A seven-time All-Star who won five Stanley Cups with the Oilers and one with the Rangers, Kevin Lowe said attitudes around offseason conditioning began to change around 1979 or 1980. "Mark Messier and I enjoyed doing it, but I remember one older veteran saying to us, 'What are you trying to do by keeping in shape? Embarrass us?'" Lowe said.

Now vice chairman of the Oilers Entertainment Group, Lowe ran, rode a bicycle and lifted weights to stay fit. He admires the dedication young players are showing today, and he admits to being envious of resources at their disposal.

"The difference is that it's what you have to do now if you expect to play," he said. "The only way to get a leg up is to work harder than anyone else."

Best known as Gretzky's bodyguard in both Edmonton and Los Angeles, Marty McSorley played in the NHL for six teams over nineteen seasons. He won Stanley Cups with the Great One in 1987 and 1988, and McSorley said he never recalls much importance being placed on physical fitness. A 230-pound forward and defenceman, McSorley accumulated 3,381 penalty minutes in his career, ranking fourth in NHL history in that category.

"Glen Sather used to kick me out of the weight room in 1987," said Mc-Sorley, who lives in Los Angeles and is married to a former beach-volleyball player. "He used to tell me, 'Don't lift any weights. You're going to lose your speed and flexibility.'

"Now look what they have the kids do today."

Today's game isn't about getting ahead of the competition. It is about staying there. Dave Lumley, a forward who won Stanley Cups with the Oilers in 1984 and 1985, said players then spent precious few hours worrying about conditioning.

In 1979–80, his first full season in the NHL, Lumley scored twenty goals and had fifty-eight points. He followed up that performance with a summer spent partying on Cape Cod, returning to Edmonton just before training camp.

"You know that extra twenty-five pounds that was supposed to help me in the corners?" he said. "I had to be able to get to the corners first for them to help me."

After a strong showing as a rookie, Lumley had seven goals and nine assists in his sophomore campaign.

"I was in the doghouse the whole year. But I had the best tan in the NHL," Lumley said.

Early in the 1981–82 season, Lumley set a franchise record that still stands by putting together a streak during which he scored at least one goal in twelve straight games. He had fifteen goals and twelve assists during that span—nearly doubling his points total from the preceding season. On December 19, he had the single best game of his career against the Minnesota North Stars, collecting three goals and three assists. As luck would have it, he was only the game's second star. Gretzky was the first.

"The little weasel had seven points that night," Lumley said.

IN CONNOR'S FIRST SUMMER WORKING WITH ROBERTS, THE VETERAN TRAINER deliberately took things slowly. He and his staff held him back, even limiting Connor's weight lifting. At the time, they didn't feel he was capable of lifting heavy amounts. Roberts's first goal was to get McDavid into a routine and make sure he understood that his fitness was a long-term proposition.

"My whole philosophy was to not try to do it in two and a half months," Roberts said. "It was something that we would be working on in some way for four years. It definitely was a process getting him into a program, but he became highly dedicated to it."

Roberts and his staff take a holistic approach to conditioning, which includes teaching players everything from how to rehydrate after training sessions, to what and how to eat, to how to rest, to the way they should present themselves off the ice.

"There's a whole lot more to it than just being a hockey player," Roberts said. "Nowadays, the game has become younger, and if you are not paying attention to all of these things, you find yourself fighting for a roster spot when you're in your early thirties. Connor is as good as he is because he made a commitment to things outside the rink—to lifestyle, longevity and success."

During the summer, it's not unusual for different groups of NHL players to work out under Roberts's watch, with Stamkos, Neal and McDavid clanking weights in the fitness centre as others participate in drills on the ice at the La Brier Family Arena. At the same time that rock music reverberates from the weight room, the air in the rink fills with a *kish-kish* sound as players streak past on thin steel blades.

Time and again, they skate, then drive the puck down the ice at blistering speed, their bodies shifting to and fro, clouds of steam billowing above them with each hard breath. The drills are similar to those kids do in cold, dank rinks across North America each winter, but pros perform them at warp speed.

From a modest starting point, McDavid began to beef up incrementally as he worked out with Roberts. On September 20, 2012, the night he made his debut with the Otters as a fifteen-year-old, McDavid measured five-foot-eleven and weighed 175 pounds. He was six feet tall and 182 pounds by the time the puck dropped for the 2013–14 season, and six-foot-one and 187 pounds by the start of his final season in the OHL.

But, despite all his progress, Connor's toughest summer was still ahead of him.

LISTED AT SIX-FOOT-ONE AND 190 POUNDS WHEN HE SHOWED UP IN EDMONTON IN JULY 2015, McDavid returned to train with Roberts for four more weeks after his time at the Oilers rookie camp. Roberts wanted to see Connor closer to two hundred pounds before he played in his first NHL game, but time was short—their training sessions had to conclude before the beginning of Connor's first official NHL training camp.

The workouts became so intense that McDavid needed to consume 4,500 to 5,000 calories per day to maintain his energy. He ate whole organic foods, and had a serving of protein, carbohydrates, fat and fiber at each meal.

In the months leading up to his first season with the Oilers, McDavid arrived by seven fifteen in the morning each weekday at the fitness centre at St. Andrew's that Roberts uses as his summer base. After dining on oatmeal, eggs and bacon or salmon, all prepared by a chef, Connor headed for the weight room for as long as two hours. When he was finished there, he joined a handful of fellow players in ninety-minute on-ice training sessions every other day.

The training didn't stop when he left the gym. Two mornings a week,

Connor visited an organic grocery with Roberts's other clients. With help from a holistic nutritionist, they shopped carefully to make sure they were eating properly. During the week, a chef and four assistants prepared eighty to one hundred meals per day to serve to some of Roberts' clients, before making box lunches and dinners for them to take home. But when the players weren't being catered to, Roberts and his team wanted to make sure that they had the skills to prepare the right sorts of food for themselves; anything less would counteract the work they were doing each day.

McDavid said his family has always been careful about what they ate, so it was not hard for him to shop properly. But, just like everyone else, on the odd day, he would eat something that he was not supposed to. When Connor lived in Erie with the Cataldes, Bob would occasionally hide vegetables in pasta and rice and other dishes he served him. Like most teenagers, Connor was not terribly fond of veggies. "I'm calling Gary Roberts right now and telling on you," Catalde would tease.

"Everyone loves pizza and wings, but that's the kind of stuff you have to look out for," McDavid said. "It's not much of a problem because I enjoy eating healthy. But every now and then I have a cheat day."

Most days it was eleven-thirty in the morning before McDavid returned home, legs heavy and muscles screaming. The weekend didn't bring much respite, either. On Saturdays, McDavid would do light aerobics that would keep his heart in the range of 140 to 150 beats per minute. He never stopped, not even when he was in south Florida for the draft. There, he would wake early each morning and exercise in his room. Sundays were the only days on which he would rest.

There was never any complaining, though; Connor understood that the fitness training was what needed to happen before his real work in the NHL could begin. For three long summers, Connor and Roberts had been laying the groundwork for exactly this situation.

"When I first met Gary he scared me, but I was young then," McDavid said. "I was just hitting puberty when I started, so some of that growth was going to occur naturally. But the hard work I've done with Gary has speeded up the process. I've never felt this strong and this powerful."

ONE DAY NEAR THE END OF JULY, FOUR SUMMERS AFTER HE BEGAN TRAINING WITH Roberts, Connor used a trap bar to dead lift 405 pounds. A few weeks later, he did three repetitions at 455. At the end of August, McDavid's percentage of body fat, which Roberts determines by pinching his skin with eleven calipers, was 12 percent. Roberts considers anything between 10 and 12 percent ideal.

"As long as I've been doing this, I don't think I have ever had a player below nine percent," he said. "You want guys to have a little fat on their body. You don't want them to be too lean."

Growing bigger and stronger under Roberts's training only made Connor's skills all the more formidable. "I don't know that this training will change what I do too much," he said. "I'm never going to be much of a physical presence. For me, it's more about taking my strength and finding a way to use it as an advantage."

McDavid's greatest weapons have always been his speed and his ability to handle the puck. From the time he was nine years old, McDavid had trained with Joe Quinn, a Toronto-area hockey instructor, to sharpen those skills.

Quinn is a renowned stickhandling coach; his lessons are used all across the league. In the summer of 2015, McDavid was one of thirty NHL players invited to participate in special clinics with Quinn, skating with a puck around, through, under and over a device Quinn had invented called the Power Edge Pro. McDavid was the youngest player there, and easily the fastest.

"The first time most players attack the circuit they're skating at thirty to forty kilometres an hour," Quinn said. "By the second or third time, they're down to seven to ten kilometers per hour. I expect them to fly right through it, because Connor can. He doesn't slow down."

Nor would he.

"I think as you progress, you realize more and more that the training is a necessity," Connor said. "There's just a point when you know you need to start going at it, and you need to get it done."

As the summer drew to a close, a new Connor emerged. While Edmonton as a whole had been gearing up for the arrival of its new favourite son, Connor had taken the time to complete his personal metamorphosis. Already, his time in rookie camp had endeared him to thousands of fans ready to see him don the Oilers' blue and orange. Edmonton had been ready and waiting for Connor for a long time; it seemed that Connor was finally ready for Edmonton.

FIVE

AFTER A SUMMER OF WORK WITH GARY ROBERTS, CONNOR McDAVID RETURNED TO Edmonton on September 8. Late in the afternoon two days later, he boarded a plane with the rest of the Oilers' rookies for a flight to Penticton, British Columbia.

In 2011, the Edmonton Oilers, Vancouver Canucks, Calgary Flames and Winnipeg Jets had established the Penticton Young Stars Classic, a tournament in which each team sends their rookies to the city of forty thousand to give prospects an opportunity to play before the start of training camp and to give fans in an out-of-the-way place a chance to see NHL hockey.

At dusk on September 10, Rick Forster sat outside his hotel room watching the sun set over Okanagan Lake, a glistening fjord carved out of the Rocky Mountains where fishermen cast for sockeye salmon and keep an eye out for Okopogo, a sea serpent around which tales have been spun for nearly a century. A retired realtor, Forster had driven nearly one thousand kilometres from central Alberta to see the tournament.

"I thought about coming here for a few years, but never got around to it," Forster said, unbuttoning the light jacket he was wearing to reveal an orange number ninety-seven T-shirt. For him and thousands of other fans that made the pilgrimage, this year was different. "Where else can you get to see Connor McDavid for ten dollars?"

A season-ticket holder for more than three decades, Forster is a throwback to the era during which the Oilers were capturing Stanley Cups one after another.

"This sort of takes me back to those amazing days," Forster said as he sat in front of the Black Sea Motel. Reggae music drifted over from a restaurant next door where patrons were sipping mojitos, downing Malpeque oysters and dining on pistachio-crusted mahimahi. "So many hockey people who know say McDavid is the real thing. It's scary how good the team could be. I think the Oilers are going to win a Stanley Cup within a couple years."

The next night, the Oilers' prodigy would play against the Vancouver rookies in front of a full house at the South Okanagan Events Centre. Edmonton's remaining games on Saturday against the Flames and on Monday morning against the Jets were also sold out. Approximately sixteen thousand fans had attended six games at the Young Stars Classic the preceding year, but this time, twenty thousand tickets were snapped up in the first few hours they were made available.

Along Penticton's pretty lakefront strip there were no rooms available in the hotels and motels, and the neighbouring communities were no more promising. There were so few rooms available that travelers were referred to accommodations ninety minutes away. A jazz festival and dragon boat regatta were also being staged that weekend, but the hockey games—or more accurately, McDavid—were the biggest draw. Bus companies brought tour groups from Alberta and a small contingent of Edmonton fans drove twelve hours one way to see Connor play.

"We knew right off that things were going to be different," Carla Seddon, the event centre's director of marketing, said. "We had tour bus companies calling from Edmonton asking for blocks of seats before they even went on sale."

Seddon said more than ninety passes—about twice as many as usual—were set aside for journalists and hockey scouts for the practice games, which typically featured only one or two players who were likely to earn a regular-season spot on each team.

The following morning, fans and players from rival teams crowded around a rink at a hockey academy beside the South Okanagan Events Centre to watch McDavid participate in the pregame skate. At times, he raced through drills so fast that the sleeves on his jersey rippled in the breeze.

"If you're an Oilers fan, there hasn't been much to cheer about, but I hope they're about to turn the corner now," said Don McKee, who months earlier had moved to Penticton from Edmonton to accept a job. "We had gotten used to winning, and what happened over the years really soured the city. We really needed this."

After an hour-long practice, McDavid filed off the ice, stopping to sign autographs for fans waiting in a roped-off area. Security officers equipped with walkie-talkies stood guard in case the crowd got out of control.

Pausing on his way into the dressing room, Connor stopped to have his picture taken with Caleb Syvenky. The seven-year-old was wearing a McDavid T-shirt and an Oilers cap.

"I wouldn't be surprised if he was wearing orange and blue underwear," his father, Greg, a magician in nearby Kelowna, said. It was the fifth year he had brought his hockey-crazed son to see the budding stars, but this time it felt different.

"It's the only time Connor will probably ever be here, so Caleb's teacher let me pull him out of school today," Greg said. "For me, it's just sound parenting."

Later that evening, in what turned out to be the only game number ninety-seven played at the Young Stars Classic, McDavid had a goal and an assist in an 8–2 thumping of the Canucks. The goal he scored was the Oilers' seventh, and although it barely trickled into the net after caroming off a defenceman, the crowd cheered nonetheless.

At the beginning of the game against the Canucks, Connor won the faceoff, stole pucks from two opposing players, connected with one of his teammates on a perfect pass and barely missed a shot as he charged toward the net. He did all that in the first thirty-five seconds.

Throughout the rest of a performance that Edmonton general manager Peter Chiarelli called "above average," McDavid showed flashes of occasional brilliance and survived a hard hit along the boards by Jake Virtanen, a bruising winger who had played alongside him on Team Canada's winning squad at the 2015 World Junior Tournament.

Most of the discussion afterward centred around Virtanen's crushing blow during McDavid's third shift. Vancouver fans roared as McDavid went crashing to the ice. For a second, he seemed surprised. As he climbed to his feet, Virtanen gave him what looked like an apologetic pat.

"I think Connor is going to have to get used to that, if he isn't already," Gerry Fleming, who was coaching the Oilers' rookies, said. "He's a good player and there are going to be guys who come at him hard and that's the way it's going to be."

McDavid seemed unfazed after the game.

"It's hockey, and stuff's going to happen," he said. Below his left eye, where he had been slapped with an opponent's glove, a welt was forming on his cheek. "It's just part of the game."

The hit Virtanen delivered was brassy but clean, but it remained a point of tension for the duration of the contest. It led to Virtanen taking a retaliatory check from Oilers winger Mitch Moroz that was followed by offsetting roughing penalties being issued to Virtanen and Edmonton's Darnell Nurse.

"I lined Virtanen up the next time we were on the ice," said Moroz, who played the previous year for Oklahoma City in the American Hockey

League. "It wasn't too bad, but it kind of set the tone for the game. I had to let Virtanen know he couldn't be doing that."

McDavid skated at both practices the next two days, but the Oilers chose to hold him out of the remaining games at the Young Stars Classic. Chiarelli broke the news to him on Sunday morning, explaining that, unlike the majority of the other first-year players, Connor did not have to earn a place on the team.

"He wasn't very happy," the Oilers' general manager said. "I told him, 'Hey, you're going to play a lot of hockey for us this year.'"

McDavid, dressed in a suit, watched while his teammates played. It wasn't often, if ever, that had been directed to sit while healthy.

"You're a hockey player. You want to play whenever you get a chance," McDavid said. "At the end of the day it's not my decision. It's their choice. That's that."

THE OILERS' ROOKIES FLEW BACK TO EDMONTON ON MONDAY MORNING HAVING LOST only one of their three games in Penticton, an overtime defeat at the hands of Winnipeg. Upon returning, they immediately readied themselves for a contest on Wednesday night against Canada's defending collegiate national champions.

Hockey and history seep through the bricks of the Clare Drake Arena. Team pictures dating back to 1909 are displayed in the lobby of the home rink at the University of Alberta, and fifty-six championship banners hang from the ceiling and line the walls. Well-worn and cozy, for a quarter of a century the old barn had played host to an annual preseason exhibition game between Edmonton's rookies and the University of Alberta Golden Bears. This year would be the first time that the game wasn't played there, though. It had been moved from its original 2,700-seat venue to Rexall Place because the campus rink was too small to accommodate the fans.

McDavid was the cause of that, and a near sellout was expected.

"It's a good thing Connor is playing," Chiarelli quipped. "Otherwise, there would be a riot."

The suggestion to move the game from the arena named after Canada's most successful college hockey coach was made early in 2015 by Stan Marple, the general manager of the Golden Bears. Each of the last two exhibitions between the teams had attracted standing-room audiences.

"I figured there were a lot of faithful Oilers fans that would like to see the prospects play and had been unable to because of the limited capacity at our place," Marple said. "I also didn't think it would hurt to expose more people to our program."

In return for moving the game, the Golden Bears received the money they would have earned had it been played on their home ice. The team splits gate receipts with the Oilers Community Foundation and uses the funds to help pay for scholarships and the salaries of its staff. Even though the game was moved to the bigger arena, only a limited number of tickets, priced at thirty dollars, were still available on game day.

Although they were a college team, the Golden Bears were likely to pose an interesting challenge. Their roster was full of players who had completed their junior careers. In the previous twenty-four games between the university team and the pro rookies, the Golden Bears had won thirteen.

But this was a deeper rookie squad than usual for Edmonton, and it was led by an electrifying prospect.

"Everybody in Canada knows Connor McDavid," said Kruise Reddick, a twenty-five-year-old centre for the university who played five seasons with the Tri-City Americans of the WHL.

Thomas Carr, a fellow twenty-five-year-old defenceman, was also looking forward to confronting the prodigy on the ice.

"I heard about him when I was playing in juniors, and I think he was only twelve or thirteen at the time," Carr, who played three seasons with the Medicine Hat Tigers in the WHL, said. "The fact that the hype hasn't died down shows how exceptional he is. As an Oilers fan, I'm excited, too."

The morning of the annual exhibition game dawned bright and chilly as temperatures in subarctic Edmonton continued their September slide. Trees were already ablaze in autumnal hues, which was simultaneously comforting and disconcerting to the city's million-odd hardy residents. Canadian Thanksgiving was only weeks away, but a cold, harsh winter would soon arrive after that.

When the doors at Rexall Place opened, spectators dressed in Oilers garb began to pour in. The lineup to get in snaked several hundred yards out the door and over the pedestrian bridge that spanned 118th Avenue. The backup was partly caused by X-ray security units newly installed at all NHL arenas, but mostly it was due to the number of fans eager to see the young star.

After driving two hours to Edmonton from rural Drayton Valley, Bill Swartz and Travis Hill were eager to settle into their seats.

"Everyone that's here tonight is here to see one guy," Swartz said.

Some fans swarmed the Oilers' souvenir store in search of McDavid sweaters and T-shirts, while others lined up to bid on memorabilia that was being sold as part of a silent auction put on by the Oilers Community Foundation.

Holding hands with his two young children, Dan Strawnychy of Edmonton headed into the rink.

"I think we all know who we're here to see," he said.

Applause erupted when McDavid's name was introduced, and from the moment the puck dropped, he had fourteen thousand fans on the edge of their seats. They roared in the first period when he broke in on goalie Luke Siemens, shifted the puck from his forehand and failed by an inch to tuck a backhand by him. They gasped when Siemens kicked the shot away with the tip of his skate as he lay sprawled across the net.

From there, anticipation grew with each shift. Midway through the first period, McDavid ignited a tic-tac-toe play, firing a pass to winger Braden Christoffer at the side of the Golden Bears' net. Christoffer redirected the puck to Leon Draisaitl, who scored. Then, just three minutes later, Mc-David collected a puck loose behind the Golden Bears' net during a power play and flicked it backwards to Alexis Loiseau through a defender's legs. Poised in front of the crease, Loiseau deposited the puck past the helpless goalie for a 2–1 Oilers lead.

Later, in explaining the blind pass he executed while facing in the opposite direction, McDavid said he never saw Loiseau, but figured somebody might be free after doing a little math in his head. He said he could feel one defender bearing down on him and saw another shadowing Draisaitl.

"I knew we had a man advantage and, as I thought about the numbers, I figured a guy should be open," McDavid said. "I just tried to throw it out there and, honestly, I got lucky. Loiseau made a spectacular play by burying the shot."

After the Bears closed the gap to 4–3 in the third period, the momentum looked like it might be turning. But McDavid was not done. Late in the game, he took off to create a two-on-one before finding Cole Sanford in front of the net for an easy goal. The Oilers won, 6–3.

"Any time he has the puck on his stick, he makes plays," said Sanford, a 159-pound winger who played three seasons for Medicine Hat. "He glides out there faster than most guys can skate."

Draisaitl, a forward from Germany drafted third overall by the Oilers in 2014, had a four-point night, collecting a goal and three assists.

"For that many fans to come out for a rookie game is pretty incredible," Draisaitl, who had taken the day before the game off to renew his visa in Calgary, said. Playing on McDavid's power-play unit had been a breeze. "He is so smart and so smooth. He makes it pretty easy for you."

McDavid had three assists, logged seventeen minutes and fifty-eight seconds on the ice and was chosen the second star of the game.

"I thought my game was a little better tonight," he said quietly. He noticed a lot of fans wearing McDavid jerseys.

"It's special to look around and see a bunch of ninety-sevens out there," he said.

As fans exited a club area on the lower level of Rexall Place, they stopped and gawked at news reporters waiting outside the Oilers' dressing room. Taking in the scene, one little boy wearing an orange number ninety-seven T-shirt began squawking like a parrot.

"Connor McDavid, Connor McDavid, Connor McDavid," he yelled. "Connor McDavid is the best."

The game against the Golden Bears marked the conclusion of the Oilers' rookie camp. On Friday, Connor would report for his first official NHL training camp.

"I'm excited, all the guys are talking about it," McDavid said. "I'm certainly looking forward to get it going."

CONNOR McDAVID BEGAN TRAINING CAMP ON SEPTEMBER 17. ON HIS WAY INTO THE dressing room at Rexall Place, he passed through shiny metallic sliding doors painted with the Oilers logo and walked straight down a hallway toward a display case that contained gleaming replicas of the five Stanley Cups the team captured between 1984 and 1990. Along the wall to his right there were pictures of Jordan Eberle, Andrew Ference, Taylor Hall, Ryan Nugent-Hopkins and Matt Hendricks; to his left there were reproductions of the Conn Smythe and Hart Memorial Trophies that had been awarded to the leaders of hockey's last great dynasty. It seemed like a million years since Wayne Gretzky and Mark Messier, barely out of their teens, ran roughshod over the league.

A young thoroughbred not unlike the one that came before him, McDavid made a slight turn around the Stanley Cups and stepped into the unpretentious area where Oilers players dress. Success had been so relatively fleeting for the team that two years earlier items that paid homage to the past were banished from the locker room, including pictures and plaques of those legendary Cup winners.

Sitting in front of his dressing stall, McDavid began taking stock of the players around him. They were a puzzling bunch. In pro sports, futility usually breeds prosperity, but it seems not in Edmonton. There had been few signs of progress in the past few years, even though at one point the Oilers had the first pick in the draft for three consecutive years. To make it more befuddling, each one of those draftees—Hall, Nugent-Hopkins and Yakupov—had performed reasonably well.

In 2014–15, the Oilers were plagued by the worst goaltending in the league. They tried to improve in the offseason by adding Cam Talbot and Anders Nilsson. But their defence had been so porous that an overhaul was needed there, too. In an attempt to get better, they traded for Eric Gryba and Griffin Reinhart, then signed Andrej Sekera, a veteran who had played nearly five hundred games for three teams in the previous eight seasons. To add depth, they also added winger Lauri Korpikoski and centre Mark Letestu, a hard-working little guy who grew up in Elk Point, a small town in northeast Alberta that once had been an outpost for fur traders.

McDavid's arrival prompted speculation that he might be invited to live with Ference and his wife, Krista, and their two young daughters. It was easy to imagine. The thirty-six-year-old defenceman had started his career playing for Prince Albert in the Western Hockey League in 1997, the same year McDavid was born. Appointing Ference to be the teenager's guardian would make sense and was certainly not without precedent. As an eighteen-year-old with the Pittsburgh Penguins, Sidney Crosby moved in with Mario Lemieux and his wife, Nathalie, and stayed five years. When he was nineteen and breaking in with the Penguins in 1984, Lemieux had done the same thing, living in in the suburbs with a couple, Tom and Nancy Matthews. More recently, Erik Karlsson moved in with Daniel Alfredsson and his wife, Bibi, in his first season in Ottawa, and Eichel, chosen directly behind McDavid in the NHL draft, found lodging in Buffalo with teammate Matt Coulson and his wife, Alicia.

The belief was that Ference, the team captain and winner of the NHL's King Clancy Memorial Trophy in 2014 for leadership and community contributions, could provide Connor with a steadying influence. In recent years, Ference had become the first pro athlete to march in Edmonton's pride parade, had served as a mentor to underprivileged inner-city youth, and had counselled gay and transgender high school students.

An undersized defenceman who helped the Bruins win their sixth Stanley Cup in 2011, Ference returned to his hometown as a free agent prior to the 2013 season. On the ice, he is resilient and tenacious. He is much beloved in Edmonton and well respected throughout the league— perhaps with the exception of Montreal. During the NHL playoffs in 2011, Ference gave Canadiens fans the middle finger after slapping a puck past Carey Price in the third game of the opening series. The celebration wasn't premeditated: Ference had never scored more than six goals in any of his fifteen seasons.

"If I played on the ice the way I am off it, I never would have made it," said Ference, who initially blamed the incident on a glove malfunction and later apologized. "You have to have an alter ego. You have to have a nut side and balance it."

Ference embodies that balance better than most. In addition to his community outreach and hockey career, he is an environmental activist, a student at the Harvard Extension School and a partner in a venture capital fund that invests in start-up companies that use sustainable technology. If Connor were to live with him, Ference would encourage McDavid to broaden his interests.

"When it comes to hockey, there isn't much, if anything, that I could teach him," Ference said, "but when it comes to real-life stuff there are things I can share. I try to tell young players that hockey doesn't have to be the be-all and end-all. If a brain surgeon can have outside interests and hobbies, hockey players should be able to. There is no excuse not to."

The other option for Connor was to move in with Hall, the team's best player and a fellow client of the Orr Hockey Group. Since being taken first in the 2010 NHL draft, Hall had finished in the top ten in scoring twice and reached eighty points in his third season. As dominant a player as Hall had become, though, he had yet to take on a significant leadership role. It was suggested that placing McDavid under his wing would help Hall grow as a person and a player, easing his transition to a team leader.

As a kid, Hall spent hours on a rink his father flooded behind their house in southern Alberta, skating around a big poplar tree in the middle that he imagined was Scott Stevens and imitating the moves of his favourite player, Jarome Iginla.

"I didn't have any brothers and sisters, so I usually was out there doodling around by myself," Hall said. "It's where I really got better and learned to play the game. I am so grateful to my dad."

A wide receiver and defensive back who could run forty yards in 4.5 seconds, Steve Hall was selected by the Edmonton Eskimos in the fourth round of the 1983 CFL draft. He reported to camp with Warren Moon, but was dealt to Winnipeg before he ever caught one of the Hall of Fame quarterback's spirals. Stops in Toronto and Ottawa followed before a testy hamstring led Hall to call it a career.

Steve settled in Calgary and became a brakeman and driver for the Canadian bobsled team, during which time Taylor was born. Although Steve wasn't a hockey player, when nobody else was around, he would play goalie for his son on the backyard rink.

"I did it until I got a puck between the eyes, and my wife told me I had to stop," he said. "I'm a brave guy. I would drive a bobsled at one hundred miles per hour, but getting hit with a puck wasn't fun."

Taylor started playing organized hockey at five, but it wasn't until much later, after countless hours of skating in the backyard, that the future NHL star began to shine.

At sixteen, Hall joined the Windsor Spitfires of the Ontario Hockey League. The team drafted him second overall in 2007, and less than a year later, he was in a *Sports Illustrated* feature that profiled athletes poised to become stars.

"Every mom thinks their kid is the best, but once he hit juniors, I knew he was special," Taylor's mother, Kim Strba, said.

In his first season with the Spitfires, Hall scored a team-high forty-five goals and was named the Canadian Hockey League's Rookie of the Year. Over the next two years, he led the Spitfires to consecutive Memorial Cup titles, and a little more than a month after the Spitfires won their second championship, the Oilers chose Taylor in the NHL draft. He was in the lineup on opening night when Edmonton took on the Calgary Flames in October 2010, and never spent a day in the minor leagues.

Despite playing on a team that consistently struggled, Hall had done well. It hadn't been easy physically or emotionally for him, however. He missed seventy-seven games with injuries in his first four seasons and had to constantly adjust to the Oilers' coaching carousel. As excited as everybody was to have Todd McLellan take over, he would be Hall's fifth head coach in as many years.

"It's hard not to get upset when you are constantly losing," Hall said. "You take it personally."

Even as the Oilers struggled to a 29–44–9 record in 2013–14, Hall was superb. Along with a career-high eighty points, he finished in a sixth-place tie with Toronto's Phil Kessel in scoring, was eighth overall with fifty-three assists and fifth in the league with a scoring average of 1.07 points per game.

"We were getting out-chanced every night, but Taylor was able to put up those numbers," said Dallas Eakins, the Oilers' head coach who was fired thirty-one games into 2014–15. "For him to have that kind of a season was impressive."

Eakins wondered if Hall and some of the team's other top prospects were served well by being asked to play immediately in the NHL. Nugent-Hopkins and Yakupov, the number-one picks in 2011 and 2012, also by-passed the minor leagues as Hall had and Connor was expected to.

"It was unfortunate for the guys in Edmonton," said Eakins, who is now coaching the Anaheim Ducks' AHL affiliate in San Diego. "All those players with little experience had the weight of the world on their shoulders. We didn't have time to let them grow."

AS CONNOR GAZED AROUND THE DRESSING ROOM, HE FOUND A FRIENDLY FACE IN Darnell Nurse. The two played against one another for three seasons in the OHL and had been teammates in 2015, when Team Canada won a gold medal at the International Ice Hockey Federation Junior World Championships.

The seventh player taken in the first round in 2013, Nurse is an impressive physical specimen at six foot four and 215 pounds. His uncle, Donovan McNabb, was a quarterback who led the Philadelphia Eagles to five NFC titles games and one Super Bowl. While attending Syracuse University, McNabb became linked with Darnell's aunt, Raquel, a four-year starting point guard who was twice named MVP of the school's women's basketball team. In 1997, she was chosen the top athlete at the school over McNabb, who went on to throw for more than forty thousand yards and 250 touchdowns in the NFL. On top of that, Nurse's father, Richard, was a third-round draft pick of the Hamilton Tiger Cats who played thirteen seasons in the CFL, and his mother, Cathy, was a standout basketball player at McMaster University. Darnell also has an older sister, Tamika, who played basketball for Canada's Junior National Team, as well as a younger sibling, Kia, who is the star of the Canadian Women's National Basketball Team. A six-foot guard attending the University of Connecticut, Kia scored thirty-three points and won most valuable player honours while leading Canada to its first gold medal in an international competition at the 2015 Pan American Games. As a reward, she was chosen to be Canada's flag bearer in the closing ceremonies.

"It was great to grow up in an environment like that," said Nurse, who also has a cousin, Sarah, who plays hockey at the University of Wisconsin. "They all had a big influence in my life."

Nurse began skating when he was very young, and chose hockey over basketball and football when he was thirteen. Years of hard work and determination led him to the NHL and put him in a position to join McDavid as one of the Oilers' top prospects. At the end of their junior careers, they faced one another in the OHL Western Conference finals, where McDavid's Erie Otters eliminated Nurse's Sault Ste. Marie Greyhounds in six games. Now they were together under the same roof, Nurse fighting for a roster spot, McDavid all but assured one.

Nurse's role would be different from Connor's, however. His size and skill make him formidable on defence. And that was something the team desperately needed.

In 2014–15, the Oilers missed the playoffs for the ninth straight year. They ranked twenty-sixth out of thirty teams in scoring and last in the league with 283 goals allowed. Their inability to stop other teams caused Peter Chiarelli, the Oilers' new general manager, to make a deal for goaltender Talbot on the second day of the 2015 draft. Edmonton gave up three picks, receiving Talbot and a late-round pick in return.

The Rangers barely missed a beat when Talbot filled in for Henrik Lundqvist during the 2014–15 season. In fact, the twenty-eight-year-old from Ontario posted slightly better numbers than the injured superstar he replaced. Talbot went 21–9–4 with a 2.21 goals-against average, and his .926 save percentage was the seventh-best in the league. More important, he helped ensure that New York made the playoffs.

Talbot's arrival in Edmonton was eagerly anticipated. The Oilers had used a number of netminders with limited success in preceding years, including Devan Dubnyk and a pair of aging Russians in Nikolai Khabibulin and Ilya Byrzgalov. Most recently, they had placed their hopes on the shoulders of Ben Scrivens.

Scrivens was an Ivy Leaguer who met his wife, Jenny, while both played goalie for their respective NCAA teams at Cornell. He had been obtained by Edmonton from the Los Angeles Kings on January 15, 2014, and after joining the Oilers posted a 9–11 record and .916 save percentage the rest of the way. On the night of January 29, just two weeks after he had landed in Alberta, Scrivens set an NHL record for most saves in a regular-season game when he turned away fifty-nine shots in a victory over San Jose. Scrivens' performance had Rexall Place buzzing and amazed McLellan, who was then coach of the Sharks.

"He was tremendous," McLellan said after the game. "He was the first, second and third star. If he wasn't, he deserved it. In all of my years in the league, I don't think I've seen anything like it."

Based on the strength of that performance and his play in subsequent games, the Oilers rewarded Scrivens with a two-year contract extension on March 3, 2014, worth $2.3 million per season. Hope for the future gave way to disappointment when Scrivens struggled in 2014–15, however. He won only fifteen of forty-one decisions and finished with a save percentage of .890, unacceptably low for the NHL.

During Scrivens' tenure as the Oilers' starter, spectators pitched jerseys onto the ice several times. Every time a sweater was tossed, Scrivens would retrieve it and use his stick to throw it back into the stands. One such incident in March 2014, during an embarrassing 8–1 loss to the rival Calgary Flames, prompted Scrivens to lash out at fans.

"You want to boo me? Go for it," Scrivens said. "You want to jeer me, call me every name; you're entitled to that. But when I see a jersey thrown out on the ice, you're not just disrespecting guys in the room, you're disrespecting all the great guys who played for this organization. It's a sacred thing for us."

At the opening of training camp, it was expected that the starting job was Talbot's to lose and that Scrivens would compete for the backup role with Nilsson, a towering Swede who had played in Russia the previous year. An unassuming guy who had played his college hockey at the University of Alabama–Huntsville, Talbot was excited to get the opportunity to be a starter in the NHL. His story was one of great perseverance. No one else wanted him, so he ended up at Alabama–Huntsville, one of only two NCAA Division I programs in the southern U.S.

"They were basically the first team to offer me a full scholarship," said Talbot, who grew up in Caledonia, a small town south of Hamilton in southern Ontario. "My family was not wealthy by any means, so getting a scholarship was important to me. It was an unusual place to go to play hockey, but once I went down there and saw the place and met people, it reassured me."

In his first two seasons, Talbot won only three of twenty-nine games. In his last year, despite facing a barrage of shots, he carried Alabama–Huntsville to a conference championship, and ranked fifth among NCAA goaltenders in save percentage. The thought of playing in the NHL never crossed his mind until late in that final season, however, and even then it was a fleeting thought.

"There were plenty of times when I was filled with self-doubt," Talbot said. "I was passed over in every draft and, even as a kid, I was never the best at my position in any age group. When things went wrong, it was always easy to question myself."

Talbot signed with the Rangers out of college, and then spent three seasons playing for the Connecticut Whale and Hartford Wolf Pack in the American Hockey League, and for the Greenville Road Warriors in the East Coast Hockey League. In 2013, he won the job with the Rangers as

Lundqvist's backup, and filled in admirably when the Swedish netminder suffered a neck injury the following season. Talbot leveraged that performance into his first shot at an NHL starting job.

"I feel more comfortable now than at any time in my whole career," Talbot said as the Oilers prepared to begin training camp. "But you can never take anything for granted. There are only thirty guys in the world that can start in this league, and only sixty spots if you include backups. You have to earn it."

Nilsson, whom the Oilers acquired in a summer trade from the Chicago Blackhawks, was a wild card tossed into the goalie race. At six-foot-five, he had the wingspan of a 747, and the twenty-five-year-old was coming off a successful campaign with Ak Bars Kazan of the Kontinental Hockey League. Nilsson had finished as the third best backstop in the KHL and took his team all the way to the championships. Nilsson's tryout in Edmonton wasn't his first taste of the NHL, though. He had played twenty-three games with the New York Islanders in parts of two NHL seasons, and had gone to play in the KHL after the Islanders attempted to send him back to the AHL.

"I didn't think that was going to help me develop my game, so I thought the best option was to go back to Europe and play in the highest league possible," he said. "I was lucky to end up with Kazan, because they had a very good team and great organization. It helped me a lot to play regularly, and I grew a lot as a goalie and as a person. Going there was a real big gamble, but it helped me achieve my goal of getting back to the NHL."

In a dressing room full of players with tattoos, Nilsson stood out. His right arm was covered with artwork, including two hockey sticks to celebrate his first professional contract, the longitude and latitude of his hometown, a clock that shows the birth year and time he was born and several renderings of the Virgin Mary. He was waiting until the offseason to add a tribute to his newborn son.

"I don't do them just for fun," Nilsson said. "I try to keep them meaningful."

His last move—to a foreign country where he did not speak the language—had been a leap of faith. As he joined McDavid at training camp, Nilsson hoped that impressing the Oilers would be easier.

AS PLAYERS JOSTLED AND MOVED ABOUT THE DRESSING ROOM, IT WAS HARD NOT TO notice the Oilers' burliest newcomer. Eric Gryba measured six-foot-four and weighed nearly 230 pounds, and was expected to bring toughness to a team in desperate need. But Edmonton got more than that in Gryba, who had spent the previous three seasons with Ottawa. They got a genuine character, who brings fun to the clubhouse.

For three years, Gryba had wielded one of the longest sticks in the league. He calls it Big Earl, just because. It is not unusual for a defenceman's stick to be lengthy, as a long stick helps them reach and control pucks. But even by those standards, Gryba's stick stands out. It was six to eight inches longer than those used by Letestu and Anton Lander, and made the one used by the rather slight Eberle look miniature.

Long before he ever put on skates, Gryba accompanied his dad on hunting trips in his native Saskatchewan. He was not yet two years old when his father strapped him into a carrier in his backpack and took him along. To keep him from being startled by gunshots, his mother stuffed little plugs in his ears. By the time he was five or six, he was put to use retrieving fowl gunned down by his father.

"We didn't have a bird dog," Gryba said.

Gryba played at Boston University for four years, during which time he won an NCAA championship and earned a business degree. He put that to use when he co-founded a company called Capital Waterfowling that manufactures duck- and goose-calling devices. A description on the company's website tells visitors, "When nature calls, you answer."

It didn't hurt that Gryba had a black beard that made him look like an NHL bad guy and a member of the cast of *Duck Dynasty*.

"That's just a coincidence," he said. "I didn't do it for effect."

The Oilers picked up Gryba in an off-season deal with the Senators for Travis Ewanyk and a fourth-round pick in the 2015 draft. In 2014–15, Gryba had established career-highs by playing in seventy-five games, recording a dozen assists and accumulating ninety-seven minutes in penalties.

When he learned he had been traded, Gryba was disappointed. When he found out he would be heading to the Oilers, he was pleased. They had Connor McDavid, a new head coach and general manager and a beautiful arena under construction.

"I thought it was a chance to play with a team that is on the rise and has unlimited potential," Gryba said. "It's exciting to be traded to a team like that."

Given the excitement that the players were feeling and the publicity surrounding all of the acquisitions, it was easy to overlook some of the quieter players, such as Letestu. A defensive-minded centre with a talent for taking faceoffs, the Oilers signed him as a free agent in the hopes that he could provide stability on a team flush with young centres. At twenty-two, Nugent-Hopkins was the oldest on the roster.

At thirty years old, Letestu was excited to return to the province in which he grew up, and where he met his wife, Brett, when they were in fourth grade. He spent three seasons playing in the Alberta Junior Hockey League with the Bonnyville Pontiacs before moving on to the University of Western Michigan for one year. Letestu never anticipated he would play in the NHL; he figured he would play college hockey, get a degree and get a job.

"I didn't believe this would ever happen," he said.

Letestu arrived for camp with 318 games under his belt. He had spent the previous four years in Columbus and had played in Pittsburgh in parts of three seasons before that. In Pittsburgh, he had played with Sidney Crosby. Now, his career seemed to be coming full circle. Letestu was entering training camp as a seasoned veteran, and it was likely that he was going to play with a rookie likened to Crosby—the kid across the room, Connor McDavid.

Of all the Oilers, the most enigmatic was probably Nail Yakupov. In his first three seasons in Edmonton, the left-handed right wing had been both the recipient of praise and the target of criticism. He led all NHL first-year players in 2012 with seventeen goals and finished in a tie for the rookie scoring title with Jonathan Huberdeau of the Florida Panthers. In the two seasons that followed, however, he totaled only twenty-four and thirty-three points and had finished a combined minus fifty-eight. That means the Oilers had given up fifty-eight more even-strength goals than they scored when he was on the ice.

Yakupov's speed and shooting ability excite fans, and his defensive lapses drive coaches batty. Dallas Eakins in particular appreciated his offensive skills but demanded that he become a better two-way player.

From the day he arrived in Edmonton, Yakupov was a fan favourite. As a teenager, he moved from Russia to Ontario to further his career, and had ended up being picked by the Sarnia Sting in the 2010 Canadian Hockey League import draft. He went on to score a McDavid-esque 170 points in 107 games, and then became the highest-drafted Muslim player in history when the Oilers chose him with the first overall pick in the 2012 draft.

That summer, in his first practice at rookie orientation camp, he was swarmed by autograph seekers and drew laughter from sports writers by pointing out that the Oilers' goalkeeper, Khabibulin, was the same age as his dad. When Yakupov was growing up, Pavel Bure had been his favorite player and, when he was older, Igor Larionov became his agent. Along with Viacheslav Fetisov, Larionov was instrumental in breaking the barrier that kept Soviet players from joining the NHL.

Always affable, Yakupov won the hearts of Edmontonians by rushing home after pregame skates to walk his dog and by showing remarkable generosity. More than once, he hopped out of his car at a stoplight to hand twenty dollars to a homeless person on the sidewalk. One time, he paid for a hotel room and bought a steak dinner at an upscale restaurant for a fellow who approached him on the street and asked for a few bucks for a cup of coffee.

"It's not that hard," Yakupov said. "For them, it's huge. For you, it is almost nothing. I think it's important to help people when they have a need."

After a difficult start in 2014–15, Yakupov had scored twenty points in his last twenty-eight games. It was hoped that he would blossom if he earned a position on the teenage sensation's right wing.

On the day that McDavid, Hall, Nurse, Talbot, Nilsson, Gryba, Letestu, Yakupov and the others reported for camp, the dressing room was full of optimism. The Oilers had suffered through nine losing seasons, but they also fielded an interesting roster full of skilled players, muckers, grinders and promising newcomers. Draisaitl, the German forward Edmonton obtained in the 2014 draft, was showing great development. Eberle was coming off seasons in which he scored sixty-five and sixty-three points. And Nugent-Hopkins had tied a career-high with fifty-six points and had represented the Oilers at the All-Star Game. It seemed like a good nucleus. After medical examinations and fitness testing, the Oilers would begin practising the following day.

Practice sessions were held at the Leduc Recreation Centre, a multiplex near the Edmonton International Airport. Fan interest was so high that the team conducted an online draw to select which spectators would get into the rink. It looked like the place would be packed each day, with everyone keen to get a glimpse of the eighteen-year-old who had graduated from high school only a few months earlier.

Connor didn't want the attention, but it couldn't be avoided. Despite his status as a number-one draft pick and predictions that he was the game's next great player, McDavid remained low key. He had done the same thing when he arrived for his first practice sessions in Erie at age fifteen. Instead of dressing in the Otters' gear, he wore his equipment from the Toronto Marlboros until he was certain he had made the team.

"You never want to show up and have anybody believe that you think you're all that," McDavid said. "I did it with the Otters, and I'm going to take that same approach again."

It wouldn't be long before McDavid was thrilling crowds in the NHL and the Oilers were embarking on a season that fans had been anticipating since the night Edmonton won the lottery. But, before that could happen, there were changes to come as the team gradually took shape. Connor decided to move into a house with Hall. Although they had strong training camps, Nurse and Draisaitl would both be returned to the AHL. Talbot won the starting job in net, and Nilsson earned the position as the backup. Even though Scrivens had looked strong in all of his preseason appearances, he was waived and sent to Bakersfield, the Oilers' American Hockey League affiliate in California. Ference was asked to accept a change, and did, joining Hall, Eberle and Nugent-Hopkins as alternate captains.

Each move was a supporting act to the main event.

SIX

RIGHT FROM THE BEGINNING, EDMONTON WAS A HOTBED FOR HOCKEY. ITS FIRST TEAM was organized in 1894, only two years after the former Hudson's Bay trading post was incorporated as a town with seven hundred residents. The first recorded game was played on Christmas Day 1894, with the hometown Thistles—made up of well-to-do men of Scottish extraction—defeating a contingent from Strathcona, a settlement on the opposite side of the North Saskatchewan River.

In 1896, nearly a decade before Alberta became a province, Edmonton's first formal hockey organization was established. The Edmonton Hockey Club consisted of two teams: the elite senior Thistles and the junior Stars. Games were played atop the frozen river against the South Edmonton Shamrocks and a team made up of North-West Mounted Police officers from a detachment in nearby Fort Saskatchewan.

A little more than a decade later, the Thistles competed for the Stanley Cup, when it was a challenge trophy awarded to Canada's top amateur team.

During that era, any club was allowed to challenge the Cup holder at any time, making it possible for several teams to capture the prized trophy—and lose it—in the same year. Sponsored by a department store merchant, J. H. Morris—the proud owner of Edmonton's first automobile, a 1903 Ford Model A—the Thistles challenged the reigning Montreal Wanderers for the trophy in 1908. The Thistles' top player and manager was Fred Whitcroft, who had played for a team from Kenora, Ontario, when it mounted an unsuccessful Cup challenge against the Wanderers the previous year. After Montreal had defeated Kenora in that series in March of 1907, the Cup was stolen and held for ransom before being returned, without a cent changing hands.

Teams played seven to a side back then, and the Thistles brought in six players with the single-minded goal of winning the Cup. Whitcroft, who had scored thirty-five goals in ten games for the Thistles in the preceding season, was the only regular in the line-up. Among the hired guns were Tommy Phillips and Lester Patrick, two of the sport's biggest stars. A left wing who was later among the original nine inductees into the Hockey Hall of Fame, Phillips had already won the Cup twice. Patrick, who is credited with being the first defenceman to rush the net and score a goal, had helped the Wanderers win Stanley Cups in 1906 and 1907, and later went on to win two more as coach and general manager of the New York Rangers.

Despite fielding a team of All-Stars the likes of which had never been seen, the Thistles lost to the Wanderers in a two-game series in Montreal. Although the Thistles led after the opening period of the first game, they lost 7–3. The real story of the game, though, was Phillips, who added to his legend by breaking his ankle, then refusing to sit out, playing the final ten minutes in excruciating pain. The Thistles managed to win the second contest 7–6 without him, but the Wanderers retained the Cup based on their higher two-game total of thirteen goals.

Two years later, the Thistles issued a second challenge, but fell in two lopsided defeats to Fred "Cyclone" Taylor and the Ottawa Senators, then members of the National Hockey Association, predecessor to the NHL. Playing at the Ottawa Arena before Canada's Governor General Earl Grey, the Thistles jumped to a 3–2 lead in the first game on January 18 before the action was halted when an Edmonton player's pants fell down and needed repairs. When play resumed, the Thistles' lead soon evaporated and they too fell, 8–4; two days later they were beaten again by a score of 13–7. By the end of the year, the Edmonton Hockey Club folded, at which point the Thistles were replaced by the Eskimos as the city's elite team.

The Eskimos fielded some great players during their proud history, including Hockey Hall of Famers Eddie Shore and Duke Keats, a centre who once collected a puck in his own end and scored a goal after skating backward the length of the ice. One of the greatest defencemen of all time, Shore played for the Eskimos for two seasons before launching his NHL career in 1926 with the Bruins, and became the league's first true superstar. Called the "Edmonton Express" because of his dynamic end-to-end rushes, Shore led Boston to its first Stanley Cup in 1929 and a second one ten years later. He still stands as the only defenceman in history to win the Hart Trophy as the league's most valuable player four times.

In 1923, Keats was the Eskimos' star when they challenged the Ottawa Senators in what would become the last Stanley Cup final contested by an Edmonton team for six decades. The Eskimos played valiantly but couldn't overcome the determined Francis "King" Clancy or the stellar goalkeeping of Clint Benedict. The Eskimos lost the first game in overtime, 2–1, and were beaten 1–0 in the second. In that game, Clancy played all six positions for the Senators, even putting on the goalie pads after Benedict was called for a penalty and had to serve it, as per the rules of the day. Later, Clancy went on to a Hall of Fame career as a defenceman, coach and hockey executive with the Maple Leafs, and, in another tip of the cap to history, Benedict fashioned a Hall of Fame career with the Senators and the Montreal Maroons. In 1930, Benedict's final season in the NHL, he began wearing a face-mask after the tip of his nose was shattered by a shot by Howie Morenz of the Canadiens. Jacques Plante popularized the use of protective facial gear three decades later, but the idea began with Benedict's splintered schnozz.

Back in Edmonton, fans desperate for information about how the Eskimos were faring gathered in the sub-zero cold outside Mike's News and Tobacco Stand, as much a popular downtown meeting spot as it was a retail business. As a practice, John "Mike" Michaels, who came to Edmonton from New York in 1912, had telegrams sent to him from distant hockey rinks where games involving local teams were being played. He would then post updates on a ten-foot billboard outside his store and, in times of high drama, read from the wires and provide play-by-play through a megaphone. At times, he even enlisted friends to simulate the action in the game.

During that 1923 Stanley Cup challenge, hockey fans spread across Jasper Avenue, the main thoroughfare through the centre of the city, to listen to Mike's commentary. The throng became so large that fire engines took detours and streetcars stopped in their tracks. Rather than being annoyed, however, the motormen simply climbed out and joined the crowd.

Mike's News Stand remained a thriving entity until the Michaels family sold the business in 1978. In its heyday, it carried three thousand five hundred magazine titles, and stocked newspapers in seventeen languages. Over the years, it also took on a role as Edmonton's largest ticket vendor, selling seats to everything from hockey, football and baseball games to the matches played by the women's basketball team that first made Edmonton the City of Champions. The Edmonton Grads won the Canadian championship in 1923, captured their first world title a year later and had won seventeen consecutive world championships by the time they were disbanded at the start of the Second World War. While long gone, they continue to hold the North American record for the best all-time winning percentage of any sports team. Over a quarter of a century, beginning in 1915, they won 502 games, lost only twenty and went undefeated in twenty-seven consecutive matches at four Olympics where basketball was a non-medal sport.

Although Edmonton was not awarded a franchise in 1917 when the

NHL was established, the city remained a centre of excellence for hockey. The Edmonton Superiors won the Alberta Senior League championship in 1931 and played the Winnipeg Hockey Club for the right to meet Hamilton in the finals of the Allan Cup, the trophy that has been awarded to Canada's amateur champion since 1909. The "Soops" lost the two games in Winnipeg as two thousand fans gathered outside Mike's to get updates. As evidence of the hysteria the Superiors created, the *Edmonton Journal* registered more than forty-two thousand calls on the telephone line it had set up for readers to check the score of the second game. The city's population at that time was less than eighty thousand, so either some fans called more than once or just about everyone in the city was nuts about hockey; most likely, it was a little bit of both.

Owned by a meatpacking company, Gainers, the Superiors went on to win senior league championships in 1933 and 1935, and then embarked on a European exhibition tour in 1932–33. After sailing across the Atlantic in November on the Canadian Pacific ocean liner *Duchess of Atholl*, the team won an international tournament in Paris and lost only once in thirty-eight games against teams from Czechoslovakia, France, Germany, Great Britain and Switzerland. Sadly, the *Duchess of Atholl* did not fare as well. Requisitioned for use as an Allied troop ship a few years later, it was torpedoed and sunk by a German U-boat off the coast of Africa on October 10, 1942.

The Superiors' captain in Europe was an Irish-born centre named Jimmy Graham. He later coached the Senior A Edmonton Waterloo Mercurys in 1950, when they won the World Ice Hockey Championships in London, as well as in 1952 when they won the gold medal at the Olympic Games in Oslo, Norway. Sponsored by James Albert Christiansen, owner of a local car dealership, the Mercurys outscored their seven opponents by a margin of eighty-eight to five at the World Championships, and upon their return, their victory parade drew a crowd of sixty thousand people—about half of the population of Edmonton. Two years later, the Mercurys went

7–0–1 while representing Canada at the Olympic Winter Games; the gold medal they captured was the country's last until 2002.

As the years went by, despite the fact that the city lacked a major professional hockey team, Edmonton had its fair share of great amateur teams. The Edmonton Athletic Club won the city junior league championships in 1934, 1938, 1949 and 1950; the Edmonton Roamers won junior league titles in 1939, 1940 and 1941; and the Edmonton Flyers won the Allan Cup in 1948 as Canada's senior hockey champions. The most famous alumni to play for the Flyers—who in 1951 became the top minor-league affiliate of the Detroit Red Wings—were Al Arbour and Glenn Hall. Arbour won eight Stanley Cups—four as a player and four as head coach of the New York Islanders from 1980–83—and Hall won three Vezina Trophies during his career with the Detroit Red Wings, Chicago Blackhawks and St. Louis Blues. He holds the NHL record for consecutive games played by a goalie with 502, and he played in thirteen All-Star games, more than any other backstop in history.

"In a lot of ways, when it comes to hockey, Edmonton really hasn't changed," Hall, who is in his eighties and owns a sprawling acreage west of the city, said. He was inducted into the Hockey Hall of Fame in 1975. "There have always been great players from Edmonton. I don't think you can find a major team in North America now without one."

AFTER YEARS OF DOMINANT AMATEUR COMPETITION, THE CITY'S HOCKEY DREAMS took a leap forward in the 1960s. A former pilot who flew Spitfires and Hurricanes for the Royal Canadian Air Force during the Second World War, Bill Hunter is considered the founding father of professional hockey in Edmonton. Equal parts showman and salesman, he coached, managed and owned a succession of teams in Saskatchewan and Alberta after the war. In 1965, he took over the Edmonton Oil Kings, a Junior A team that had been originally bankrolled in 1950 by Christiansen, the same man who had sponsored the world-champion Mercurys. While playing in different leagues and for different ownership groups, the Oil Kings contended for national championships ten times over twenty-six years, and won Memorial Cups in 1963 and 1966. In the latter season, their opponent was the Oshawa Generals, whose lineup included a promising defenceman in Bobby Orr. A year after taking over the Oil Kings, Hunter founded the major junior Western Canadian Hockey League, now known as the WHL, before setting his sights on the real prize: acquiring an NHL team.

After being rebuffed in attempts to land a franchise when the NHL expanded in 1967 and 1970, Hunter made an offer to purchase the Pittsburgh Penguins, a struggling postexpansion team, which the league likewise refused. Miffed, Hunter joined forces with American promoters Gary Davidson and Dennis Murphy, the same starry-eyed dreamers who started the American Basketball Association, World Football League and World Team Tennis, and, in September 1971, the World Hockey Association was born.

The ABA had been a qualified success, with four teams absorbed by the National Basketball Association. Those four franchises—the New York Nets, Denver Nuggets, Indiana Pacers and San Antonio Spurs—were ultimately success stories, but other organizations were more questionably run. Murphy had been the general manager of the Miami Floridians, who were eventually renamed the Floridians as they played home games at seven arenas in six cities around the state. The franchise became best known for scantily clad ball girls and wacky promotions: Giveaways included panty hose on Ladies Night, live turkeys at Thanksgiving, potatoes on Irish Night and vats of gefilte fish to appeal to the Jewish fan base.

The WHA founders knew that they needed to establish credibility quickly. So, at the urging of Hunter, owners of the original dozen WHA franchises pooled resources and convinced Bobby Hull to play for the new Winnipeg Jets. Embroiled in contentious contract negotiations with the

Blackhawks, Hull joked that he would move to the WHA for one million dollars. Seeing it as an opportunity, the league made him an offer that was unheard of in that day: a salary of $1.75 million over ten years, plus a one-million-dollar signing bonus. Just as quickly, the Philadelphia Blazers fired another shot across the NHL's bow, stealing Derek Sanderson from the Bruins by paying him $2.6 million. That was more than the world-famous soccer star Pele was earning at the time, and it made Sanderson the highest-paid player in all of professional sports.

From the beginning, the WHA was a nuisance to the NHL. In the first year alone, sixty-seven players followed Hull and Sanderson to the upstart league for higher salaries. The WHA made itself even more attractive by doing away with the reserve clause that had long annoyed NHL players, because it effectively bound players to one team for their entire career. All the concessions and perks offered by the WHA were intended to strengthen the league's position as a viable competitor of the NHL. But for many of the owners, the WHA was merely a means to an end. When the WHA began play in 1972, the hope was that, as with the ABA, the strongest franchises would eventually be invited to join the established rival league; Hunter fully intended that his franchise in Edmonton would be one of them.

Hunter originally named his team the Edmonton Oilers, a tribute to the city's economic engine and the nickname for the Oil Kings in the 1950s and '60s. Just prior to their first season, though, the planned Calgary franchise for the WHA folded, so the Oilers were renamed the Alberta Oilers as Hunter planned to split home games between Calgary and Edmonton. But the team ended up playing all of its home games that year in Edmonton and, at the start of their second season, the name would revert to the Edmonton Oilers.

Hunter immediately set out to promote the team in any way he could. He created a stir by snatching the Alberta-born Jim Harrison away from the Toronto Maple Leafs. On the day he signed Harrison, the flamboyant team owner rolled a shopping cart jammed with seventy-five thousand dollars in cash up to Harrison's front door in Bonnyville; in his previous year in Toronto, Harrison had earned twenty thousand dollars.

The Oilers' first captain was Al Hamilton. A speedy defenceman, he had played for the Oil Kings for three seasons and exchanged end-to-end rushes with Orr during the 1966 Memorial Cup. Signed by the New York Rangers as a teenager, Hamilton played a few games for them in 1966, but spent most of the next two years in the minor leagues. He finally cracked the Rangers' lineup in 1969, but was left unprotected in the 1970 NHL expansion draft and selected by Buffalo. He immediately became a Sabres mainstay on defence and led the team's blue-liners in scoring in both of his seasons there.

When the WHA was established, Hamilton was both bemused and curious about the rival new league.

"The first thought I had was, 'What the hell is this? Another one of Bill Hunter's wild schemes?'" Hamilton recalled.

In May 1972, Hunter invited Hamilton to meet him in Ottawa where the Oil Kings were playing in the Memorial Cup. They discussed the possibility of Hamilton returning to Edmonton to play for the newly hatched Oilers.

"He was pretty convincing in telling me the WHA would work," Hamilton said. "He was one of the all-time characters. He was a promoter who had big dreams, and the absolute ability to convince other people to spend their money on his dreams."

The first player the team selected in the 1972 WHA draft was a thirty-eight-year-old left winger, Val Fonteyne. A veteran of thirteen NHL seasons, Fonteyne grew up an hour south of Edmonton and played for Hunter in the early 1950s in the Western Canada Hockey League. Fonteyne was set on returning for another season with the Penguins when Hunter called. The Penguins even offered Fonteyne a position in the organization once his playing days were over, but all those plans went out the window when Hunter stopped by his home in Wetaskiwin.

"He was not shy, that's for sure," said Fonteyne, who, at eighty-two, is the oldest surviving member of the original Oilers. "He wanted to have local players, and the nucleus of the team was formed from guys he had been associated with. That was his main idea."

The league got off to a rocky start. Teams had financial difficulties and logistical problems, sometimes switching arenas or cities as a result. But the on-ice product was dynamic.

"There were all sorts of twists and turns, but we had fun," Hamilton said. "The first exhibition game we ever played [on September 29, 1972, against the Los Angeles Sharks] took four hours and twenty minutes because about twenty fights took place. The safest thing on the ice was the puck."

In their first year, the Oilers were mediocre on the ice but, in other ways, they were a smashing success. Because Hunter had loaded the roster with players from the Oil Kings and other local teams that were familiar to fans, the team soon developed a devoted following. The excitement generated in that first season also helped persuade the local Edmonton Exhibition Association to build Northlands Coliseum, the arena that opened in 1974 and would serve as the Oilers' home for the next forty-two years.

While the Coliseum was being built, the Oilers played their first two seasons at the since-razed Edmonton Gardens, a dilapidated rink that was constructed in 1913 as a stock pavilion on the city's fairgrounds. A rose long past its bloom, the Gardens was famous for terrible sight lines, uncomfortable seats and oily wooden floors. Bob Hope entertained there once and poked fun at the place as part of his stand-up routine. Another time, the Moscow Circus showed up but, upon seeing the place, its acrobats and tightrope walkers threatened to leave. On event nights near the end of the Gardens' reign, the Edmonton Fire Department would station seven firefighters in the building, with three assigned to keep an eye out for fires in concession areas and dressing rooms.

However, as bad as it was, the Gardens was nowhere near the worst rink in the WHA. The former Cleveland Arena used chicken wire to separate the playing surface from the crowd, and it was located in such a rough neighbourhood that five players had cars stolen out of the parking lot in the first two years. And the New Jersey Knights played in a building in Cherry Hill that had no showers in the visitors' dressing room, so opposing players had to bathe and change at a Holiday Inn two miles away.

"Sometimes, in that first season, we would play a team on the road in one rink and when we went back a month later they would already be in another one," Fonteyne said. "It was quite an experience."

Jim Harrison led the Oilers in scoring in their first season with eighty-six points, and became the first player in modern history to score ten points in a game when he had a hat trick and seven assists against the New York Raiders at the Gardens on January 13, 1973. A hard-working, defensive forward, Fonteyne had thirty-nine points in seventy-seven games and, astonishingly, was flagged for just a single two-minute penalty in the entire season. Perhaps the most gentlemanly player in the history of pro hockey, Fonteyne went without a penalty in five NHL seasons and received only thirteen penalties in 969 games in the NHL and WHA.

"It's tough to explain," Fonteyne said. "All I can think of is that I was a good skater, and because of that, I usually wasn't trying to catch guys so I didn't get called for tripping or hooking very often. I was a small guy so I didn't take to fighting, either."

With Hunter acting as owner, general manager and, eventually, head coach, the Oilers managed a 38–37–3 record in their first season. They finished with a record identical to that of the Minnesota Fighting Saints, only to lose to Minnesota in a wild-card game staged to determine who would receive the fourth and final spot in the playoffs. The New England Whalers beat Hull's Jets in the first WHA championship series, after which the victorious team skated around the ice without a winners' trophy because the one ordered by the league had not yet been delivered.

The WHA started and ended its first season with a dozen teams. There were too many problems to count, but it survived, contrary to predictions from the NHL. Some fans had been hesitant to support the Oilers initially for fear that the league would not last. After it was clear the team would be back for another season, the fans quickly came around and, by the start of the team's second year, season-ticket holders filled nearly half of the Gardens' uncomfortable seats.

Despite the chaos that struck other organizations, the Oilers established themselves as one of the most financially stable franchises in the league. A record WHA crowd of 15,326 turned out for their first game at the Northlands Coliseum on November 10, 1974. That night, Edmonton's forty-five-year-old goalie, Jacques Plante, outdueled Cleveland's Gerry Cheevers, and the Oilers won.

The Oilers struggled to win consistently over the next two seasons, however, and, in both years, Hunter fired coaches and ended up climbing back behind the bench. Eventually, he bowed out of the picture in 1976, giving control of the team to Nelson Skalbania, a real-estate entrepreneur. Skalbania, in turn, sold half his shares to Peter Pocklington, a young, self-made millionaire then running a busy Ford dealership in Edmonton. The $700,000 agreement between them was scribbled on the back of a dinner napkin from the Steak Loft in Edmonton. As a down payment, Pocklington slipped a $150,000 diamond off his wife's finger, then completed the deal by giving Skalbania a canvas by French landscape artist Maurice Utrillo and three Rolls-Royce convertibles, including one that had been used in the film *The Great Gatsby*.

Pocklington knew little about hockey but a lot about turning a buck. As a kid, he sold his Christmas presents to friends; as a teenager, he sold the family's Oldsmobile 98 out of the driveway while his unsuspecting father was on a business trip. Within a year, Pocklington bought out Skalbania and, in 1978, he engineered the deal that brought the seventeen-year-old Wayne Gretzky to Edmonton.

The Oilers' last season in the WHA was their best. With Glen Sather behind the bench, Gretzky winning rookie of the year and goalie Dave Dryden chosen the league MVP, the team finished first for the only time. Although they reached the league championship series, they lost in six games to the Jets.

The following year, the Oilers realized Hunter's dream when they were invited to join the NHL. In March 1979, they joined the Jets, Nordiques and Whalers in hockey's most famous league. The WHA was on its last legs by then, but it had inflicted terrible damage on its rivals. Due to the competition, the average salary in the NHL had soared from a little less than thirty thousand dollars to nearly ninety-two thousand over seven years. In addition, the NHL racked up nearly twelve million dollars in mostly futile court actions against a league that had Hunter's handprints all over it.

"Without Bill Hunter, it would have been a long time before we ever had an NHL team in Edmonton," Hamilton said.

Although he wasn't associated with the Oilers when they joined the NHL, Hunter did not give up. In 1982, he heard the St. Louis Blues were for sale, and quickly set about attempting to buy the team and move it to his hometown, Saskatoon, Saskatchewan. It seemed like an absurd notion, but a man like Hunter, who charged through life with bluster and charm, was not easy to dissuade. In a matter of months, he secured a $32 million loan from the provincial government to help pay for construction of an eighteen-thousand seat arena, and he received an equal number of season-ticket applications from expectant fans.

That was good enough for St. Louis's owners. In April 1983, the Blues' ownership group stunned fans and irritated NHL executives by announcing that they had reached a deal to sell the team to Hunter for about twelve million dollars. From the beginning, the league was aghast at the idea of moving an established team in a major U.S. market to a relatively small city on the Canadian prairies. "Who the hell wants to go to Saskatoon, anyway?" the Maple Leafs' bombastic Harold Ballard raged. "I don't want to be taking dogsleds to get around."

On May 18, 1983, Hunter and his associates made a presentation in New York to the NHL Board of Governors at the Helmsley Palace Hotel. The board rejected the sale, breaking Saskatoon's heart and angering the Blues' owners. As part of the ensuing chaos, suits and countersuits were filed, St. Louis lost general manager Emile Francis to the Hartford Whalers and, because it was feuding with the league, the Blues sent no representative to the annual entry draft. It is the only time in NHL history that a franchise voluntarily forfeited its picks in the draft.

Irrepressible, Hunter tried one last time in 1988 to become an NHL owner. His efforts to bring an expansion team to Saskatoon collapsed two years later, when the Saskatchewan government refused to guarantee a twenty-million-dollar loan that his group of investors needed. That was the end of Hunter's quest to own a professional hockey team; in 2002, Hunter died of cancer in Edmonton. But, thanks to his early efforts, hockey in Edmonton was forever changed.

Over the next ten years, the Oilers, who had never won a championship in the WHA, won five Stanley Cups, Gretzky became the greatest player the sport had ever seen, and a dynasty was born. The first year the Oilers won the Stanley Cup, Pocklington bought all the players golf clubs. Another time, he bought everyone on the team trips for two to Hawaii. He once gave a Ferrari to Gretzky as a present and, when Gretzky broke Phil Esposito's single-season NHL scoring record on February 24, 1982, Pocklington gave a Mustang convertible to Gretzky's girlfriend, Vicki Moss. Generous as those gifts were, Pocklington saved his grandest gestures for the most important occasions.

In the spring of 1982, just minutes before the Oilers took to the ice for Game 6 of the Division Semifinals against the Los Angeles Kings, Pocklington visited the dressing room at the Northlands.

"I walked into the dressing room with a duffel bag and emptied one hundred thousand dollars on top of their ping-pong table," Pocklington said. "I told them, 'This is yours, but you gotta win the game.' The players loved it. They went out and tore them apart. The NHL fined me ten thousand dollars or something, but I didn't care. I gave a shit and wasn't interested in ever losing."

Ken Lowe, the Oilers' medical trainer from 1989 to 2010, remembers that night for several reasons. The players were gathered in the clubhouse when Sather suddenly announced Pocklington wanted to address the team.

"Nobody knew what to make of it because a team owner never does that," said Lowe, who spent seven seasons as a trainer for the Edmonton Eskimos of the Canadian Football League before joining the Oilers. "He walked in with this big bag with carrots sticking out of the top of it and everyone wondered what the hell was going on. Then he tipped it over on the table and piles of cash fell out. It worked out to thirty-three hundred dollars a man. I don't think I had ever seen that much money before. It was like winning the lottery."

After that long period of big wins and big spending, the Oilers fell on hard times in the 1990s. Crippled by a lengthy strike at his meatpacking plant and saddled with other growing debt, Pocklington was forced to sell the team. The franchise was saved not once, but twice, by Cal Nichols.

A small-town guy from St. Walburg and Paradise Hills, Saskatchewan, Nichols learned about community involvement when he served as a town councilor and as head of the chamber of commerce. A hockey player in his youth, Nichols moved to Edmonton with his wife in 1969, and quickly became a huge fan of the Oilers. In the team's first two seasons, Nichols attended games at the Gardens and became a season-ticket holder after they moved into Northlands Coliseum.

The team was struggling and failing at the box office in 1996 when Nichols co-chaired an effort to recruit thirteen thousand season-ticket holders, the minimum number required for Canadian teams to receive equalization payments from the league. The subsidies became necessary as the dollar hovered in the sixty-cent range, allowing U.S. franchises to acquire the best talent.

With Nichols leading the charge, the Oilers more than doubled their season-ticket holders in less than a year, and the team received its much-needed infusion of cash. A year later, however, with the team still hurting financially and the dollar remaining weak, the Alberta Treasury Bank called in a loan it had extended to Pocklington. The Oilers were on the verge of being sold to Houston Rockets' owner Les Alexander when Nichols put together a group of investors to make a bid to buy the team.

"Winnipeg and Quebec City had just lost their teams, and I figured somebody needed to lead the charge here, so I rolled up my sleeves," Nichols said. "I went everywhere in the city and had the door slammed in my face a few times but I never gave up. It was probably the biggest challenge I have ever taken on."

Selling shares of the team in units starting at one million dollars, Nichols was able to raise sixty million dollars. That, in turn, allowed him to secure a fifty-million-dollar loan and match the offer made by the group from Houston.

"When the smoke cleared, we ended up with thirty-eight people in what became known as the Edmonton Investors Group," Nichols said. "I look back at it now and I'm very proud. What I kept saying was that Edmonton was a way better place with the Oilers than without them, and I told people to just look at Winnipeg and Quebec."

Nichols owned and governed the Oilers as chairman of the Edmonton Investors Group from 1998 to 2008, at which point Daryl Katz purchased the team. Nichols said one of the reasons he led everyone in and out of ownership was that he anticipated a new generation of buildings being constructed around the league. He knew the Oilers needed a new home and that deeper pockets would be required to make that happen, and bought into Katz's concept of using an arena as the catalyst for a downtown revitalization project.

"I knew it was going to require somebody with horsepower," Nichols said. "That in part led to the sale of the team to Katz. The coliseum had many great characteristics, but the leg room was not adequate and the concourses were not close to what we were seeing in so many new buildings. As great as it had been, we knew we were going to have to do better."

More than a century after the first amateur teams began playing on the city's frozen rivers and fans had gathered around the billboard outside of Mike's News Stand, Edmonton was finally poised to take its place among the world's hockey elite. With a flawless pedigree and a devoted fan base, there was no place better for hockey.

SEVEN

THERE WASN'T AN EMPTY SEAT ON SEPTEMBER 18 WHEN THE OILERS OPENED TRAINING camp at the Leduc Recreation Centre, a rink south of Edmonton near the city's international airport. Seven thousand fans had entered an online lottery in hopes of getting one of three-hundred wristbands that were distributed on each of the three days that camp was open to the public.

The reason fans gathered in such great numbers was no mystery. It was the first time Connor McDavid would skate with the full team under the direction of Todd McLellan, who was seen as the answer to Edmonton's coaching problems. Since accepting his first head post in 1993 with the Battlefords North Stars of the Saskatchewan Junior Hockey League, McLellan had experienced just one losing season. In twenty-two years of coaching, including three as an assistant in Detroit under Mike Babcock, the teams he was associated with missed the playoffs only twice.

It didn't take long for McLellan to lose patience, not with McDavid, but with a number of the other fifty-eight players on the ice. Confused at the start of a drill, two groups of players gathered in the same corner. They should have gone to opposite sides of the rink. Exasperated, McLellan blew his whistle and swore. People in the stands laughed. They love the Oilers, but they also realize theirs isn't the tightest-run ship.

"This is going to drive me crazy all year," the new sheriff barked. "This is about detail. This is about being fucking alert. You are responsible for this, not us coaches."

It was only a practice session and the start of the regular season was still three weeks away, but two things were clear: McLellan was far more detail-oriented than the stream of coaches that came before him, and McDavid was better than anybody that had worn an orange and blue uniform in years.

The crowd that filled the place spoke to that, and so did the flock of journalists. There were so many reporters that two scrums had to be arranged with players and coaches: one for print writers, the other for television and radio.

"When these types of things happen in a community, within an organization and pretty much a country, because everybody has got their eyes on this young man, it speaks of his talent, his skill and his ability," McLellan said after that first practice, addressing the extraordinary interest in McDavid. "When you have that skill set and you have had it that long, this is the environment that is created."

After the on-ice session, Connor was surprised to learn that his arrival had caused so much excitement. He is unpretentious, bordering on naïve. He never telegraphs to others what a gifted player he is.

When he attended his first OHL training camp in Erie, Connor refused to wear an Otters' jersey. Asked to explain why by the team's general manager, the then-fifteen-year-old said he wasn't certain he was good enough to earn a roster spot.

"If you don't make the team," Sherry Bassin told him, "I'm moving to China."

After watching the teenager for the first time, many of McDavid's new Oilers' teammates gushed about him.

"Even though I'm older, I kind of look up to him because of how good a hockey player he is," Teddy Purcell, a forward who played with Steven Stamkos, Martin St. Louis and Vincent Lecavallier on other teams, said. "I was pretty wide-eyed out there."

McDavid continued to impress during practices and scrimmages over the next two days, and then McLellan started trimming the roster. Before the regular season opened in St. Louis on October 8, 60 percent of the invitees would return to college programs or be shipped off to the minor leagues.

The Oilers played their first of eight preseason games on September 21 at Rexall Place against the Calgary Flames. For the most part, exhibition contests are affairs between players with unrecognizable names. Veterans see just enough action to freshen their legs, and prospects skirmish for the rest of the way in tedious encounters. Even before training camp, all but one or two positions on many teams are already locked up.

At the beginning of his career, Gretzky said players reporting for camp rarely received new gear. Typically, the best that most could hope for was to convince an equipment manager to find them a slightly lesser-used pair of skates.

"My first year in the NHL, I think I got a pair a shoulder pads a guy wore for seven years," Gretzky said. "Larry Robinson once told me that he was given Rocket Richard's old shin pads during training camp one year in Montreal. He said, 'Wayne, they didn't even cover my knees.'

"You didn't get new equipment. You got gear that had been passed down for twenty-five years."

In his first NHL exhibition game, McDavid helped set up third-period goals on wrist shots by Draisaitl and Yakupov. The Oilers beat their rivals, 4–2. With Connor's arrival, speculation had risen that perhaps the Battle of Alberta, once one of hockey's most contentious rivalries, would become interesting again.

A feud has always simmered between the province's two largest cities. Edmonton and Calgary are separated by 300 kilometres but, on top of that, there is a cultural and political divide. They squabble constantly, whether it is over sports teams or the placement of the capital building or dollars for school construction. The Conservative Party is deeply entrenched in Calgary; Edmonton, by comparison, is its left-leaning foil.

For decades, the cities have engaged in constant games of one-upmanship. In 1978, Edmonton hosted the British Commonwealth Games in its newly constructed, twenty-one-million-dollar football stadium; ten years later, Calgary hosted the Winter Olympics at its freshly built two-hundred-million-dollar Olympic Park and one-hundred-million-dollar hockey arena, the Saddledome. In the most recent display of gamesmanship, as construction continued on the Oilers' four-hundred-and-eighty-million-dollar downtown rink, plans were proposed in Calgary in August 2015 for a nine-hundred-million-dollar downtown project that would include a covered football stadium, a hockey arena and a multisport field house. Since then, the Calgary Sports and Entertainment Group has been asked to downsize its proposal and consider a site other than the one it selected on a plot of land that formerly was home to a creosote plant. The cost of remediating the soil alone was estimated at $140 million dollars.

Hockey has long played a role in the disharmony. The rivalry dates to 1895, when a brigade of Calgary firefighters travelled to Edmonton and trampled a team drawn from local detachments of the Mounties. It wasn't until nearly a century later that the Oilers and Flames came along, and they showed great disdain for one another from the start. The discord became especially bitter in the second half of the 1980s, when both ranked among the game's elite. One or the other reached the Stanley Cup Final each year from 1983 to 1990, and the games between them became more a tale of the tape than a tale of two teams.

"When we met, it was like the Red Sox versus the Yankees, only worse," said Dave Lumley, the winger who played in nearly four hundred games for

Edmonton over seven seasons beginning in 1979. "It was the only time I ever thought someone might actually die on the ice."

Once, the Oilers and Flames combined to take 177 minutes in penalties—in a preseason contest. On another occasion, players on both teams dropped their gloves three times and collected seventy penalty minutes in the first thirty-four seconds of a game.

"We were like two forces pounding at one another—an explosion of some sort had to occur at one point or another," Kevin Lowe, a great defenceman for Edmonton in that era, said. "The games were so tough; we didn't look forward to them. We had to rise to a whole different level when we played them. They had the firepower and toughness to compete with us. The only ones that had fun were the fans."

The battles between the teams were desperate because for each, winning a championship was unattainable without conquering the other. In 1984 and 1988, the Oilers turfed the Flames from the playoffs en route to winning the Stanley Cup. In 1986, Calgary eliminated Edmonton in seven games in the division final. The Flames lost to the Canadiens in the Stanley Cup, but they had won the bragging rights in Alberta.

In later years, as both teams struggled, the series lost its oomph. With Calgary returning to respectability in 2014–15 and Edmonton landing the game's most exciting newcomer in a generation, there was hope that those good, bad old days would return again.

There wasn't a single fight in the split-squad meeting between the Oilers and Flames that night. A sense of history is lacking in NHL wannabes. The last time the teams had met in the playoffs was six years before Connor McDavid was born.

On the night McDavid made his preseason debut, he played more than twenty minutes, set up two goals, won most of his fourteen face-offs and was chosen the game's first star. He was getting used to the NHL game but still was not being genuinely tested.

"It's a different pace and different guys, but I felt a lot better as the game went on," McDavid said. "I was a little nervous at the start, but I guess that's to be expected with all of the hype that has occurred. It takes a little while to settle down."

McLellan was as pleased with the teenager's effort as the crowd, who applauded him at the end of each shift.

"We got what we expected," the coach said.

Connor sat out against Winnipeg on September 23 and 25 as the coaching staff assessed other players, and then returned to the lineup on September 26 against the Minnesota Wild. The game was played in Saskatoon, where more than 7,500 fans showed up to cheer his every move.

The game had been brought to the SaskTel Centre by John Graham, a Toronto-based promoter. Ticket sales soared when it was announced the day before that McDavid was going to play.

On Saturday afternoon, the rookie thrilled a large number of fans wearing his trademark jerseys by notching a third assist in the first period on a goal by Anton Slepyshev, a big Russian forward who played the preceding season in the KHL.

In the 3–0 victory, McDavid put on quite a display, showing off his speed on two breakaways and providing teammates with numerous scoring opportunities, including one no-look pass from behind the net that brought the crowd to its feet. On Slepyshev's goal, McDavid started the play by stripping the puck from a Minnesota player behind the goal and passing it to Draisaitl, who then found Slepyshev open for a one-timer.

"What Connor doesn't get enough credit for as an eighteen-year-old is his ability to play on both sides of the puck," McLellan said. "A lot of times you see these types of offensive players cheating. I like what he is doing.

"He has a number of breakaways or partial breakaways and I don't know how you can score when you are going that fast, so we have to figure that part out, too. But he obviously has proven he can do it."

On September 29, his best game to that point, Connor set up the fourth goal as the Oilers beat the Coyotes, 4–0. That night, Brian McDavid, who was in town to help Joe Quinn put on a coaching clinic, saw his son play in an Oilers uniform for the first time.

Connor gave his parent an eyeful, streaking down the ice in the first period and breaking in on the net with the puck at the end of his stick. Sprawled across the goalmouth, Anders Lindback redirected the shot with his toe. The crowd roared anyway, and the teenager pretty much ran the Coyotes ragged the rest of the night.

McDavid was credited with one assist, on the second of three successive goals by Anton Lander, but, with any luck, he could have had a handful.

"Sometime in the first or second period, I sent a text to my wife," Brian said as he waited for Connor outside the Oilers' dressing room. "All it said was, 'He belongs.' "

It was something Connor's dad had suspected all along. But now, he was certain.

"I wanted to see it with my own eyes before I leaped to any judgment," he said. "Now I know that he can skate and play with these guys."

Quinn, who had served as Connor's stickhandling coach since he was a kid, was as thrilled as his dad.

"When I met Connor, he was ten or eleven years old," Quinn said. "I still remember him as a freckle-faced little boy. It's like watching my own son grow up."

With the victory, the Oilers improved to 6–0. It was the first time they had won six games during the preseason since 2006 and only the second time in twenty-five years. The team's prospects were indeed looking bright.

On the first of October, Mark Messier stopped by to take a peek at the first overall draft pick. Messier had met McDavid in the summer at a playoff game in Chicago and they filmed commercials together for Rogers, the NHL rights holder, but he had only seen him play on television.

"Great players possess great skills all the way across the board," said Messier, who was in Edmonton to launch The First Shift, a how-to-play program sponsored by Bauer and Hockey Canada. "The four fundamentals you have to master in hockey are skating, shooting, stickhandling and puck handling, and he obviously does those very well. Being able to think the game and see it differently and slow it down is also a critical component, and we have seen all the best players do that. They have a way to find open ice and an ability to do great things at great moments, and again, Connor is no different.

"I expect Connor to transition pretty smoothly to the pros. His off-ice demeanor, his commitment, his work ethic, all the things that make great players great, he obviously has. With that comes expectations and pressures and all of the things great players have to burden, but they find a way to take it in stride. I don't see Connor handling it any differently than Wayne Gretzky, Sidney Crosby, Mario Lemieux or any of the other great players that came before him."

An advisor to the Oilers, Messier sat in the stands and watched as McLellan put the team through its pregame paces. Later that night, with Messier watching from a suite with team executives, McDavid set up his fifth goal when Hall tapped in a rebound of one of the rookie's shots little more than a minute into the game. The Oilers lost, 5–2, then closed out preseason on October 3 with a 3–2 loss in overtime at Vancouver. They concluded their practice schedule with a 6–1–1 mark. Although the record was meaningless, it helped to further energize their loyal fan base. Each fall, hope springs eternal in Edmonton. Then the NHL season starts and ruins everything.

Before putting preseason to bed, McLellan spoke after the Vancouver game about the progress his team had made and the proficiency demonstrated by its young star.

"He is ready," the coach said. "He gets credit for being offensive and fast and dynamic, but what I have learned about him is that he is very intelligent, too. I think he understands his toolbox. He knows his speed can create open ice, but he also has that sense of when to slow things down, when to delay and when to make a play. He's fun to watch."

On the morning of October 5, the Oilers made their final moves to reach the requisite twenty-three players allowed by the NHL. In the biggest surprise, they kept Slepyshev and sent Draisaitl to Bakersfield. Among the other prominent players cut were Darnell Nurse and Ben Scrivens.

Draisaitl, who had a goal and three assists while shuffled between centre and wing, took the news hard.

"What we told Leon this morning is that he did everything we asked him to do," Chiarelli said after watching the confirmed team practice for the first time. He was joined that day in the stands by Daryl Katz, the Oilers' media-shy owner. "What we told him, and I'm not sure how much he heard, is that he has to look at the big picture. It was a tough decision and he was upset, and we went through the same process with Darnell. We want to make sure that their games are smoothed out so that when they come back up here, they are here for good."

Scrivens stopped 93 percent of the shots directed at him in preseason, but he still lost the battle for the backup role to Nilsson. The imposing Swede went unscored upon to earn the job behind Cam Talbot.

"The decision on which goalie to keep wasn't easy," Chiarelli said. "I had a conversation with Ben in the summer, and asked him to focus on a few things, and he did everything we asked. At the very least Ben will provide depth for us, but I think he will be somewhere else at some point."

After practising the next morning in Leduc, the Oilers boarded an Air Canada Airbus for a three-and-a-half-hour flight to Springfield, Illinois, a little more than an hour's drive from St. Louis.

It was the first of innumerable charter flights the team would take during the course of the regular season. Over the next six months, the Oilers would travel nearly one hundred thousand kilometres and spend eighty-eight days on the road during their eighty-two-game campaign. As the plane barreled down the runway, there were five thousand pounds of hockey equipment in its belly, alongside medical equipment and glove-drying and skate-sharpening machines.

As he settled into a business-class seat with an Oilers logo on the headrest, Connor McDavid was a little more than twenty-four hours from realizing his lifelong dream.

A FRUITFUL HOCKEY CAREER IS A COLLECTION OF MOMENTS STRUNG TOGETHER BY the physical feats they require and the objects involved in making them happen. The sweater worn for a first shift in a first game in a first season. The puck that found the back of a net for a first goal. The stick that puck was shot with. Skates that helped carry a Stanley Cup. For athletes, the items are keepsakes that link material and memory. For fans and collectors, they represent their love of a player or team, a moment in time, an investment even. For the Hockey Hall of Fame, they are pieces of history.

A player like McDavid comes along rarely. If he performs and develops as expected, there could be scoring records, Stanley Cups and individual awards to go along with an abundance of other, smaller milestones. His first game seemed like a shrewd time to start putting pieces away. The Hall of Fame already has a jersey he wore with the Erie Otters. The Hall will likely soon find itself with much more.

"Normally, we ask for a particular item at the completion of a season, or if there is a milestone of note we are aware of," Craig Campbell, the manager of archives for the Hall of Fame, said leading up to the start of the 2015 season. "It's better to plan now than to try to go back and find things twenty years later."

After Gretzky announced his retirement in 1999, sticks from his final few games at Madison Square Garden were collected. At the end of a shift or during a stoppage in play, number ninety-nine would hand them to one of the Rangers' equipment managers to be set aside.

Panic grips the hockey world when one of these prominent mementos suddenly goes missing. Reebok offered a ten-thousand-dollar reward and set up a tipline after Sidney Crosby lost a glove and a stick in the aftermath of scoring Team Canada's winning goal in the gold-medal game at the 2010 Olympics in Vancouver. The stick was found, mistakenly placed in a shipment of items headed for the International Ice Hockey Federation Hall of Fame in St. Petersburg, Russia. One of Crosby's teammates, Patrice Bergeron, discovered the glove in his equipment bag. In 2005, one of Crosby's jerseys went missing after Team Canada's gold-medal victory at the World Junior Championship in Grand Forks, North Dakota. Some significant articles never show up after they go missing, but luckily, Crosby's jersey was found in a mailbox outside a post office in Lachute, Quebec.

In the days before Connor's first game, the Oilers discussed grabbing a piece or two of his equipment following the match, either as a souvenir for him, the Hall of Fame or for their own purposes. The team planned to have an exhibit of historic Oilers items at their new arena, and something from McDavid would fit nicely along with the Stanley Cup banners and retired sweaters, connecting the past with the future.

Brian McDavid had already considered the implications of his son's first game.

"We have his first pair of skates, every jersey he has ever played in, all of his trophies," he said.

Jennifer Bullano Ridgley, the senior director of communications for the Penguins, said Crosby was given the jersey and stick from his first game. The Islanders, meanwhile, saved a few items from the night in 2009 when John Tavares made his regular-season debut.

Jeff Jackson, McDavid's agent, said one of the prodigy's game-worn sweaters had to be retained as part of a contractual obligation with Upper Deck, the official trading-card licensee for the NHL. After McDavid scored his first goal, the puck would be retrieved by one of his teammates, handed off to somebody on the bench and then given to him later.

Jackson, who played in 263 games and scored thirty-eight goals in nine years with the Maple Leafs, Rangers, Nordiques and Blackhawks, still has the puck from his first goal, scored against Steve Weeks of the Hartford Whalers on December 2, 1985.

"I can still recall it in my head," the former left wing said. "You never forget your first NHL goal."

LAURI KORPIKOSKI HEADED DOWN A TUNNEL BENEATH THE STANDS AT THE SCOTTRADE Center in St. Louis early in the day on October 8. Spying a pack of news-hounds waiting outside the Oilers' dressing room, the Finnish winger stopped and flashed a smile.

"I know you guys are waiting for me," Korpikoski joked. "This happens in every city I go to."

A team of little consequence in recent seasons, the Oilers had been drawn back into the spotlight for one reason only: the eighteen-year-old whiz kid who was about to make his professional debut.

Only a few months removed from high school, Connor McDavid looked unruffled during the Oilers' morning skate. Sitting on the bench as the Zamboni slowly groomed the ice, he chatted casually with Mark Let-estu and Andrew Ference, two guys with nearly twenty opening nights be-tween them.

Taking to the rink, he circled it slowly, juggling a puck on the blade of his stick. After stretching and practising face-offs with Ryan Nugent-Hopkins, Connor participated in a few light drills, at one point accepting a sweet pass across the goalmouth from Hall and burying it in the net.

Appreciating his fast hands and accuracy, teammates banged their sticks against the ice.

"There is a bit of a wow factor when you watch him," Matt Hendricks said.

In the dressing room afterward, the Oilers were animated and eager for the season to begin.

"We are about as prepared as we can be," Hall said. "We have high hopes for our team this year."

The Blues, who play tough, old-time hockey, would offer a steep challenge. The Oilers lost all three games to them in 2014–15, as well as all three the year before that. In the last twenty-one games between them, Edmonton had won only four.

"I'm not sure it can be any tougher than this," Hall said. "I'm looking forward to seeing how we handle it."

Hall, who had just taken in McDavid as his roommate, said the rookie seemed fine. They would play together that night on the second line, with Slepyshev on the other wing.

"We've all seen what Connor do, but he's still eighteen and there are going to be trials and errors," Hall said. "I'm twenty-three, and I still have bad games."

A few minutes later, McDavid met with the media in a room down the hallway. The space is usually reserved for interviews after Missouri Valley Conference basketball games. On those occasions, the crowd gathered is a little more intimate.

His hair wet and messy, and with beads of perspiration on his forehead, Connor stood surrounded by journalists and answered questions. So quiet were his responses that the throng pushed closer to hear.

"You only get to do this once," he said. "Certainly I'm a little bit nervous, but I feel pretty good. I'm just really excited to play. It's something you work hard for all of your life."

In his hotel room the night before, McDavid slept like a log.

"It wasn't until I woke up this morning that it hit me that I was playing in my first NHL game," he said. "It's obviously at a little different magnitude. You want to do the best you can."

That morning, Brian and Kelly McDavid flew from Toronto to St. Louis. Kelly had not seen her son since Labour Day.

"I just can't wait," she said. "This is the longest I've ever gone without seeing him."

In Erie, Bob Catalde planned to watch the game at home with his family. He had originally planned to drive ten hours to St. Louis to take in the contest with eleven-year-old Nico, but a last-minute scheduling conflict scuttled those plans.

"I've been asked by friends to join them at a bar, but I don't want to dilute the experience by drinking beer and analyzing every move Connor makes," Catalde said. "I'm going to enjoy it with my family. I'm letting my son stay up late."

Nico was crestfallen when McDavid moved out. Catalde was nearly as broken up as his son.

"It was very difficult when Connor left," he said. "It's the closest I can ever imagine becoming to someone else's child."

That morning, McLellan said he was keen to see how McDavid would respond in his first game.

"This is a new adventure for all of us," McLellan said. "I've never had a player whose arrival has been anticipated like this. There is a lot of external pressure on him along with shouldering his own expectations and those of his teammates, coaching staff and city.

"I talked to Sid [Crosby] about his experience, but with social media, things have even changed since then. What's really different in Connor's case is that national, international and worldwide eyes are on him."

Ken Hitchcock, the veteran St. Louis coach, said his team had not spent much time scouting McDavid. The rookie should expect a long night, Hitchcock suggested.

"If you think we're going to make it easy on him, you're crazy," he said.

CONNOR McDAVID'S FIRST NHL GAME WAS PLAYED BEFORE A FULL HOUSE ON A WARM night a few blocks from the Mississippi River. The catfish weren't jumpin', but the crowd was.

Before the puck dropped, thousands of Blues fans gathered in the shadows of the Scottrade Center for a pep rally. On their way into the building, they posed for pictures beside bronze statues of the team's greatest players: Al MacInnis, Bernie Federko and Brett Hull.

Wearing a Connor McDavid jersey, Kyle Levicki of Edmonton stood in a line inside waiting to get through a security checkpoint. A paving superintendent, Levicki was part of a group of seven friends who had travelled from Alberta for the game.

"I came because of McDavid, but I'm excited because we got [general manager] Peter Chiarelli, and made coaching changes as well," Levicki said.

On the April night when the Oilers won the NHL draft lottery, Levicki was in a hotel room in Banff with fifteen of his gentleman's league hockey teammates.

"It was about ten days after the Oilers had finished with the third-worst record in the league," he recalled. "All but two of us were jumping around and screaming when the Oilers won. The other two guys were Leafs fans."

Lining up against the Blues' physical defencemen, it took Connor a few shifts to adjust to the speed and flow of the game. Playing in front of his parents and before a prime-time national television audience on *Hockey Night in Canada*—a rare weekday slot for the Oilers—he showed bursts of his incredible speed. All told, in his first NHL game, McDavid was on the ice for eighteen minutes and seven seconds over twenty-two shifts. He struggled in the faceoff circle, winning only three of thirteen draws, but generally played well. At times he looked dangerous, once missing a breakaway when he was barely offside. Defensively, he held his own, poking a puck away from the man he was covering once, stripping one another time.

With the game tied at 1 in the third period, Connor nearly scored twice. The first time, he blew past Blues defencemen Jay Bouwmeester and Alex

Pietrangelo before having his wrist shot rejected by Brian Elliott. Seventy-three seconds later, McDavid made a deft spinning move in front of the net and fired a backhand that required Elliott to stretch out his arms to make the save.

"That McDavid is going to be a good player," Pietrangelo said. "I'm pretty impressed."

The Blues triumphed, 3–1, with the winning goal scored midway through the third period by the Blues' Robby Fabbri. It was first of the nineteen-year-old rookie's career. He and Connor had been friends since they were kids and had been teammates at the World Junior Championships.

"I guess I've got some bragging rights," Fabbri said good-naturedly. "We'll see how long that lasts."

Afterward, McDavid looked sullen in the dressing room as he packed his bag. A few minutes later, he talked about the night he had been waiting for all his life. It had not been bad by any means, but it certainly did not end the way he had hoped. His voice was so soft that it was barely audible.

"I did some good stuff and bad stuff along with the rest of the team," he said. "There are some things to improve. I had a couple of chances that I needed to score on."

His coach and teammates were less critical.

"I thought he held his own," Hall said. "When you're eighteen years old, you're playing against guys sometimes twice your age, and not every play and every game is going to be easy. I think you saw a lot of pushback from him, and that's great."

McLellan was especially impressed with McDavid's energy.

"I thought his best period was his third," he said. "If you lose your composure or lose your focus, that tends to be your worst. So that says a lot about him as a young player. When we needed him to be an offensive threat, he was."

At one point, McDavid used his speed to try to split Blues defencemen

Kevin Shattenkirk and Carl Gunnarsson. Although he was able to advance the puck into the offensive zone, he wasn't able to squeeze through them as easily as he had against opponents in the OHL.

"There were moments where I'm sure he would have pulled away from junior players, but tonight they were strong enough to tug him and hold him back," McLellan said. "That's all experience. It is sixty minutes into what will probably be a fifteen- or twenty-year career. He is going to get a lot better."

In a few minutes, the Oilers would head for the airport and take a short flight to Nashville, Tennessee. Two nights later, Connor would play against the Predators in the second game of his career and then, after a stop in Dallas, the Oilers would return home for their first game at Rexall Place on October 15.

"I certainly enjoyed the day," McDavid said before boarding the team bus. He was dressed in a smart gray suit with a matching purple shirt and tie, and he looked tired. "I'll remember this for a long time."

Then he paused.

"I'm glad it's over," he said.

THE FIRST WEEK OF CONNOR McDAVID'S NHL CAREER CONTINUED ALONG ITS THREE-game swing through steamy American cities where hockey is pretty much an afterthought. In St. Louis, the fans had been deafening but their hearts had been with the Cardinals, then still trying to knock the Chicago Cubs off their October run. When the Oilers arrived in Nashville, the downtown teemed with football fans in town for that weekend's clash between the Titans and the Buffalo Bills. Looking ahead to their game a few days later in Dallas, Texas, with the Cowboys and Rangers playing back-to-back games, a hockey game in Texas did not seem like it would be a starring attraction.

After their game-day skate on Friday, the Oilers gathered in front of a television in their dressing room and cheered wildly while watching the

Blue Jays take on the Rangers, a game Toronto would lose in extra innings. Edmonton would lose later that night as well. McDavid spent much of the game shadowed by the Predators' All-Star defencemen Shea Weber and Roman Josi, and was crushed against the boards by Cody Hodgson midway through the second period. As Hodgson slammed into Connor, the sellout crowd, many of whom were wearing old-style foam rubber hockey helmets given out before the game, roared.

With his opening-night nervousness behind him, McDavid looked slightly more relaxed against Nashville. During a break in play, he and Benoit Pouliot stood side by side on the Oilers' bench, tapping their sticks in a show of respect for a U.S. Armed Forces member who had served in Afghanistan. Despite Connor settling down, though, the Oilers as a whole still couldn't find a way to win. The outcome hinged on a single mistake—a turnover at centre ice by Andrej Sekera that turned into a breakaway goal by Craig Smith. An error by Ference led to another Nashville tally and, when the game ended in a 2–0 defeat, McDavid and Nugent-Hopkins stood and stared at the ice. The team's only goal in its first two games had been an accidental own goal by the Blues.

McLellan continued with his patient assessments.

"We need to score goals to win games," he said outside the dressing room at Bridgestone Arena. "We had looks, but we were not really strong around the net. Some of the things we did on the power play were right, but we killed that with our execution."

McDavid had a few strong moments, backhanding a pass to Korpikoski that ended with a shot that was too soft, then teaming with Yakupov to create several late scoring chances.

"I thought that line was the best we had out there," McLellan said.

On a night when the team suffered for lack of offence, McLellan preached patience when asked about McDavid.

"He just played against two of the top defensive teams in the NHL," he said. "It's going to take some time."

After flying to Dallas late Saturday night, the Oilers had a union-mandated day off on Sunday. McDavid used the free time to join a handful of teammates at the Cowboys' afternoon game against the Patriots, then went to watch the Jays beat the Rangers in Arlington that night. After the game, the group posed for a picture in Toronto's clubhouse with Josh Donaldson.

"It was great for sure," Connor said. "I got Blue Jays fever. I think like a lot of people I got right on the bandwagon."

The players were refreshed at their morning practice on October 12 at American Airlines Center, but they were perhaps distracted, and McLellan was impatient with their effort. At one point, he stopped a drill to chew out Hall for not heading up ice fast enough. In another moment, he chided a defenceman for a shot that had little steam.

"For a goalie, that's as easy as picking apples off a tree," the coach said.

With no game Monday night, some of the Oilers went to watch the Jays again; others spent a few hours exploring Dallas. Ference, Hendricks and Yakupov visited Dealey Plaza, where John F. Kennedy was assassinated on November 22, 1963. There is a museum there, and an X is painted on the street where Lee Harvey Oswald shot the president while he was riding in the back of a limousine.

"Andrew brought it to my attention a couple of days ago, and I decided I wanted to see it," Hendricks said. "I'm a history guy, and I try to put myself in other people's situations. It was an eerie feeling."

Standing in front of his dressing stall after practice, McDavid said he was enjoying his first trip through the United States' heartland.

"They're all beautiful cities," he said. "It's a little different from Sault Ste. Marie, that's for sure."

The Oilers were rested the following night when they took to the ice against Dallas. Unfortunately, as a team, they played their worst game of the road trip. They were outshot fifty-two to twenty-eight and were fortunate to lose to the Stars by only a 4–2 margin. Anders Nilsson made forty-eight saves to keep it close.

"The other two nights we were prepared and ready to engage," McLellan said. "Tonight we had some key people that weren't engaged in the game and others that were overwhelmed and that's the result we are going to get when that happens."

While his teammates struggled, McDavid had his best outing yet. His early efforts had not been flashy, but his progress had been clear. Playing with his jersey tucked into the back of his hockey pants, the way Gretzky used to, Connor flexed the muscles he had developed with Gary Roberts the previous summer. He backchecked hard, sent the Stars' Johnny Oduya flying with a body check and set up his teammates for multiple scoring chances. At one point, McDavid even poked his head into a scrum around the net, a show of feistiness that might have given team management the vapours. But his biggest accomplishment came with 7:42 left in the second period, when Connor tipped in a slapshot from the point by Sekera for his first NHL goal.

After the puck flew past Kari Lehtonen, Connor pumped his fist, raised his arms, breathed a deep sigh of relief and skated past the front of Edmonton's bench, smiling broadly as teammates offered fist bumps.

As with Gretzky and Crosby, the goal came in McDavid's third NHL game. Equipment manager Jeff Lang wrapped the puck in white tape and used a black Sharpie to mark down the details. "1st NHL goal vs. Stars" is what it said.

"Is Connor McDavid old enough to be prime minister?" one fan asked on Twitter.

For McDavid, scoring was like opening a pressure valve. "I was excited, but a lot of what I felt was relief," he said. "It's been a bit of a stressful time for me. There's been a lot of pressure. It's good to get it out of the way."

The day before, McLellan pulled Connor aside and told him not to feel that he shouldered the responsibility for the entire team.

"Connor getting his goal was a nice reward," the coach said. "I know he has been squeezing the stick tight and I am sure he has felt the pressure to score. He has to understand that he is a very important piece to our organization and our team, but the weight isn't on his shoulders. We have to remind him that's not how we are looking at it."

At home in the Toronto suburbs, his mother, Kelly, was elated. "I am so happy for him," she said.

The Oilers started the season with three losses in six days, each against a tough opponent destined to make the playoffs. It was a trip that would have tested anybody, much less an unproven team and an introverted teenager shouldering comparisons to Wayne Gretzky and Sidney Crosby. Connor's goal was a sign that he was growing more comfortable. With the team heading back to Edmonton to play their first game before a raucous home crowd, it seemed that the good times were only just getting started.

EIGHT

AS A KID GROWING UP IN THE SUBURBS OF EDMONTON, ANNE-MARIE BROWN SLEPT IN
Oilers pyjamas. On her way to bed each night, she walked down a hallway
past framed photographs of Stanley Cups.

On the morning of October 15, she stood at the exit of the players'
parking lot at Rexall Place, clutching a sign she made herself in team colours. "Lifelong fan from London, Ont.," it read. "May I please get an autograph?"

It was hours before the Oilers home opener, the most exciting game
in Edmonton in years. The franchise's bleak recent history was an afterthought.

"I think this is a first step toward a return to the Oilers' glory years,"
Brown said. A friend passed on their season tickets so she could attend the
game. "I'm excited for the city."

Brown waved her sign and Teddy Purcell stopped and rolled down the
window of his Tahoe. A minute later, Justin Schultz pulled up in a Range

Rover and did the same. Luke Gazdic came next in a 4×4 Chevy pickup, with Hall and Mark Fayne riding shotgun.

Then came McDavid, sitting beside his mother at the wheel of a rented Kia. Kelly, Brian and Connor's brother Cameron flew into Edmonton from Toronto that morning, leaving behind a city glued to the Blue Jays' playoff run. Rolling down the windows, Kelly chatted as fans surrounded the vehicle, getting autographs and photographs with her youngest son.

"This is sick," one fellow said, inspecting his number ninety-seven jersey, now sporting a fresh signature.

Twenty minutes earlier, outside the Oilers' dressing room, Brian McDavid held a scrum for newsmen. There were thirty reporters, give or take, scribbling notes and jabbing microphones in his face. It was not the sort of thing that happens in hockey every day.

"I'm just really happy for Connor," Brian said. "To watch him play in the NHL, words can't describe the way I feel. It's what we all want as parents: We want our kids to be happy, fulfilled and to be living their dreams. To see him get to this level is unbelievably rewarding.

"The hardest part is that this is playing out on a stage that's so visible."

Connor and his dad talked every day and after every game. "He doesn't like to lose, so that's the tough part," his father said. "This sort of looks like his first year in Erie, where his team only won nineteen of sixty-eight games. But he was part of the turnaround there, and certainly I think it will be the same thing here."

At the Oilers' morning skate, Bob Nicholson watched from the stands at one end of the rink. Peter Chiarelli sat at his elbow. It would be the Oilers' final home opener in Rexall Place, and they were expecting a standing-room crowd of nearly seventeen thousand fans.

It had taken Tony Mazzotta thirty-four hours, including flight delays and a missed connection in Toronto, to get from his home in Lago, Italy, to Edmonton the previous week. A dozen years ago, the city's former pizza king had turned the business over to his son and nephew, but he still came back every year for the Oilers' first home game. He sat drinking coffee and mulling a slight conflict. His son-in-law was arriving in Edmonton early in the evening and expected to be picked up at the airport. If Tony played chauffeur, it would likely cause him to miss the game.

"Oh, to hell with him," he said finally. "He can get a cab."

ON THE NIGHT BEFORE THE OILERS' OPENER AT REXALL PLACE, CONNOR McDAVID SAT at home in the living room with Hall and Gazdic, where they watched the Blue Jays beat the Rangers in Game 5 of the American League Division Series. They cheered as Jose Bautista launched a three-run blast and defiantly flipped his bat in the bottom of the seventh inning. The dramatic home run sent Toronto to the American League Division Series for the first time in twenty-two years, and Bautista's accompanying theatrics caused the benches to clear.

The game had a little bit of everything, including something no one had ever seen.

In the top half of the seventh, with Rougned Odor of the Rangers on third base and Shin-Soo Choo at the plate, Toronto catcher Russell Martin attempted to throw a ball back to Aaron Sanchez. The throw hit Choo's bat and caromed toward third base as Odor raced home and scored. Even though the home-plate umpire initially appeared to declare the play dead, the decision was reversed after an eighteen-minute delay, during which various consultations were held, the replay was reviewed and fans tossed cups of beer onto the field. When play resumed, Sanchez got the third out and the Blue Jays rallied behind Bautista's towering shot.

"It was one of the craziest sporting events I have ever seen, and probably the most intense baseball game I ever watched," McDavid said.

The next night, with a deafening crowd aching to crown him its new king, McDavid was fairly well shut down by the Blues' suffocating defence.

He failed to register a shot and was on the ice for three of St. Louis' four goals in a 4–2 defeat.

"The fans were rockin'," Connor said. It seemed like two-thirds of the crowd was dressed in McDavid jerseys. "It's too bad we couldn't give them something to cheer about."

He showed a few flashes of his trademark speed, flying down the wing, but the Blues' defence kept him in check.

"I'm thirty-four and it's difficult for me to play against a team like that," Hendricks said. "They're a heavy, hard team, but you're going to find a lot of teams like that in our division. Connor is a very heady player, though. He's learning. He's definitely becoming the player we need him to become."

In their first four games, the Oilers couldn't win. They had managed to score only five goals.

"I'm sure Connor feels that a large chunk of our 0-4 record probably falls on his shoulders," McLellan said. "With the focus that's on him right now, I bet he's taking a little more [responsibility] than he should be."

After four consecutive games against tough teams, the Oilers headed to Calgary on October 17. At 1-3, the Flames were also struggling, but the Oilers had failed to beat their rivals once last season.

The game was televised by *Hockey Night in Canada*, mostly because of McDavid's presence. Even the Flames were keen to see him.

"I've skated with him a few times over the summer in Toronto," Calgary captain Mark Giordano said the day before. "Right away, you realize why there's so much hype. He is just that good."

At the Young Stars Classic the previous month in Penticton, Bob Hartley, the Flames coach, got up early one day specifically to watch McDavid skate.

"I made sure I found out what time the Oilers' rookies were practising so I could see for myself," Hartley said. "Not only is he going to be a great player, he's also going to be an attraction for twenty-nine other NHL cities."

With Flames fans booing every time he touched the puck, McDavid scored his second and third NHL goals in a 5–2 pounding of Calgary. In a surprisingly one-sided victory, each of the Oilers' first overall draft picks scored as they combined for nine points, with McDavid notching his first multipoint game.

"I think first and foremost the team played very well," he said. "When the team has success that's when individuals start to have success, and I think you saw that tonight."

The triumph was the Oilers' first over Calgary after seven losses in a row, and was McLellan's first victory as the Edmonton coach. McDavid scored the go-ahead goal in the second period, then sealed the victory on a power-play in the third with assists to Hall and Sekera.

"It was the best game yet from Connor," McLellan said. "He made an impact throughout the night and had an impact on the score sheet. I think he finally let himself go and gave himself permission. As a young player, you don't have to give way to the veterans all the time. You are allowed to take charge and I think he did that tonight."

After the game, the Oilers flew to Vancouver, and the next day they played their second game in two days. McDavid set up a goal by Yakupov on a power play early in the first period, then Korpikoski scored on a break-away in overtime to give the Oilers a 2–1 victory.

"He is really fast and he is really smart," Yakupov said of his younger linemate. "With this guy, you have to be ready all of the time."

The Oilers returned home for a few days of rest, after which they would play six of the next seven games at Rexall Place. Things were starting to click for Connor and the team and it appeared that the anticipation fans had so long been feeling might finally be paying off.

AFTER A SHORT OPENING STRETCH IN WHICH THE TEENAGER WAS FEELING HIS WAY along against rugged, playoff-calibre opponents, Connor began to turn into the wunderkind everyone expected. In a stretch of a little more than two weeks, McDavid scored his first goal, had his first multipoint game, registered his first game-winner and put together a scoring streak that spanned seven games. He was smiling and relaxed on November 2, the day the NHL announced he was named Rookie of the Month for October.

"I didn't set any numbers as goals," Connor said as he stood in front of his stall. The crush of reporters chased teammates away from lockers on either side of him. "I just wanted to feel as good as I could and get more and more comfortable as the month went on.

"I feel more confident now, and know what to expect going into a game. The overall comfort level makes the difference."

Hope and expectations went hand in hand. Although the fans in Edmonton had looked to Connor to start off the season with prolific goal-scoring and consistent highlight-reel moves, McLellan had been careful not to saddle him with expectations that were too lofty. But even he couldn't help but be enthused.

"You don't think an eighteen-year-old is going to advance that quick, but his game has matured in a lot of different areas," the coach said. "He has gone from being a player to a catalyst on the team."

As Connor's confidence grew, the organization's excitement continued to build, and the city was riding the crest of that wave. Fans were gushing about Connor on social media, and T-shirts emblazoned "McJesus" were being sold across the city. The talk was all about how far the Oilers could go; there was nothing to suggest that hockey's most star-crossed team was about to be dealt anything like the cruel blow it suffered on the evening of November 3.

It happened in a matter of seconds. Near the end of the second period of a game against the Flyers, McDavid tore down the left wing on a short-handed breakaway and fired a shot that was turned away nicely by goaltender Michal Neuvirth. As momentum carried Connor past the net, one of his skates turned inward and he crumpled to the ice. In the collision that followed, McDavid crashed shoulder first into the end boards beneath the weight of Brandon Manning and Michael Del Zotto, the Philadelphia defencemen who were chasing him.

Thrilled seconds earlier by Connor's high-speed rush, the crowd in Edmonton gasped and held its collective breath. For a moment, as McDavid lay motionless, Manning stood over him. From the press box overlooking the ice, Oilers executives Bob Nicholson and Kevin Lowe stared in silent worry.

As everyone watched, the eighteen-year-old climbed to his feet, leaned and collected his stick with his left hand. As he skated slowly back to the bench, he kept touching his jersey below the left collarbone with the fingers on his right hand.

"I could see the pain in his face," Nicholson, the Oilers' CEO, said. "I knew it was serious."

Back home in Ontario, Kelly McDavid leaped out of bed. She and her husband had just retired for the evening, and Brian was already dozing off as his wife watched the game.

"Connor's hurt!" she yelled.

Brian startled awake in time to see his son lean down and pick up his stick. If he was significantly injured, his father reasoned, he would be unable to do that.

"He's okay," he told Kelly.

"No, he's not," she shot back. A mother knows. A mother always knows.

Then they both watched, crestfallen, as Connor skated, touching his collarbone again and again.

"Oh, no," Brian said.

McDavid sat with teammates on the bench for the final 104 seconds of the period. As soon as the intermission began, trainers and doctors checked him over. McLellan was immediately alerted that his young star would not return to the game. The examination revealed that the new face of the franchise, if not the National Hockey League, had fractured his left clavicle. The information was then passed along to the Oilers' top brass.

"As soon as we got the information, my first job was to reach out to Connor's family," Nicholson said. "I phoned his mother and father and promised we would move on it as quickly as possible."

As soon as Connor was injured, Kelly had sent an email to Nicholson asking for details. At the same time, Brian had sent a text to J. J. Hebert, the Oilers' communications and media relations director. Nicholson tried to call Kelly right back, but in the commotion, she somehow missed his call. Nicholson then called Brian and gave him the news.

By the time the third period began, Connor's left arm was in a sling. Speculation over the severity of his injury swamped social media. Anxious fans took to Twitter and posted messages, using hashtags that included #PrayForConnor and #PrayForMcDavid.

Out on the ice, Connor's teammates rallied and scored three third-period goals to beat the Flyers, 4–2. At any other time, it would have been a feel-good moment for the struggling team. The injury, though, had rocked everyone in the organization.

"You never want to see a guy out of the lineup, especially one just starting his career and doing so well," Hall said in the Oilers' hushed clubhouse. Unlike after other victories, there was no music, no banter, no smiles. "He was becoming a leader in our locker room, even though he's only eighteen.

"It's never good when someone doesn't come back in the game, and he is a guy that would be out on the ice if he could. It doesn't bode well."

During his postgame news conference, McLellan was sombre. He said doctors and trainers were still evaluating the lightning-quick centre, but they had already told him that McDavid would be out long term.

"I saw Connor for just a moment and told him to keep his head up," McLellan said. "He is disappointed he got injured. It's his rookie year and things are going very well. I have a nineteen-year-old and I can't imagine how he would feel if he got hurt in his first year in the NHL."

McLellan rejected any suggestion that Manning or Del Zotto, who drove McDavid into the boards after he shot the puck, had deliberately hurt him. Combined, the two defencemen weigh 390 pounds.

"Connor went to the net hard like he always does, and the three of them got tangled up in the corner," said the coach, whose brief playing career as a defenceman ended as a result of recurring shoulder injuries. "It was a hockey play."

Through the night, Nicholson repeatedly called and texted the McDavids with updates. X-rays indicated that Connor had sustained multiple fractures. He would spend the night in the hospital and have surgery that day.

At home in the Toronto suburbs, Connor's distraught mother was heartsick for her youngest child. From a teenager living his dream, he had been pitched into a nightmare by one unlucky turn of a skate.

"I knew right away, as soon as he hit the wall, that something was wrong," she said.

As she contemplated the unexpected and ugly twist of fate, her husband made arrangements to catch the first cross-country flight that he could to Edmonton.

"I couldn't sleep," Kelly said.

WHEN PARENTS FIRST TIE SKATES ON THEIR YOUNG SONS' AND DAUGHTERS' FEET ON dreary winter mornings in cold, dank rinks, nobody imagines it will end like this. Through hundreds of hours of drills and countless forgettable games, tens of thousands of parents warm their hands and stomp their frozen feet as their cherry-cheeked youngsters partake in a pastime that becomes a life-long obsession for many and an avocation for few.

There is great joy in seeing children learn discipline and sportsman-ship through hockey, and to watch them grow through the jubilation and pain of winning and losing, but there is not much hope that it will turn into a profession. Nearly a half-million youths are registered to play organized hockey in Canada each year, and there are fewer than seven hundred players in the NHL. Among them, only about half are Canadian, which means that for every one thousand kids playing the sport, there might be one or two whose talent is noteworthy.

In minor hockey, responsibilities fall on the shoulders of parents. Day after day, they lug gear, drive kids to practice in the frigid darkness before dawn, tie their skates and pay prodigious amounts for gear that is outgrown from one fall to the next. The days when a twenty-dollar wooden stick would do are long gone; today's generation of budding McDavids prefer light, composite instruments that cost in the range of two-hundred seventy dollars.

Parents split and share duties any number of ways. Along with the dads who tote their kids' bags into stuffy arenas, there are armies of moms who play roles every bit as critical.

As Connor McDavid grew up, it was his father who helped develop his hockey skills, and his mother who nurtured his heart.

"We used to drive long distances with our boys, and that provided great opportunities to talk," Kelly McDavid said at home during the summer of 2015 before her son embarked on his NHL career. Brian was at work that afternoon, Connor was golfing with friends and his older brother, Cameron, was serving an internship in Toronto with an investment firm. "With Connor, sometimes it would take a while, but things would come out. I was the one he would talk to when something was bothering him.

"I would tell my husband and he would say, 'He didn't tell me that.' I think boys sometimes are afraid to talk about certain things with their father. They don't ever want to disappoint them."

Kelly and Brian were introduced by Brian's sister, who was dating one of his beer-league hockey buddies at the time, and the couple has been married since 1989. He fashioned a career as a business strategy and operations consultant and former retail executive with the Hudson's Bay

Company. She became the human resources director for Miele, a high-end German appliance manufacturer whose Canadian headquarters is just north of Toronto.

Connor was born in Richmond Hill, another Toronto suburb, and he was turning a year old when the family moved into its house in Newmarket. Connor's steady rise to stardom transformed the initially quiet neighbourhood. By the time he made the NHL, strangers would occasionally knock on the door, hoping to catch a glimpse of him or wrangle an autograph. In the town where late comedian John Candy and actor Jim Carrey grew up, the teenage hockey sensation became its most famous resident.

"Whether we deserve it not, I think everyone here feels an immense sense of pride," John Taylor, the town's deputy mayor, said. He confesses to having a McDavid jersey hanging in his office. "Everyone in Newmarket was converted into Edmonton Oilers fans very quickly."

A native of Newmarket who remembers the city from when it was a hamlet in the middle of cow pastures, Taylor has hosted a fundraising golf tournament for years. In 2014, Connor played, but when he sat and signed autographs afterward, not everyone sought his signature. In August 2015, after Connor had been chosen first in the NHL draft, he played in the tournament again. That year, he was swamped with autograph requests.

"People treated him like he was a rock star," Taylor said. "This is a town where people live and breathe hockey."

Connor embodied that obsession. As a youngster, when he played ministicks in the basement at home with his friends, he would direct everyone to congregate in a room off to the side before the game, pretending it was their dressing room. From there, the boys would march out together single file and sing "O Canada" before they played.

"Connor always had a great imagination," Kelly said. "He would get his stuffed animals and put them around the room, and when I asked what he was doing, he would tell me, 'Those are the fans.'"

As she worked in the kitchen, Connor would yell to her up the stairs. "Mom, I just scored the winning goal in the Stanley Cup Final!"

"That's nice, dear," she would say.

The unfinished basement in the family home, the arena where Cameron and Connor had engaged in fierce roller hockey battles as children and where Connor had teams of his friends singing their national anthem, was later converted into a family room, and photos of both Connor and Cameron cover the room.

"We were always down there until our parents got it finished," Cameron, a finance student at the University of Western Ontario, said. "It's nice now, but we really hated them for doing it for a long time."

In one photo in the family room, a three-year-old Connor beams as he stands atop the rink his father flooded for him and Cameron in the backyard. At four, in his first official hockey picture, his broad grin radiates through his facemask.

"That one is my favourite," Kelly said. "Isn't he cute?"

Just a little further along the wall is a framed copy of Connor's first newspaper clipping from 2009. Near it sits a framed copy of the *Hockey News* in which, at age fifteen, Connor's name had first appeared. There are winning team photos from the 2013 U18 World Championships and the 2015 World Juniors, as well as a picture of him standing on the stage in an Oilers jersey after his name was called at the NHL draft.

"That was quite a night," Kelly said. "We didn't want it to end."

Connor's rise to the NHL might not have been possible if it weren't for his brother. Before Connor began his preternatural ascent to hockey stardom, Cameron had been a talented player for the hometown Hurricanes of the Ontario Junior A Hockey League.

"He always looked up to Cam and wanted to do the same thing," Kelly said. "It made him feel a little older."

Playing against his older brother proved a good challenge. As a child,

Connor competed only against players who were at least one year older than he was. In his first season with the Bantam AAA Marlboros, he struggled a bit with the transition.

"He'd get quiet, and I would worry," Kelly said. "He's a thinker."

Eventually, an appointment was arranged for Connor to see Brian Shaw, a sports psychologist and adviser to the Toronto Blue Jays. Like many elite athletes, McDavid is a perfectionist, complete with the enormous emotional burden that brings. Coping with defeat was especially difficult, especially when he was young. He often agonized over it and felt as if he had let his older teammates down. Shaw told Connor there was nothing wrong with being upset after a loss or a bad game but, at a certain point, he had to let those feelings go.

"He told him, 'That is what makes you who you are,' and taught him techniques to help him get over it more quickly," Kelly said.

Connor and his mother would talk in the car on the way to the appointments, attend the sessions together and then have another lengthy conversation on the drive home.

"He would probably tell you that he didn't think it always helped him, but I could see him settle down right away," she said.

From the time Connor was young, Brian McDavid, doting dad and youth hockey coach, had told his wife their youngest son was a whirlwind well beyond his years. Kelly would nod, and then she'd suggest to her husband that he was a tad touched.

"He kept saying, 'He's special,'" she said, smiling at the memory. "I would say, 'Oh, for goodness sakes. Every parent thinks their kid is going to play in the NHL. Get that thought out of your head.'"

It wasn't until Connor was about twelve years old that Kelly recognized that he was different. Two years later, in his second season with the Marlboros of the Greater Toronto Hockey League, she began to believe what Brian had been saying.

"I remember sitting in a rink in and saying, 'Wow, that was really good,' and 'Geez, that was impressive,' and then it started to hit me," she said. "He was able to do things other people couldn't do. I started thinking that maybe Brian was onto something."

Through all those years of hockey, McDavid had mostly managed to avoid harm. Of course, there was the occasional mishap. When he was eight, Connor knocked out two front teeth while playing with a friend during one of Cameron's games. Connor was wearing Heelys, shoes with wheels embedded in each sole, when his friend gave him a shove to see how fast he could go. Instead of taking off, Connor toppled right over and smashed his face against the concrete floor.

When he got up, he had no idea he had lost any teeth. "Am I all right?" he asked his playmate, mouth agape. "I think we better go see your mother," his terrified friend said.

By the time Connor approached Kelly, who was sitting in the stands with other moms, he was crying.

"He walked up to me with his hands over his mouth," Kelly recalled. "I could see blood. I told him to show me what happened. He said, 'Mom, just fix it.'

"We went into the bathroom and I cleaned the blood off. When I took a look, I realized we had to go to a dental clinic right away. It was late on a Friday afternoon, so they were shorthanded. I had to play the role of assistant, and I couldn't even look in his mouth. But Connor was fine all the way through it. He's tough as nails, that kid."

As Connor's hockey career progressed, the number of trips he took to the dentist increased dramatically. Over the years, he broke a few teeth, and, after being struck in the mouth a few times with a puck, had to have root canals on others.

"My dentist knows me well," McDavid said. "Every time I leave his office, my bite is different."

Connor's only major injury came in his final season in the OHL, when he missed six weeks after fracturing a bone in the pinkie finger on his right hand.

The injury occurred November 11, 2014, during Connor's one and only hockey fight, a row with Bryson Cianfrone of the Mississauga Steelheads. After exchanging slashes behind the net, the former hockey-academy classmates dropped their gloves. McDavid pummelled his smaller opponent, but in the process, one of his haymakers slammed into the glass above the boards.

At home, watching the game with her parents, Kelly wondered if Connor had lost his mind.

"I remember saying, 'Oh my God, what is he doing?'" she said. "I sat here on pins and needles until Brian called and confirmed he had broken his hand."

After being taken to a hospital for X-rays that night, McDavid was examined by a specialist in Toronto the next day. Doctors decided surgery was unnecessary but, for the next four weeks, he had to wear a cast.

As fans across Canada worried that he would miss the World Junior Championship, Connor kept in shape by doing bag skating, grueling drills during which players sprint for short distances, then stop and start, again and again. The cast came off only days before the tournament, at which point Connor enhanced his growing reputation by leading Team Canada to a gold medal. Serving as one of the team's alternate captains, he had a tournament-leading eight assists in seven games and was chosen for the All-Star team.

"The interest and attention in him progressed, starting with when he broke his hand," Kelly said "After the World Juniors, it really took off."

In his final abbreviated season with the Otters, Connor recorded a point in forty-five of forty-seven games and finished third in scoring in the Ontario Hockey League. Despite his productivity, though, it was his teammate Dylan Strome, a fellow 2015 first-round draft pick taken by Arizona, who won the scoring title.

"Connor's special gift is that he makes players around him better," Kelly said.

On the night that Connor got hurt in Edmonton, everyone in the hockey world shared his mother's anguish. Whoever the Oilers put on a line beside him, Yakupov and Pouliot included, had been racking up points.

The next morning, Brian flew to Alberta.

"If Brian couldn't have gone, I would have been the one," Kelly said. "It made sense for him to go because he wasn't working."

Because of work commitments, Kelly would wait until Friday afternoon to fly to Edmonton. Until then, her heart and mind were miles away.

ON THE MORNING OF NOVEMBER 4, PETER CHIARELLI HELD A NEWS CONFERENCE AT Rexall Place and talked about McDavid's injury for the first time.

"He will be out indefinitely, not week to week," Chiarelli said. "We're talking about months. We don't have a particular time frame."

Chiarelli fielded a few halfhearted questions about what could be done to prop up the team in McDavid's absence. He spoke about teammates having to step up and the necessity for everyone to move on, but then attention returned to his young star. Under the circumstances, ruminating about shuffling line combinations seemed trite.

"The human side is that there is an eighteen-year-old kid that had a significant injury and who was very upset after the game," the Oilers general manager said. "Connor is such a special player, and at such a young age, it's disappointing. We won last night, but today it feels like a loss."

Trying to find a sunny side, one journalist asked Chiarelli if the Oilers felt fortunate that McDavid had suffered a broken collarbone instead of a dislocated shoulder.

"No," the front-office executive replied tersely. "This is not better than a separated shoulder."

As he watched McDavid plough shoulder first into the boards, Chiarelli said he knew, "This isn't going to be good.

"As a rookie in this league, he has done a lot of things, and he has also done a lot of things as a player in general," Chiarelli said. "He's a bright-eyed kid that comes into the dressing room and makes everybody's day. He's always happy, so that's going to be missed."

Just hours after the game the night before, McLellan had received text messages and emails from medical staff confirming that McDavid had suffered a serious injury. As Chiarelli fielded questions from the press, McLellan was mulling how Connor's loss would affect his team. The Oilers were off to a 5–8 start, but had won five of their last nine games, during which Connor had accumulated eleven points.

"Connor is important to our hockey club, he's important to his teammates, he's important to the city of Edmonton, he's important to the National Hockey League and he's important to the hockey world in general," he said. "But our lives go on right now and we have to put our team back together and get ready to play. That's just the way it is."

Already, residents of Edmonton were in a tizzy. Don Iveson, the city's mayor, called McDavid's broken collarbone "serious business." On *Oilers Now*, a local sports-talk radio program dedicated to discussing the team, Bob Stauffer fielded call after call from tortured fans despondent for Connor, the Oilers, their own suffering and the second-unit power play. After watching replays, some fans were convinced that the injury had been inflicted intentionally. One bemoaned the loss of the star by simply tweeting, "I wanna be sedated (until McD gets back)."

In previous years, fans had had ample opportunity to obsess over injuries if they'd so chosen. Nugent-Hopkins and Hall had each undergone surgery for torn labrums, and Jordan Eberle was convalescing at that very moment from a shoulder injury. But McDavid was not like the others. He had never been like any other. Fans were suspicious.

"You could watch the video one hundred times and there's nothing dirty about it," McLellan said, trying to restore calm. "It's very clear if you watch it and slow it down that Connor caught a rut in the ice with his skate or lost an edge. When the pile of three went down, all three of them were in a dangerous position with the boards coming at them very quickly. I don't think there was anything malicious about it."

Even if their hopes for rising out of the cellar in the NHL's Pacific Division were not completely dashed, the Oilers had just had their legs cut out from beneath them.

"He is going to come back strong, but that doesn't negate the fact that we are going to be without a great player for a long time," Hall said. "There are only a few players in the world who have Connor's skill so, collectively, we are going to have to be better. He's a guy who was really coming on for us personally, and driving the team. It is just bad timing all around."

Matt Hendricks, who took on the role of alternate captain after Eberle was injured during preseason, said McDavid had surprised teammates with how well he had played.

"Since he came here, everyone, including myself, has been saying what a great person he is," Hendricks said. "He is easy to talk to, he wants to learn, doesn't have a big head on his shoulders, is just a great kid. And then he starts playing as well as he had been and you look at him as the guy to start following. To lose a kid at that age, and with how well he was playing, you could see how bad it hurt him emotionally."

As news spread about Connor's injury, players and legends shared their disappointment.

In February 2013, when McDavid met Sidney Crosby, his hockey hero, for the first time, the sixteen-year-old had addressed Crosby as "Mister." Connor's injury came just two days before the two were supposed to play against one another in the NHL for the first time.

"You could tell he was really starting to get comfortable and feeling good out there, so it's definitely unfortunate," Crosby said after the Penguins' morning skate on November 4. "It's one thing to go into the boards like that, but most times you don't have two guys following you up to have that happen. It's kind of fluky."

Speaking to EPSN that same day, Gretzky weighed in.

"He had already shown everybody that he belongs in the NHL, and he's an elite player," the Great One said. "Every time he is on the ice, he makes something happen. Just as important, he thrives under the microscope."

Chicago's Patrick Kane suffered a similar injury when he was driven into the boards in February 2013. He returned in only seven weeks and helped the Blackhawks win their third Stanley Cup in six years. When Connor went down, he also chimed in.

"I was in a little different situation where I was trying to get back for the playoffs," Kane said. "With Connor, it seems like he has a little bit of time to make sure everything is right. If I was giving advice to him, it would be to do everything he can to do it right and not to rush anything."

Clavicle fractures are not uncommon in the NHL, and they generally occur when a player falls on the point of their shoulder with great force. In cases in which there is a simple, clean break, an operation is not necessarily required. But in situations where a bone is broken in multiple places and the pieces are some distance apart, the treatment most often involves surgery.

After making an incision over the middle part of the fracture, doctors cut through the muscle covering the clavicle, then repair it by connecting the broken bones with a collarbone-shaped titanium plate that has holes punched in it for screws. The recovery period varies depending on a variety of factors, including the age and physical attributes of a patient, and the severity of the injury.

That afternoon, as Brian McDavid worried in the waiting room, Connor's broken collarbone was repaired. Now, all the teenage hockey star could do was wait for his bone to heal.

Mark Messier (*left*) and Wayne Gretzky (*right*) celebrate winning their fourth Stanley Cup on May 26, 1988. *Mike Blake/Reuters.*

Mobbed by fans, Wayne Gretzky hoists the Stanley Cup during the Oilers'
1984 Stanley Cup parade through downtown Edmonton. *Material republished
with the express permission of* Edmonton Sun, *a division of Postmedia Network Inc.*

Wayne Gretzky wipes tears from his eyes during a news conference
announcing his trade from Edmonton to Los Angeles on August 9, 1988.

Material republished with the express permission of Edmonton Journal, *a division of Postmedia Network Inc.*

Connor McDavid beams in a family photo taken during his youth in southern Ontario. *Courtesy of the McDavid family.*

Brian McDavid and his two hockey-playing boys, Cameron and Connor, on a visit to the Hockey Hall of Fame. *Courtesy of the McDavid family.*

Connor and Kelly McDavid at home in Newmarket, Ontario, in the summer of 2015. © *Kevin Van Paassen.*

Connor at home in Erie with his billet family (*left to right*): Camryn, Nico, and Caisee Catalde sit beside Connor; in the back are Stephanie and Bob Catalde.
Courtesy of Bob Catalde.

The McDavid family celebrates at the NHL draft in 2015 (*left to right*): Connor; his mother, Kelly; his father, Brian; and his brother, Cameron.
Courtesy of the McDavid family.

Connor McDavid poses on stage after being chosen by the Oilers with the first overall pick in the 2015 NHL draft. *Bruce Bennett.*

Oilers executive Bob Black leads Connor McDavid and other prospects on a tour of the construction site of the new downtown arena on July 4, 2015. *Andy Devlin/Oilers Entertainment Group.*

An aerial view of the under-construction Rogers Place, the anchor of a $2 billion development project in downtown Edmonton. *Jeff Nash/Oilers Entertainment Group*.

Megan Classens, an engineer with the firm hired to build Rogers Place, at the arena site in the winter of 2016. *Shane Jones/PCL Construction.*

Thousands of fans gather outside Rogers Place for a sneak preview on a minus-20-degree morning on January 16, 2016. *Andy Devlin/Oilers Entertainment Group.*

Die-hard Oilers fans Cheryl and Brian Stuart at home
in the suburbs of Edmonton. © *Amber Bracken.*

Fans were eager to anoint
Connor McDavid the
franchise's saviour.

*Material republished with the express
permission of* Edmonton Sun, *a
division of Postmedia Network Inc.*

Con Stavropoulos, restaurateur and character, presides over Fireside Steak and Pizza during the Oilers' last season at Rexall Place. © *Jason Franson.*

Built in the months preceding the opening of the Northlands Coliseum, Fireside Steak and Pizza has welcomed hockey fans for more than forty years. © *Jason Franson.*

Connor McDavid poses for a photo for EA Sports during the NHLPA
rookie showcase in Toronto on September 1, 2015. © *Kevin Van Paassen.*

Left to right: Connor McDavid, Jordan Eberle, Ryan Nugent-Hopkins and Taylor Hall glower during a loss in the 2015–16 season as Oilers coach Todd McLellan (*standing*) looks on. THE CANADIAN PRESS/Darryl Dyck.

Connor McDavid speaks with the media in Edmonton for the first time after fracturing his left collarbone. *THE CANADIAN PRESS/Jason Franson.*

Connor McDavid celebrates after scoring a highlight-reel goal against the Columbus Blue Jackets in his first game back on February 2, 2016. *Andy Devlin.*

Oilers players past and present salute the fans at Rexall Place at the last home game played in the arena on April 6, 2016. *Codie McLachlan.*

CONNOR McDAVID'S FIRST OFFICIAL NHL ROOKIE CARD WAS RELEASED ON NOVEMBE
2015, one day after he underwent surgery to mend his broken collarbo.
Edmonton hockey fans were despondent over the young star's condition, b
it didn't keep them from lining up at sports and collectibles stores around tl
city.

A line was already forming outside West's, a shop on 118th Avenu
near Rexall Place, when Jim Amerey arrived for work nearly two hour:
early. Normal hours were 11 a.m. to 10 p.m., but Amerey opened at
9:30 a.m. that day. By the time he closed fourteen hours later, his voice was
hoarse and his inventory of new Upper Deck Series 1 Young Guns cards
was depleted.

"I have never had a single day like it in twenty-six years," Amerey said.
"Customers who usually buy packages were buying boxes, and people who
usually buy boxes were buying cases. It was crazy."

Collectors went through 2,400 boxes of cards at one hundred dollars
apiece in one day. A number spent $1,080 each to buy a case in hope of
maximizing the likelihood that they would find a prized McDavid rookie
card. Months later, cases of the same cards were selling for $1,800, if you
were lucky enough to find them.

"The demand that he drove in the market was insane," Chris Carlin,
the senior marketing manager for California-based Upper Deck, said. "It
exceeded anything we saw in 2005 when Sidney Crosby entered the league.
In terms of value and interest, it was an amazing year for him."

As the NHL's lone licensed trading-card partner, Upper Deck sells
products all over the world. The two busiest shops it supplies with hockey
cards are both in Edmonton: West's and Wayne's Sports Cards & Collectibles.

That says something about the thirst of Oilers' fans in general, and also
about the furor Connor McDavid created, injured or otherwise.

Before his first professional season, the then-eighteen-year-old had

signed an endorsement contract with equipment manufacturer CCM for a reported $1 million per year. The five-year deal was the richest ever signed by an NHL rookie, and was second in the league to Crosby, who received $1.4 million annually from CCM to hawk its products. McDavid also represented Adidas training shoes and sportswear; the sports energy drink BioSteel; Rogers; a hockey training device, the PowerEdge pro; a Toronto-area memorabilia business, AJ Sportsworld; Canadian Tire's Jumpstart program; and CIBC.

Connor's endorsement choices weren't entirely financially motivated; in many cases, it was his history with the company that persuaded him to support them. His first set of hockey gear was a hand-me-down that his Dad bought from Canadian Tire for his older brother, and CIBC was the bank with which he established his first savings account when he made a ten-dollar deposit at age eleven.

"I was excited because I got a bank card, even though there was no point because there was no money in the account to speak of," he said. "I remember how grown-up it made me feel."

McDavid opened his first chequing account in December to pay rent to Hall. Until then, he had never had any bills. Despite the number of paycheques he deposited, he didn't make any major purchases.

"I'm probably the most boring guy ever," McDavid said.

To fans and the companies that clamour for his attention, though, McDavid is anything but that.

"We approached *him*," Landon French, the executive director of Canadian Tire's Jumpstart Charities, said. The program covers the cost of sporting goods, registration and transportation for kids from low-income families. "We had been watching him since he was fifteen."

Andrew Goldfarb, owner and founder of AJ Sportsworld, signed an exclusive agreement with McDavid in 2012 when he played for the Erie Otters. For the next three years, his company provided retailers from coast

to coast with merchandise signed by McDavid. He also has deals with Jack Eichel and Aaron Ekblad, among other exciting young NHL players.

"To get someone like Connor, who's bigger than the rest of the players in terms of marketability, has been an amazing experience," Goldfarb said. "He's a special case in terms of him coming into the NHL. The hype and demand for his memorabilia is overwhelming."

Although fans were disappointed when McDavid's rookie season was interrupted after thirteen games, they kept buying his jerseys and anything else they could get their hands on. He had played so well so early that they remained patient and hopeful even as he waited for his cracked clavicle to heal.

Kelly Hodgson, the brand and events manager at a sports specialty shop in Edmonton, United Cycle, said he began receiving orders for McDavid jerseys from the moment the Oilers won the lottery. The league and NHL Players Association prevented him from selling items until he was selected in the draft, however. Then, he was deluged.

"With him playing as well as he has at every level, the value keeps going up and up," Hodgson said.

On National Hockey Card Day, more than 250 fans were waiting for the doors to open at Wayne's Sports Cards & Collectibles. As part of a promotion staged by Upper Deck, customers at Wayne's received a free pack of cards for entering the store and a second pack with the purchase of any merchandise. Customers waited as long as three hours to get into the shop across from the West Edmonton Mall that Wayne Wagner has operated for twenty-five years.

"I've never seen anything like it," Wagner said.

The hockey trading-card business changed when Crosby arrived on the scene, Wagner said. And now the same thing is happening again, only more so, with the arrival of McDavid. There was no lull in sales when he got injured, and buyers were in a frenzy at Christmas.

"We are usually busy in November and December, but this year sales went crazy, obviously because of him," Wagner said. "There was never an ex-asperated gasp of 'Oh no' when he got hurt. By then he had already shown flashes of brilliance and had a points-per-game average that was unheard of for a rookie. People just couldn't wait to see what was going to happen when he came back."

THE OILERS WERE WEARY AS THEY WAITED ON THEIR BUS ON THE TARMAC AT LOS Angeles International Airport in the wee hours of the morning on November 9. They had lost to the Blackhawks, 4–2, in Chicago on Sunday night, and were exhausted after a four-and-a-half-hour flight aboard an Airbus operated by Air Canada. (The airline's in-house charter carrier, Air Canada Jetz, is used by all Canadian teams, as well as the Colorado Avalanche.)

The game at Chicago's United Center had gone poorly. Edmonton fell behind fifty-eight seconds after the opening faceoff, and they mustered only two shots over the first seventeen minutes as they fell behind, 2–0. If that wasn't bad enough, a piece of the roof actually fell onto the ice at one point during the game.

As the Oilers traveling party sat in the dark—players in one bus and TV, radio and website reporters in another—a fellow emerged from a fancy private jet parked nearby. It was nearly two in the morning, and no one could make him out. He wore a hoodie wrapped around his face as he approached.

"I bet that's Bieber," someone said, eliciting chuckles.

Dressed in long, baggy bright blue shorts, the mysterious stranger strolled up to the bus carrying the media, motioning to the driver to open the door.

"We all wondered who it was," said Tom Gazzola, a reporter with the website Oilers TV.

As curious as everyone else, the driver flipped the doors open, at which point Justin Bieber climbed aboard. The Canadian singer, who has a home in Beverly Hills, had landed at LAX minutes earlier on a return trip from France.

"I just want to wish the team good luck," he told J. J. Hebert, the Oilers' director of communications and media relations.

Acceding to Bieber's request, Hebert attempted to take the entertainer to the players' bus for a fast visit. U.S. Customs agents intercepted them en route and would not allow it, however, because Bieber had just deplaned from an international flight.

It was probably for the best. Celebrities and sports are an iffy proposition. Pretty much every team Drake supported in 2014 lost. Mick Jagger has a history of announcing he is rooting for soccer teams, only to have them stumble following his pronouncement. And with Connor's injury still fresh in their minds, the Oilers didn't need any additional bad luck.

Two nights after their near meeting with Bieber, the Oilers celebrated a rare victory in Anaheim. Edmonton clawed back from a deficit three times, and the game was decided in overtime on a goal by Purcell, making it Edmonton's first triumph at the Honda Center since April Fools' Day 2012. It seemed like the U.S. border officials had done the Oilers a favour; with Bieber in the team's rearview mirror, it looked like things might finally be taking a turn for the better.

SPORTING A MOVEMBER MOUSTACHE—WHICH PROMOTES TESTICULAR CANCER awareness—and free of an arm sling, Connor McDavid spoke publicly about his injury for the first time on November 16. For a guy whose clavicle had been re-assembled only twelve days earlier, he looked good. And he announced that he had done an upper-body workout that morning, and had been riding a stationary bike for more than a week. That's the difference between an elite athlete and the rest of us, who would never think about exercising so soon after a major operation.

"I feel really good," Connor said at a rink in northeast Edmonton where his teammates were holding practice; a rodeo had temporarily evicted the Oilers from Rexall Place. "It's definitely way better than I thought it would be at this point. If there is anything positive, it's that the injury occurred to a bone, and bones can heal."

The young centre said he knew that something was wrong as soon as he struck the boards. But when he bent over and retrieved his stick, he had no idea his clavicle had been broken apart like a wishbone at Thanksgiving.

"I was in a little bit of shock and it was definitely painful, but I wasn't going to make too big of a deal out of it," he said.

Describing the incident, McDavid said he was skating hard and simply lost his footing after taking the shot.

"I had a lot of weight coming in behind me, and that's all it took," he said. "Any time three guys are going into the boards at that type of speed something is bound to happen. I was the guy that actually hit, so I guess I got the worst of it."

When asked if he thought Del Zotto and Manning had deliberately hurt him, Connor sidestepped the question.

"I don't really want to touch on that too much," he said. "I know there has been a little bit of debate."

McDavid's reluctance to discuss the issue fueled speculation that he blamed the Flyers' players. The truth is that he avoided the question out of respect for Don Cherry. He did not want to contradict the former NHL coach and popular TV host.

On November 7, Cherry expressed outrage over the incident on a segment of *Hockey Night in Canada*.

"I'm steaming," he told a national audience before showing a video clip of the crash. "People are saying that it was just a hockey play, but I'm telling you [Del Zotto and Manning] meant to drive Connor McDavid into those boards. He was hurt, and he was hurt on purpose."

Understanding the serious nature of the accusation, Cherry's co-host, Ron MacLean, offered the outspoken presenter an opportunity to recant. Cherry, who is as opinionated as he is entertaining, wouldn't budge.

"They never give him a chance," Cherry said of the defencemen. "They should have let up a little. The league can't do anything about it because they can't prove it. But hockey guys like me know they drove him into the boards."

There was no penalty assessed and no formal review was ever conducted by the NHL, but outraged fans began lashing out at Manning after Cherry's remarks.

"People said they hope I get AIDS," he said. "There was all kinds of stupid stuff."

McDavid said he was disappointed at the time of the injury, but had since begun to focus on his recovery.

"I was upset, but at a certain point you have to put it behind you," he said. "It's a fast game, and people get hurt. It's unfortunate, but I'll be back out there as soon as possible. These things happen."

Later that day, McDavid had his first postsurgical appointment with doctors. It was just one of many office visits that would occur as the Oilers' medical staff obsessively monitored every aspect of his progress.

"Connor is convalescing and is not in any pain," his agent, Jeff Jackson, said. "He's chilling out and trying to relax, which is tough to do at his age. It's just a matter of letting the bone heal. But he'll pick up where he left off, I know the way he is. I don't have any doubt that he will hit the ground running."

NINE

AS HE WAITED FOR HIS COLLARBONE TO HEAL, CONNOR WAS FORCED TO WATCH KEY moments pass by. He missed the first game he was to play against Sidney Crosby, and his long-awaited homecoming in Toronto against the Leafs. That one hurt the most. Old-timers had anticipated McDavid's debut in the centre of the hockey universe in much the same way as Wayne Gretzky's appearance at Maple Leaf Gardens in January 1982. When Gretzky arrived, it marked the Oilers' fifth visit since they joined the NHL in 1979, but Gretzky's first as a celebrity with widespread appeal.

When Gretzky arrived, the great tenor Luciano Pavarotti was in town to perform at Massey Hall, but his presence barely created a ripple of excitement. Tickets to the opera were scalped for $150; last-minute seats to the Oilers-Leafs game sold for $250. There was so much interest that Gretzky called a news conference at a downtown hotel the day before the game. That a twenty-year-old would summon the media was unheard of back then. But it was easier for him than granting the 132 interview requests that the Oilers had received.

"In terms of a single visit, there is nothing that can compare with it," said Bill Tuele, who was then the Oilers public relations director. "I don't know anybody who wasn't there, in terms of major media."

Journalists reporting for every publication from *Life* to *Sports Illustrated* were in the audience when Gretzky held court for ninety minutes in Toronto on January 15, 1982. He was in the middle of a historic 212-point season, and his fame had spread far beyond sports. The year before, he had even landed a cameo role as a Mafia enforcer, Wayne, on his favourite soap opera, *The Young and the Restless*.

Standing before five TV cameras, nineteen microphones and a massive assembly of journalists, Gretzky invited questions.

The first: As someone with roots in Eastern Europe, how did he feel about Lech Walesa's labour solidarity movement in Poland?

"Everyone groaned, but Wayne answered it like a career diplomat," Tuele said. "Anyone else would have pooh-poohed it."

Gretzky held a second news conference the following morning, and then began to scramble to get tickets for that evening's game. At the time, the NHL made fifty available to visiting teams. In most cities, that would be enough to satisfy the players' needs. But so many of the Oilers were from Ontario, and there was so much interest in Gretzky, that fifty was nowhere near enough. By the time the game rolled around, players had made requests for more than one hundred thirty tickets, with Gretzky needing thirty to forty alone. Worried that some friends might be left at the door, Gretzky handed over one of his Titan hockey sticks to Tuele, who sent it out with a member of the Oilers' training staff to swap with scalpers for tickets. The Oilers got clobbered 7–1, but Gretzky was mobbed by teenage girls as he exited the arena.

Absent from the lineup, but never far from mind, McDavid created a similar stir on November 30 during his first visit to Toronto as an Edmonton Oiler.

While his teammates participated in a morning skate, the eighteen-year-old entertained questions in a room down a winding hall beneath Air Canada Centre.

Gathered in a tight circle, a pack of fifty journalists surrounded him. There were so many that one videographer climbed atop a table to get an unobstructed view. McDavid never envisioned that he would return to the hotbed of hockey while nursing an injury, or that he would watch the game from a suite high above the ice.

"It hurts a lot," McDavid said about his situation. "This is a building I grew up with, and I've seen a lot of games here. I wanted to play."

The Oilers had won only three of eleven outings since the rookie's season crashed to an unexpected halt.

"It's a big hit for us," Todd McLellan said. "Connor was already one of our top players despite his age. He was a catalyst who provoked strong play from his teammates. Some of those others are just finding their way back now."

The Oilers were beaten 3–0 that night in one of their feeblest performances of the season. With James Reimer unavailable due to a lower-body injury and Jonathan Bernier struggling to stop pucks, the Maple Leafs started rookie Garret Sparks in the crease. Called up days earlier from the Toronto Marlies of the American Hockey League, Sparks recorded twenty-four saves in a game in which there were few good chances generated by the Oilers. He became the first goalie in Leafs history to earn a shutout in his first game. Only a year earlier, the twenty-two-year old was toiling in the minor leagues for the Orlando Solar Bears. As the clock expired, his parents stood and cheered. Sparks sobbed with joy.

"They've been playing hockey here for a long time, so I think that's pretty cool," Sparks said. "I can't even describe the way I feel."

Despite Sparks' gutsy performance, Connor and his long road to recovery were still the most talked-about part of the evening. It would be another few weeks before Connor resumed skating, a month before he re-joined his teammates at practice and longer still before he participated in contact drills.

During the time in between, he visited pediatric patients at an Edmon-ton rehabilitation centre on December 8, an annual tradition for the Oil-ers, and attended a dinner in honour of former coach and general manager Glen Sather, who had a banner raised at Rexall Place on December 11. That night, the Oilers chased Henrik Lundqvist from the net while extending their winning streak to five games, their first since February of 2008. Lauri Korpikoski scored twice in the first period and added an empty-netter to seal the 7–5 victory and register Edmonton's only hat trick of the season.

"It reminded me of one of those games in the eighties," Korpikoski said in the dressing room, where he was congratulated by fellow Finn Jari Kurri, who had travelled to Edmonton to pay homage to Sather.

A number of other Oilers' greats had participated in the event before the game. As fans gave Sather a standing ovation, a banner decorated with five Stanley Cups and his name beneath them was raised to the ceiling.

"The success we enjoyed could not have been achieved without being surrounded by exceptional people," Sather, who spent twenty years as gen-eral manager and fourteen as head coach, told the crowd. "It is difficult to put into words my gratitude for this honour. It's not a coach that makes a team, it's a team that makes a coach. I never expected them to be putting my name up there."

Former players said Sather, who played for three seasons for the Oil Kings before embarking on a ten-year career in the NHL and WHA, was too modest.

"He is basically the guy who taught us all," Grant Fuhr, the Hall of Fame goalie, said. "He was our friend as much as our coach. For me, it's a time of great reflection. You can't help but be overwhelmed. There is a tremendous number of people he affected along the way."

The Oilers won their sixth straight game on December 12 on an overtime goal by Sekera in Boston, but then lost the remaining three games on the road trip. After watching a 3–1 victory over Winnipeg on December 21, Connor caught a redeye from Edmonton that landed in Toronto early the next morning. Instead of heading home to rest, he went directly to the old Maple Leaf Gardens—now Ryerson University's Mattamy Athletic Centre—to surprise a group of Pee-Wee hockey players.

Dressed in blue jeans, Stan Smiths and a red track jacket, McDavid signed autographs and offered advice to the eleven- and twelve-year-old girls from the Leaside Wildcats and boys from the Leaside Flames, who were gathered for a friendly scrimmage.

"I'm betting on you to beat the boys," he told the girls, who seemed delighted and a little awestruck. When McDavid visited the neighbouring dressing room, the boys lost their minds, whooping and hollering as he charged around high-fiving and fist-bumping them.

"I try to make it as memorable a day as I can," said McDavid, who made the appearance on behalf of Canadian Tire's Jumpstart program. "I try to leave them with something to think about, whether it is something I've said or something I've done. The kids get so excited to see you that you can't help getting excited, too."

After entertaining the kids at the tournament, McDavid went home to the house he grew up in to enjoy Christmas. The family had been unable to celebrate together in the previous two years when Connor was playing at the World Junior Championships.

"I can't remember a Christmas where we weren't rushing off to a hockey tournament," Kelly said. "The year before last, we flew to Sweden on Christmas Eve, landing there on Christmas Day, and didn't get to see him. Last year, we opened presents on FaceTime so we got to see each other, but it's still not the same."

Upon returning from his holiday break, McDavid joined the Oilers at practice for the first time in months on January 1. He looked so good during the skate that rumours began to circulate that he was about to rejoin the team. On January 9, McLellan quashed the swirling hysterics by announcing that Connor would remain sidelined until after the All-Star break.

Because of odd scheduling, the Oilers had ten days off between their final game of the first half of the season on January 23 and their first game of the second half on February 2.

"We've got maybe the strangest All-Star break in the history of the league," McLellan said. "We've got an Olympic break versus an All-Star break, and we have determined that Connor is not physically ready to play for us between now and then.

"Even if he was ready on the last day or two, it doesn't make a lot of sense for us to play him and then give him ten days off. Connor would love to play tomorrow and we would want him to play, but Mother Nature dictates a lot of it, and common sense does, too."

McDavid, who felt that his recovery was well ahead of expectations, expressed slight disappointment.

"You want to play as soon as possible, but you have to play when it's safe," he said. "It's a little frustrating when you feel good, but it's for the best and will give me extra time to heal. It will probably help in the long run."

The next night, he watched as his teammates battled against a future Hall of Famer, Florida's Jaromir Jagr. Jagr was forty-three, and had scored 257 NHL regular-season goals before McDavid was even born.

"It would have been cool to play against a legend like him," McDavid said.

Four days later, Connor celebrated his nineteenth birthday on the road with the Oilers in San Jose, California. Little was planned in the way of a party; he didn't feel much like one anyway.

"It sucks to be in the spot I'm in right now," he said. "When we lose, I wish I could do something to help. When we win, I feel like I'm not a part of it. Playing in the NHL has been my life's goal, so this has really been hard for me."

McDavid acknowledged frustration with his long layoff while having lunch with his agent during the Christmas holidays.

"It's hard for anyone to sit around, especially a first-year player who's eager to prove himself," Jeff Jackson said. "It's a really messed-up place to be mentally.

"He looks great, but there is a big difference between practising, taking shots and lifting weights, and getting crunched against the boards by a two-hundred-twenty-five-pound defenceman and having guys fall on you in the corner. Everybody is anxious for him to come back because he is one of those types of players. But there is not a scenario in the world where the Oilers would rush him."

They didn't want to push him, but the Oilers did find clever ways to keep Connor engaged. It went beyond the monotony of rehabilitating his injured left collarbone. To keep the talented teenager from feeling left out, the team handed him responsibilities off the ice, including helping with scouting. Jackson said the Oilers' proactive approach helped Connor return with his head firmly in the game.

"He was upset and disappointed he was missing so much time, and wanted to be ready to come back," Jackson said. "Sometimes, when a player is injured, it's easy for them to feel marginalized. The Oilers deserve a lot of credit for having a plan and the right one."

After being idle for so long, McDavid began his final push to get ready for his return against the Columbus Blue Jackets on February 2. He participated in the Oilers' skills competition at Rexall Place on January 24, then spent a few days participating in contact drills with the Bakersfield Condors, the American Hockey League affiliate. He could not have been more excited to come back, and he wasn't worried about suffering another injury.

"What happened was a bit of a fluke," he said. "I have made that same play one hundred times before and have never got hurt. Once you start holding back, you hesitate, and I think that's when you have an accident. I am going to come back healthy and I am going to come back strong."

In fewer than three weeks, Connor would make his return before a full house in Edmonton. What he did that night against the Columbus Blue Jackets was hard for even his biggest fans to believe.

AFTER THREE LONG MONTHS, CONNOR McDAVID RETURNED TO PRACTICE WITH THE Oilers at full speed for the first time on February 1. He had spent the previous week participating in contact drills in Bakersfield, and he was excited that Monday morning when he arrived at Rexall Place. His exhausted teammates, who had rested their bruised bodies and egos during the All-Star break, welcomed him back.

The Oilers had won only fourteen of thirty-seven games in Connor's absence, and the team had tumbled so low that they were perilously close to missing the playoffs. They scored two or fewer goals in twenty of the games that he missed and were in desperate need of a boost, both offensively and emotionally. It is not often that an NHL team gets that from a teenager who has played thirteen games, but McDavid already commanded a level of respect usually reserved for experienced veterans.

"When he walked through the doors today, I can tell you, there were a lot of open arms," Matt Hendricks, one of the Oilers' emotional leaders, said. "We've got the big guy back, and that's going to give us some confidence. I think he is going to bring us some energy and a lot of spark offensively. We have really struggled lately."

Upon rejoining his teammates after the All-Star break, McDavid didn't show much rust. He was bumped a few times and fell once during his first practice, causing the Oilers' collective pulse to rise for a few anxious moments before he got up from the ice. Afterward, Connor admitted to a bit of nervousness about his anticipated return against the Blue Jackets the following night.

"I feel a little more comfortable than I did going into my first game because I have thirteen games' experience now," he said. "You're not starting from scratch necessarily, but you certainly are at a lesser point than a lot of other people. But I'm definitely excited. How could you not be after missing so much time? It's a big day to come back and be healthy again."

McLellan announced that McDavid would centre a line the next night with Eberle and Pouliot on the wings. Pouliot had teamed well with Mc-David in the early going, but had cooled since then. Eberle was an even bigger conundrum. He had been hurt at the beginning of the season and returned to practice just one day before McDavid was injured. Eberle scored seventy-six points in seventy-eight games in 2011–12 but had played inconsistently since returning to the lineup from his injury in 2015; he had only scored three times in the previous eighteen games.

When the Oilers took to the ice on February 2 for their morning skate, McDavid's return was the buzz of the NHL. Without him, the season had started to feel dreary. The biggest stories of the first half were the success of the Capitals and the Panthers and the poor play of the Cary Price–less Canadiens. There was no arguing that Jack Eichel and some of the other promising young prospects had done well, but none of them stirred emotions like McDavid. When it came to generating excitement, the kid from Newmarket was in a class of his own. In Edmonton, radio talk shows were alive with callers predicting amazing things for Connor's first game back.

Following the morning skate, McDavid was surrounded by newsmen in the dressing room at Rexall Place. The mood in the room was decidedly upbeat, with the atmosphere more like a playoff game than a contest between the NHL's two most underachieving teams.

As mysterious as they might seem to fans, dressing rooms are generally dull. A few players entertain questions at their stalls, but most disappear into unseen treatment rooms to be tended to by trainers, masseurs and medical staff. It is the farthest thing one can imagine from the old days where stars sat around telling unhurried stories with cigar-chomping scribes. To some players, the media is a necessary evil, and serious journalists do not consider themselves to be boosters of the team.

That morning, the media presence was so unusual that the crush of reporters chased an exasperated Anton Lander, one of the Oilers' centres, away from his stall. Korpikoski feigned disappointment when he was bypassed by the mob. Hendricks' eyebrows raised when someone approached. "On a day like today, you want to talk to me?" he said, chuckling.

McDavid answered all of the same questions that he had been asked the day before. He said he wasn't worried that his collarbone wasn't strong enough or that doctors might not allow him to play. "I've done everything possible to come back and be one hundred percent healthy again," he said. "I have nothing but faith in the doctors. They say it's safe for me to play, so it must be safe."

Always engaging and folksy, McLellan held court before a standing-room crowd in a bare concrete room beside the locker room. He did not plan to gradually work McDavid back into the lineup. Connor would start on the first line.

"I'm going to open the door and say, 'Go,'" McLellan said. "The way he skated at practice today, I'm not as worried about him as the nineteen guys who have been off for a week."

On game days, the home team participates in a brief skating session first, followed shortly by the visitors. The skates are light workouts designed to let players exercise their legs and loosen their muscles. It was invented in the old days to keep players from partying too hard the night before a game. As the Blue Jackets took part in their session, John Tortorella answered questions beneath the stands at Rexall Place. The coach was unable to join his players on the ice because he was recovering from ribs broken when he was accidentally bulldozed by one of his players during practice. When asked about Connor's return, Tortorella said he was looking forward to seeing the young star play for the first time.

"I've only seen him on tape," Tortorella said. "He's at the top of the list of many good young players in the game right now. I think having him back will give Todd and the Oilers a jump right away."

Tortorella's words came true just a few hours later. When the doors to Rexall Place opened, fans wearing McDavid sweaters poured through and lined up to bid on McDavid memorabilia that was being sold as part of an auction by the Oilers Community Foundation.

Brian Stuart came with his wife, Cheryl. "I have been nervous for him all day today," Cheryl said. "I can't even imagine how he is feeling. I feel like his Alberta mother."

McDavid didn't just return to the lineup; he blew through the confused Blue Jackets team like a hurricane. As soon as the puck dropped, he charged down the ice and drew a penalty. He directed a power play that recorded five shots within a minute. Then he scored an eye-popping goal. In that one play, it took McDavid just four seconds to skate through the Columbus defenders at full speed and deposit the puck past the confused goaltender. By the time he got to poor Joonas Korpisalo, McDavid was thundering like a runaway train, his body and head juking in opposite directions. After scoring his sixth goal of the season, McDavid slid across the ice on his knees and pumped his fist three times. Back in Newmarket, his mother, Kelly, leapt up from the couch, cheering. Connor burst into a smile as he skated to the bench where he was mobbed by teammates. It had been ninety-one days since he fell into the boards, and he picked up right where he left off.

"I'd spent three months of waiting around and there were a lot of grumpy days, so it felt good to get that one," McDavid said later. "I think a lot of frustration on my part came out there."

He later added two more assists as the Oilers went on to a 5–1 victory. Late in the game, the crowd wouldn't stop chanting the number-one draft pick's name. Fans wearing number ninety-seven jerseys hugged beneath the stands and sang "Sweet Caroline" to him when he came out to take his bows as the first star of the game. It was the first time the crowd had spontaneously broken out in song all year.

For the rest of the night and the following morning, McDavid's goal was replayed on TSN and Sportsnet, two of Canada's major sports networks. Fans couldn't get enough of it. "I'm convinced he hypnotized those three Blue Jackets," one fan exclaimed on Twitter. "Totally Obi-Wan'd 'em. Is there a rule against that?"

Teammates were no less awestruck and, in the dressing room, even Connor had trouble explaining it.

"I'm lucky I didn't get killed," he said. "Maybe it was a little bit of luck, a little bit of this and that, but it felt pretty good."

The Oilers headed home that night feeling better about themselves than they had in a long time. It was the happiest night in Edmonton since that Saturday in April when they won the NHL lottery draft. The game was a reunion of sorts, and everyone but the Blue Jackets was delirious. Relief flooded both the dressing room and the city at large, with one fan summing it up perfectly on Twitter: "All hail McJesus."

The morning after Connor's return to the lineup, the Oilers flew to Ottawa to start a four-game road trip. You might never have known they were the away team, though; the lobby in their hotel in the suburbs was packed on the day they got into town. An employee was posted at the base of the escalator to stop autograph seekers from knocking on the rookie's door, and a corner inside the hotel's entrance was cordoned off to keep the crowd at bay.

Sixteen-year-old Nehemiah Bosum was there that morning. Nehemiah and his dad, Harry, had driven 750 kilometres the day before from the Oujé-bougaomou Cree Nation in northern Quebec. Nehemiah was waiting in the hotel lobby to see his hero walk to the team bus; he had already had his number ninety-seven sweater signed a few hours earlier during the Oilers' morning practice at Canadian Tire Centre. "When my wife heard he got his autograph, she cried," Harry said.

The Oilers' game-day skate had been a raucous affair. Henry Burris, the quarterback of the CFL's Ottawa Redblacks, sat rinkside with his children, who were clamouring to see McDavid. Boys wearing hockey sweaters snapped selfies with Connor seated on the bench in the background.

Bob Stauffer, a long-time fixture on Edmonton's sports scene, witnessed the commotion in the lobby that day. Born and educated in Edmonton, Stauffer came aboard as the Oilers' colour commentator in 2008 and, in the years since, had missed only one game while suffering from an abscessed tooth. After watching the pack of fans react at the chance for Connor's autograph, Stauffer said he suspected the hysteria over the young player would grow as the team travelled from city to city.

"Without him, and with the team not in the running for the playoffs, there has been a relevancy issue," Stauffer said. "He has made the Oilers relevant again.

"There's a certain magnetism and energy about him. He's so grounded; it's unbelievable. He has incredible maturity for a kid. It's really off the charts. There wasn't another player who could have done what he did the other night. Chris Knoblauch, his old coach in Erie, texted me and said, 'I've seen that goal before, and you're going to see that again.'"

Jack Michaels, who has combined with Stauffer on radio doing play-by-play since 2010, had seen few goals that generated so much excitement.

"I waited to reserve judgment on Connor," said Michaels, who grew up near Erie in Meadville, Pennsylvania, once known as the zipper capital of the world. "I didn't want to go head over heels over him, but he has made a believer out of me. Those people that think it is too late for him to win the Calder Trophy are out of their mind."

Before the game, there was still much talk being dedicated to Connor's highlight reel goal two nights before. Craig Anderson, the Senators goalie, suggested that McDavid's goal was lucky.

"If the defenceman doesn't fall down there, it's a different story," Anderson said. "It's just the way things unfolded for him."

A few hours later, Anderson had to eat his words. He was replaced in the net after giving up three goals on ten shots. McDavid collected two assists in the first eleven minutes, with Eberle scoring both goals. Eberle was clearly thankful for Connor's return to the lineup, as he had three goals in McDavid's first two games back. Fifteen of the Oilers' eighteen players recorded points. Gryba had two fights against his former team, and Darnell Nurse threw haymakers as the Oilers rolled over the Senators, 7–2.

After the game, the Oilers boarded their plane for a short flight to Montreal, where the Canadiens were reeling without Price and looked ripe for the picking.

MONTREAL IS A SPECIAL CITY, A VIBRANT PLACE WITH A EUROPEAN FEEL AND CITIZENS with cosmopolitan personalities, a deep hockey history and an appreciation for the game, even for opponents. It's beautiful any time of the year, but it truly sparkles in winter. There is no better place to watch a hockey game than the Bell Centre, and no smarter fans.

A few hours before the puck drop, Jill Lean of Fredericton stood on the snowy street in front of her hotel proudly wearing a McDavid sweater. She and her husband had driven seven hours the day before, part of a caravan of New Brunswick hockey fans who had rolled into town to see the rookie play.

"For me, it's all about McDavid," she said. As she spoke, actor Billy Bob Thornton walked out of a building across the street dressed as Kris Kringle, filming a scene for *Bad Santa 2*. His presence did nothing to distract her attention. "I want to see him skate circles around the Habs."

She wasn't the only one expecting magic from the young star that night. "Every now and then a superhero comes along in hockey, and we got one again," Bob Cole, who has called games on *Hockey Night in Canada* since 1969, said. "And he's in Edmonton. Just like the eighties."

At eighty-two, Cole remembered the first game he worked, a Stanley Cup semifinal between Montreal and Boston that went into double overtime. He has seen countless great players, and was looking forward to seeing McDavid for the first time in person. The nineteen-year-old had asked to meet the broadcast legend and, before the game, Cole and Connor chatted outside the Oilers dressing room. "I watched Tuesday night's game," Cole said. "That goal happened so quickly and beautifully. I wasn't surprised, it just reassured me of everything I had heard about him."

P. K. Subban, a Montreal defenceman, admitted that he was impressed. Subban and McDavid had tangled once in the season already, and the rookie had gotten the best of him. After a tough battle near centre ice, McDavid had broken free of Subban for a moment in the third period and lunged to tip a puck toward a streaking Pouliot. Pouliot deposited the puck past Price, who was playing in his last game before he went down to an injury, tying the score at three. The Oilers, who had been trailing 3–0, then scored in the final minute to complete a 4–3 victory. Subban was determined that this meeting be different.

"He's a special kid," Subban said. "What he's done is no surprise. I'll have my work cut out every time I step onto the ice with him."

As savvy as they are impassioned, Canadiens fans arrived at the Bell Centre eager to eyeball the game's newest and youngest star over Sauvignon Blanc and smoked meat.

The Habs slapped around the erring Oilers, winning 5–1, but McDavid drew gasps with his sleight-of-hand trickery in the final minutes. Charging at the net from an angle, he passed the puck between a defenceman's legs, then fired it back through his own legs at the net. Somehow or other, Ben Scrivens, the former Oiler goalie, deflected the shot. McDavid wasn't showing off, he just never stops trying.

The move caused Guy Lapointe to jump out of his seat in the press box. A Hall of Fame defenceman who won six Stanley Cups with the Canadiens, Lapointe now serves as chief amateur scout for the Minnesota Wild.

"Oh my God, I can't believe what just happened," Lapointe said. "This kid is unbelievable."

Paul Messier, an Oilers scout and the brother of a certain Edmonton Hall of Famer, was seated beside Lapointe. "Even in some of the first games of the season, Connor had me on the edge of my seat, and I watched Paul and Wayne play," Messier said.

Despite the praise his stickhandling garnered, McDavid had a frustrating day. He set up teammates for a handful of shots, but the Oilers had nothing to show for it. When Connor was on the ice, much of the game had been played in Edmonton's end, limiting his chances.

Things were no better the next afternoon, when the Oilers played their worst game of the year, losing 8–1 to the Islanders in Brooklyn. McDavid scored his team's only goal. Two nights later, in New Jersey, on the same evening that the Devils raised Martin Brodeur's sweater to the rafters, the Oilers lost. Once again, McDavid was a part of the Oilers' only goal.

The team returned home after that, having just a single win in the four games. After winning their first two games following Connor's return, it looked like their faint chances of making the playoffs were slipping away. If they were to have any chance at all, they had to turn things around in their next six games, all at home. The Leafs were in town next, another match-up between the two worst teams in the league, and with time running out, the Oilers looked to their bright young star to lead the way.

TEN

A GOAL HORN BLARES FROM THE BASEMENT OF A SHOW HOME ON THE NORTH END OF
Edmonton. Replicas of five Stanley Cups are displayed in a cabinet at the
bottom of the stairs. Along one wall, there are three flat-screen televisions
with an electronic ticker streaming sports scores above them, while opposite them sits an autographed goalie mask once worn by Grant Fuhr. A
framed black-and-white picture of Wayne Gretzky hangs behind a bar with
cold beer on tap and a popcorn machine in one corner.

For hockey fanatics, the basement is heaven. For Coventry Homes, an
Edmonton builder in its fortieth year, it's just smart business.

In February 2016, Coventry Homes launched a marketing program to
woo the city's rabid hockey fans. The company was experienced in providing specialized construction layouts: They had packages with options for
chefs that included a souped-up kitchen with rubber flooring and a glass-
front fridge, and another for athletes that sported a home gym with mirrored walls, a home spa with heated ceramic tiles, a body spray shower, a

sun-tanning tube and framed mirrors. But what really set Coventry apart was that they were the only manufacturer in the country that offered fan caves as one of its standard options. Base packages that celebrate the Oilers cost an additional fourteen thousand dollars. From there, the price rises depending on how large and elaborate a buyer's fan cave is.

"We have a base package, but after that it is really à la carte," Tara Van Horn, the marketing manager for Coventry Homes, said. "Pure fans want to see what we've done, and others who are in the market for a new home come in to see the fan caves, too. If people want to go over the top, we will do it for them."

If it sounds a bit crazy, it is. But so, too, is the team's fan base. For years, all of the Oilers' home games were sold out, and in 2015, more than 10 percent of their season-ticket holders dated to 1979. Demand for the rooms was so enthusiastic that in the spring of 2016, one model home with a fan cave was purchased on the spot, forcing the firm to build a replacement. Even though the Oilers managed to hit an iceberg every year, interest in the team not only remained consistent, but continued to spill over into life outside the arena.

"The market has definitely been tighter than it has in the past," Van Horn said, referring to the economic downturn in Alberta tied to weak global oil prices. "It definitely helps if you have a marketing strategy. We launched a partnership with the Oilers because we were looking to do something unique. We wanted to celebrate our love for the team, and see if that would help set us apart."

Coventry entered a partnership making the company the Oilers' preferred builder. The conditions of the deal stipulated that Coventry use only licensed NHL merchandise in the fan cave, and that all the memorabilia be certified as authentic. The Oilers organization provided a few items, including hockey sticks signed by the entire team. The home-building firm introduced its fan caves with a video at one of the Oilers' games at Rexall Place during the 2015–16 season, and held open houses a few weeks later.

For months afterward, gawkers visited the fan cave each time an advertisement appeared.

"If the Oilers show the promotional video during a game, we have crazy traffic the next day," said Yolanda Grant, the area sales manager for Coventry, at a model home on the north side of Edmonton. "We get tons of fans. They bring their family to see the fan cave, and right away the kids are hanging on to the goal horn."

The company has two show homes on opposite sides of the city, each with a distinct theme. The show home in southwest Edmonton features a basement designed to celebrate the current team. Jerseys signed by McDavid, Hall, Nugent-Hopkins and Eberle hang in dressing stalls built into one wall. A colossal Oilers ottoman sits in front of a sectional sofa with orange-and-blue accent pillows. Padded Oilers stools are lined up against a corner bar, and there are display cases full of memorabilia on each side of a big-screen television. Beside the bathroom door is a hockey stick and four framed photos and, to top it all off, there is a Stanley Cup Champions plaque above the commode and a miniature of the trophy on the counter beside the toilet.

For the team's older fans, the cave in the model home on the city's northwest side is dedicated to Oilers teams of the 1980s. Replicas of each of the five Stanley Cups are on display, with an empty spot set aside for one more. The retro fan cave has a comfy leather couch with pillows bearing the names of players whose jersey numbers had been retired—Glenn Anderson, Paul Coffey, Fuhr—and there is an autographed photograph of Fuhr and Andy Moog in one corner. The lights in the bathroom are strung from wooden Sher-Wood sticks, while the shower curtain is decorated in Oilers colours. And, of course, the room features a horn and light that can be activated every time the Oilers score. It is the stuff of dreams for passionate hockey fans.

Born and raised in Edmonton, Kyle Snowden counts himself among the team's most dedicated fans. He was only six months old the last time the team won a Stanley Cup, but he does not hold a quarter-century-long losing streak against them. They came close to winning again in 2006—damn those Carolina Hurricanes—and he has not forgotten the magic of that postseason run.

"I remember how super exciting it was coming home after school and watching their playoff games with my dad," Snowden said.

On a Saturday late in the 2016 hockey season, Snowden wasn't buying a house, but he was spying.

"We just bought a new home down the street, and the basement isn't finished," he said, perusing the surroundings in one of the show homes. "I came here to get some ideas of how to decorate it. I'd love to do something like this. It would be pretty wicked to have even half of it."

Snowden's wife, Michelle Carabeo, smiled as she listened to him.

"I wouldn't mind if he did something like this," she said. "It is just so cool."

Only a dozen games remained in the Oilers' season. For the past decade, as the snow thawed, fans had been saying, "There's always next year." But, finally, the onset of spring was bringing optimism instead of resignation.

"That Connor McDavid is something else," Snowden said. "I can't see any reason why we won't make the playoffs. It's amazing what one guy can do."

OLDER FANS HAD PLENTY OF EXPERIENCE IN THE POSTSEASON DEPARTMENT, AND they had never missed a chance to plan for a championship celebration. The new generation of Edmonton fans was desperate for their team to get back in the playoffs, so that they might have the same opportunity, but history showed them the danger of planning too far ahead.

Plans for a victory parade in Edmonton had been quietly made, then scuttled, back in 1983. Playing in their first Stanley Cup Final, the Oilers had been swept in four games by the Islanders, who then went on to win the last of their four straight Stanley Cups—a reign that has since gone unmatched in the NHL. It was a frustrating series for the upstart Oilers, who had easily won the Smythe Division and got 196 points from Wayne Gretzky in his fourth of nine straight MVP seasons. New York goalkeeper Billy Smith limited their high-powered offence to six goals and shut out Gretzky, while also earning the team's wrath for a slash across the knee to Anderson.

Sather, Edmonton's coach and general manager at the time, unsuccessfully complained that Smith deserved an attempt-to-injure match penalty, then suggested that the Oilers might retaliate. Smith, who also took a dive in the series to draw a penalty against Anderson, responded by warning that if they did, blood could be spilled. "The victim could be Gretzky," he said.

After their defeat in Game 4, the Oilers walked past the Islanders' dressing room and noticed that many of the New York players were exhausted and covered with ice packs. Later, Mark Messier said that seeing the broken-down Islanders gave the Oilers inspiration when the teams met in a rematch the following year.

As the Oilers rolled through the playoffs in 1984, plans were again tabled for a parade. The team reached the finals by sweeping the Jets and North Stars, with a hard-fought seven-game series against the Flames in between. At that point, only the Islanders and their old nemesis, Billy Smith, stood between the Oilers and their first Stanley Cup title.

It was around that time that Don Clarke, one of the parade organizers, approached Sather to discuss plans for a celebration. Clarke had a colourful past. He had moved to Edmonton in 1959 and became a cop and, over his storied career, he had a knack for being in the right place at the right time. In 1965, he and his partner apprehended a Communist sympathizer who had just blown up three U.S. F-84 fighter jets that had been at an Edmonton airstrip for overhaul. Years later, he helped the FBI to bring in a member of the infamous Patty Hearst gang. He was also befriended by Johnny Cash, threatened with a punch to the nose by a member of a tartan-clad pop band, the Bay City Rollers, and berated over the phone by Fidel Castro for refusing to stop a couple of Cuban defectors. After his career as a policeman, Clarke had become an executive with the group that ran the Northlands Coliseum, and was excited at the prospect of planning a celebration for the team.

"Don't even think about mentioning it to them," Sather, who was superstitious, snapped at him.

"They didn't want anyone to know," Clarke recalled. "They were afraid it might jinx them."

Fuhr recorded a shutout and Kevin McClelland scored the only goal in the first game of the 1984 finals on Long Island. When the Oilers beat the Islanders in Game 1, it ended the Isles' record nineteen-game postseason winning streak. The Islanders rebounded to win Game 2 at home, but then lost three in a row at the Northlands Coliseum. Gretzky scored twice and had an assist to lead the Oilers to a 5–2 victory in the fifth and final game on May 19.

It wasn't until the final buzzer had sounded and the Oilers were hoisting the Cup at centre ice that Clarke received permission from Sather to announce that a parade was going to be held through downtown Edmonton. Hardly anyone in the dressing room heard him.

"They didn't pay much attention," Clarke said. "Guys were pouring wine down the front of each other's pants."

Three days later, on a mild afternoon, 150,000 people gathered along Jasper Avenue to take in the victory march. The weather had been lousy for several days leading up to the parade. However, on that Tuesday morning, the skies cleared, as though they dared not rain on the Oilers' parade. The turnout was equal to about a quarter of the population of the entire city, and drew a larger audience than processions held when Queen Elizabeth II and Diana, Princess of Wales, had come to town. Laurence Decore, the mayor of the day, called it the largest gathering in Edmonton since VE Day.

Some might have thought that level of excitement impossible, but this was hockey in Edmonton, and the Oilers had just become the first western Canadian team to capture the Stanley Cup. They did it in only their fifth season in the NHL, fulfilling a prediction made in their first year by Peter Pocklington, the team's owner. When he promised that Edmonton would bring home the Cup within its first five years in the NHL, it had been more of an angry retort by the vitriolic millionaire than a promise, made in response to a Toronto sportswriter who he thought was disrespecting his team. But, no matter the origin, it was right, and the Oilers brought pride and attention like never before to an unassuming and unpretentious northern outpost that had seen its share of suffering. At its best, the oil industry creates great wealth and, at its worst, is the cause of great economic hardship. The parade that day was a reminder that sometimes it did one good to step outside that cycle and bask in the moment.

The parade route stretched ten blocks and ended downtown near the steps of City Hall. With a pipe band marching at the front, a cavalcade of convertibles crawled along Jasper Avenue. Players sat atop the rear seats, waving to fans. To get a better view, some spectators climbed atop lampposts and shimmied up power poles. Soon, the crowd pushed its way within a foot or two of its heroes, reaching out to touch them to try to shake their hands. Streams of paper fluttered down from the tops of buildings.

"Nobody, including me, had any idea it would be that crowded," Clarke, now an octogenarian, said in 2015 while watching a tape of the festivities in his home on the south side of Edmonton. "You couldn't raise your hand to scratch your nose."

Around the city, extra police officers were called in, but not to work the parade. Administrators feared that, in the midst of the celebration, a bank would get knocked off.

Pocklington and Sather sat side by side in the lead white convertible, beaming. The players then followed, mostly two to a car, with Kevin Lowe and Lee Fogolin, the top defencemen, first in line. Wearing sunglasses and looking every bit the star, Messier rode in a vehicle with his Stanley Cup MVP trophy at his feet. He had flowers pinned to his shirt: not a corsage, but whole flowers. Other stars followed: Kurri, Coffey and Dave Semenko, who chugged from a can of beer. It looked as if the big, bearded winger, who served as Gretzky's bodyguard, might not have slept since Saturday night.

The Great One was all the way at the rear, wearing an immaculate white suit and holding the Stanley Cup. Fans rushed so close to him that his car was barely able to inch along. As the parade passed, the spectators who lined Jasper Avenue began to follow and made their way toward the square, as though Gretzky were the Pied Piper, bringing his faithful to the town centre. It took fifteen minutes for him to travel the final half block with a police escort.

Churchill Square was decorated with orange, blue and white balloons, the team colours, and there was a stage set up at one end. Clarke acted as emcee while, in front of him, fans waved Stanley Cup pennants and towels over their head, lit sparklers and blew horns. The theme song from *Chariots of Fire* was playing in the background, but no one heard; the music was drowned out. Looking out over the throng, Clarke momentarily began to panic.

"I stood there with the microphone trying to convince people at the back to stop pushing forward because the people at the front had nowhere to go," he said. "It was on the verge of getting out of control. It's just a wonder that somebody didn't get seriously hurt."

Players and coaches and team staff members were invited onto the stage. Paul Lorieau, a local optician and tenor who sang "O Canada" and "The Star-Spangled Banner" at Oilers games for more than twenty years, opened the ceremonies. As he started "O Canada," 150,000 voices joined his. When the singing had died down, Mayor Decore, who proposed placing the words "City of Champions" on welcome signs a few years later, spoke. The microphone was then turned over to Bill Tuele, the Oilers' public relations director, who introduced coaches and players one by one.

"Last summer, I ate a lot of crow from Billy Smith," Sather told the exuberant crowd. "This summer, he is going to eat a lot of duck from us."

On stage, the Oilers basked in the adulation. Fogolin, the first player introduced, still had one black eye from the playoff run. Kurri, introduced as "the greatest right winger in the game today," drew huge cheers. He had 113 points that season, the second year in a stretch where he had 100 or more points in six of seven years.

Of course, the loudest response was reserved for Gretzky, who was introduced last. It wasn't for dramatic effect, but because they were called up in numerical order. Number ninety-nine was last, and it was as though the crowd had been saving itself for that very moment. The din was deafening as fans thanked the Great One for finally bringing home the Cup they so badly wanted.

ONCE WAS NOT ENOUGH, AND THE OILERS RETURNED WITH A VENGEANCE IN THE 1984–85 season. They won the Smythe Division again, beating the Jets and Flames in a tight race and led the league in average home attendance for the fifth straight year.

In a spectacular season, Gretzky reached two hundred points for the third time in four years, set a league record for assists in a season with 135 and won his sixth straight Hart Trophy as the NHL's most valuable player. That same year, Mario Lemieux made his debut and scored one hundred points and was the league's top rookie.

The Oilers finished with the second-best record in the league, with Philadelphia taking top spot. The Oilers steamrolled the Kings, Jets and Blackhawks in the playoffs, and then met the Flyers in the Stanley Cup finals. It was exactly as it should have been—the league's top two teams facing down for the ultimate prize. Edmonton lost the opening game at the Spectrum, then won three tight games in a row to put them on the verge of their second straight championship.

Game 5 was back at the Northlands, and it was all Edmonton that night. Messier and Coffey scored two goals apiece and Gretzky, the playoff MVP, added a goal and three assists to lead the Oilers to an 8–3 pounding of Philadelphia. It had been a postseason to remember. Kurri tied a record by scoring nineteen goals, and Coffey set records with most goals by a defenceman (thirteen) and most assists (twenty-five).

In Edmonton, there was no doubt a second victory celebration was in order, but this time, for safety reasons, organizers moved the event into Commonwealth Stadium, the 56,000-seat bowl that was built ahead of the 1978 Commonwealth Games.

Once again, the weather was gorgeous when the parade commenced on June 2, with the Pipes and Drums of Edmonton Transit marching ahead of the players in convertibles. Pocklington and Sather came first again, with Coffey and Gretzky in a red Jeep at the front of the procession of players. Sitting atop the back seat, the Great One hoisted the Stanley Cup and kissed it several times. A few feet away, his Conn Smythe Trophy was sitting in the front seat. The emotional conscience of the team, Messier stood at the back of his car with his hands raised overhead. Pat Hughes and Mark Napier, who were brothers-in-law, rode in another vehicle together, as did the goalies, Fuhr and Moog.

A smaller crowd of about forty thousand people showed up for the victory party, cheering all of the players but saving their loudest applause for a few. They loved Fogolin, who had only an hour of sleep the night before the Stanley Cup final. He had been suffering from an infection. Unable to ignore it, he had gone to the hospital in the middle of the night and had one ear drained, but played that night as if nothing was wrong.

Donald Clarke served as the emcee again, and the organization pulled out all the stops. The program was delayed a bit when the SkyHawks, Canadian Forces parachute team, battled winds gusting to thirty miles p hour on their descent. One jumper missed the field entirely, landing in upper deck. Caught by the breeze, he was dragged across rows of seat

his orange parachute until he came to a sudden halt against a concrete wall. But that minor disruption didn't stop the celebration.

Players walked from the cars, which were parked on the track that circles the stadium, and climbed up on the stage. Billy Carroll, a centre the Oilers acquired that season from the Islanders, stood smiling. He had teeth on either side of his mouth, but there was a long, empty gap in between where the others had been knocked out.

"It's a wonderful city to be champions in," Pocklington said that day. "With all of the things people have said about Edmonton, I don't think there is a better city for a sports franchise to be in."

Decore, still the mayor, thanked the Oilers for bringing great distinction to the city, and Sather thanked the fans.

"On behalf of the team, I want to let you know that you touched every one of us with the noise and the excitement of coming out here," he said. "I hope next year we can bring the Stanley Cup back here again."

For the second time in as many years, a Stanley Cup Championship flag was raised in Edmonton.

The Oilers never again staged a Stanley Cup parade. In 1986, the team was upset by the Flames in the Smythe Division Final. In one of the greatest series ever contested in the Battle of Alberta, Calgary won Game 7 when Steve Smith, an Oilers rookie, accidentally banked a cross-ice pass off of Fuhr and into his own net. Smith, who celebrated his twenty-third birthday that day, sobbed as he stood in line during the postgame handshakes, and continued weeping in front of his locker.

That loss interrupted two straight Oilers Stanley Cup championships, which were followed by another pair in 1987 and 1988 and then a fifth in 1990. The excitement and the interest in the celebrations steadily waned after the first two. Winning had become routine. Twenty-five years later, fans would have done anything to experience it again.

AFTER WINNING THEIR FIRST TWO GAMES IN FEBRUARY, WHILE STILL ENERGIZED BY Connor's return, the Oilers entered one of their most difficult stretches of the season. McDavid was playing better than anyone could have expected. However, as the month wore on and the dog days of the season set in, a seeming lack of effort on behalf of some players began to miff McLellan. He had never coached a losing team in seven years in San Jose and had won a Stanley Cup in Detroit in 2008 as an assistant under Mike Babcock. He wanted to see his players hungry to win.

The Oilers were tired and battered when they arrived for practice at Rexall Place on the morning of February 17. They had suffered a tough loss at home the night before, with Anaheim scoring two empty-net goals a little more than a minute apart to seal the victory. As the players sat at their stalls, mulling a season of promise that was fast slipping away, McLellan walked into their midst with an eight-year-old boy beside him. A novice hockey player from northern Alberta, Kohen Flett had been diagnosed with an inoperable tumour on an optic pathway at fifteen months old and had undergone seventy chemotherapy treatments by the time he was three years old.

"He's tough, he's resilient, he's inspiring and all of us can learn a lesson from him," McLellan told his team.

Invited to skate with the Oilers through the Make-A-Wish Foundation, Kohen dressed at a stall beside McDavid and walked onto the ice accompanied by Hall. After leading the team in stretches, he spent the next hour practising face-offs with assistant coach Jim Johnson and won a shootout against McDavid and Eberle, his shots just barely eluding the goalies, as the players slapped their sticks against the ice. Afterward, Kohen sat beside Darnell Nurse as he answered questions during a scrum with newshounds. A tough guy who had exchanged punches with the Kings' Milan Lucic early in the season, Nurse joked that Kohen "had beaten me up" during a wrestling match on the ice.

"The heart that he has and the battle that he goes through daily put our lives into perspective," Nurse said. "We're fortunate to be where we are."

Wearing a number sixteen Oilers jersey and seated at a stall in the club-house with his name above it, Kohen proclaimed that it was the best day of his young life.

"This is just an amazing experience the Oilers have given my son and whole family," Doug Flett said. "It touches your heart. Kohen is over-whelmed and amazed. He has been through a lot. I am happy he doesn't remember a lot of the hospital things he has been through."

For the Oilers, all the bruises that were adding up and all of the aches and pains that were taking a toll suddenly didn't hurt as much. They were there to entertain the youngster, but he lifted their hearts as much as they did his.

"We're happy he came out," Matt Hendricks, a dad himself, said. "He brightened our day. Your bodies are beat up and a little weary, and then you see what he has gone through. I know this is going to be a big day in his life, and it was great for us, too."

When that morning's activities were done, Kohen plopped down be-side McDavid. The rookie patiently unlaced the youngster's skates and slipped them off his tiny feet. As he had all season, and well before that when he was playing for the Otters in Erie, Connor demonstrated that he has a soft spot for kids.

"It has been a little tough lately," McDavid said. "He definitely lifted our spirits."

THE GOOD VIBE DIDN'T LAST. THE OILERS CONCLUDED A FORGETTABLE HOME STAND against Ottawa on February 23. They entered the game with four straight losses, and they faded rather badly in the last two against Minnesota and Colorado. As the defeats stacked up, a few players continued to work hard, McDavid especially, but there was an apparent lack of effort on the part of others.

On that morning before they took on the Senators, Peter Chiarelli sat in the stands watching the Oilers skate at Rexall Place. At times, he spoke earnestly into his phone, presumably with general managers from other NHL organizations seeking to bolster their rosters for a playoff run.

The Oilers were not officially eliminated, but they were edging closer each day. On game nights, scouts for other teams sat in the press box high above the ice in Edmonton, scribbling in notebooks. The previous week, John Ferguson Jr., the director of player personnel for the Bruins, had witnessed the Oilers suffer their tough 5–3 loss to Anaheim. The former general manager of the Maple Leafs, Ferguson had also driven four hours to Brooklyn on the morning of February 7 and watched Edmonton's worst loss of the season, the embarrassing 8–1 dismantling by the Islanders. In that game, McDavid scored the Oilers' only goal and played as hard at the end of the game as he did at the start.

Whether the Bruins or any other contender could find a player capable of significantly helping them on Edmonton's floundering ship was doubtful. The Oilers were 3–8 since the All-Star break and had lost eight of their previous nine games. Unbelievably, despite the addition of McDavid and Cam Talbot, who was doing a respectable job in net, they once again ranked last among the league's thirty teams.

The NHL trade deadline was less than a week away that morning as Chiarelli watched the Oilers go through their paces. With that in mind, he agreed to accept questions from media and provide a general synopsis of the team. It wasn't pretty, and Chiarelli didn't try to paint it that way.

"I'm disappointed where we are in the standings," he said. "In this last little stretch, I felt our energy level and work ethic waned a bit. There was a time this year where we were close in a lot of games and could feel good about that and the effort. Lately it hasn't been there, and that's disconcerting."

Chiarelli pronounced that he would be among the sellers on February

29, the trade deadline day, but only if a deal made sense. He said he did not expect a blockbuster deal that would include any of the team's top young players: Hall, Nugent-Hopkins, Eberle or Yakupov. McDavid, of course, was deemed untouchable.

"We have some players that have underachieved, and we have players that may need a new venue," Chiarelli said. "If certain players are still around [after the trade deadline] it's because the deal wasn't right, or we feel there is a future for them with us. The sky isn't falling as much as it feels it is. There is ability to make this team a contending team, and you can do in a hurry."

With another standing-room crowd watching, the Oilers played poorly that night. They were outworked by the Senators, who were battling to make the playoffs, and struggled badly to get the puck out of their own end. The Oilers coughed it up a staggering fifteen times in the first period, and they were fortunate to head into the intermission trailing by only one. The Oilers' defence didn't improve in the ensuing periods, and the Senators pulled away with a 4–1 win.

More distressing than the score was that, for the first time all season, the home crowd began to get noticeably restless. They jeered when the Oilers had trouble advancing on a power play and booed every time Justin Schultz touched the puck. The Oilers had been shopping the defenceman to other teams with no success; the worse he played, the more difficult it had become to trade him, despite the fact that Schultz was twenty-five and had only a one-year contract.

Once again, the lone bright spot was McDavid, who set up Edmonton's only goal, a chip-in by Eberle off a rebound, and was the team's most dangerous player. Eight of the Oilers' scoring chances occurred when McDavid was on the ice, and he won six of the eight face-offs he took, showing significant improvement from early in the season.

In the quiet dressing room afterward, Hall sat stone-faced in front of his stall. After a few minutes composing himself, he stood, pulled a baseball cap on, and talked disconsolately about the team's fifth straight loss at home, this time to a team they had steamrolled a few weeks earlier.

"That's not the way you want to play in front of your home crowd," Hall said. "We had to crawl back from behind. That's a tough way to play and it seems like we're doing it all the time now. Losing sucks. I feel culpable for sure."

Hall said he didn't feel as if anyone had quit, but Todd McLellan wasn't so sure. Edmonton's coach choked back anger. His tone had become more and more cutting recently during post-game addresses, not so much because the Oilers were losing but because he was frustrated with their effort.

"There are some players that should be embarrassed," McLellan said during what was one of his more intemperate news conferences. "Individually, there has to be ten guys that have so much pride that they pull the rest of the guys along. It's got to get better or we are going to make some huge, huge changes."

Even as the losses had piled up, McLellan had chosen his words carefully. But on this night it seemed like he couldn't take it anymore.

"Right now, I am really disappointed," he said. "I am concerned about the spirit of our team. It is not where it needs to be. I think there are a lot of guys waiting for something, what that is I don't know. If it's changes coming, if it's them leaving, if it's new guys coming in, whatever, that's a dangerous, dangerous thing."

McLellan even took a swipe at Schultz, who played a team-leading twenty-one minutes and twenty-five seconds as the Oilers tried to showcase him for a trade.

"This was pretty disappointing tonight for him as an individual, and it affected our team," McLellan said. "I can't justify any of the first three goals (the Senators) scored. I can't explain them at all. The third one broke our spirit. It completely broke our back."

When asked what it might take to get better results, the coach pondered for a second, and then gave a grim response.

"Maybe we get rid of players," he said.

The trade deadline was six days away.

DESPITE McLELLAN'S OMINOUS HINTS, THE DEADLINE CAME AND WENT RELATIVELY quietly for the Oilers, as it did for the rest of the league. The team acquired a handful of players—defenceman Adam Pardy and wingers Patrick Maroon and Adam Cracknell—and the new arrivals injected a bit of life into the dressing room and brought positive results on the ice. Heading into a home game against Arizona on March 12, the Oilers had won four of six games.

Two nights earlier, McDavid had scored his fourth game winner when the Oilers ambushed the Wild in St. Paul, Minnesota. Blazing down the ice, the rookie had accepted a perfect outlet pass from Zack Kassian and muscled a wrist shot under the arm of Darcy Kuemper with 7:29 remaining to steal the game.

"I'm glad I don't have to defend against him, because I know I couldn't catch him," McLellan said afterward. "But it's not much of a surprise anymore. He's very deceptive in his last three or four strides. When you think you have him, he's still pulling away."

The victory was only the Oilers' fifth in their last twenty-six games at the Xcel Energy Center, and it stunned the Wild, who were battling with the Avalanche for a wild-card position.

"It feels good," McDavid said. "They're a desperate team and had a couple of days off, so we knew they would be well rested. It's a good win for us."

The Coyotes looked like roadkill when they arrived in Edmonton for the second of back-to-back road games. The one bright spot was that Mike Smith would be starting in the net in his return from an abdominal injury that caused him to miss forty games. It seemed like the game was Edmonton's for the taking.

But if there was anything fans had learned, it was that nothing was ever certain with the Oilers. The Coyotes may have been playing poorly, but they entered the game having never lost to Edmonton in regulation time in five years.

The sell-out crowd was in fine spirits early. While a flag was unfurled and a military band played "O Canada," the crowd gave a standing ovation to the three hundred soldiers attending the Armed Forces Appreciation Night. But two hours later, those same fans were grumbling after witnessing another disappointing effort. The Oilers lost 4–0, despite outshooting the Coyotes forty-four to twenty-nine. It was Edmonton's seventh defeat in eight games in the last month at Rexall Place and their second straight shutout on home ice.

McLellan was uncharacteristically terse in remarks in a room down the hallway from his team's quiet dressing room. The way the Oilers fell apart was becoming all too familiar, and his disappointment resulted in a tirade.

"I would tell you that the smarter team won tonight, hands down," the coach said.

Then he began to list the Oilers' shortcomings, and it was a very long list.

"There were reckless pinches on defence, times where we left guys uncovered. We gave up a breakaway on our power play. We took a slashing penalty about fifteen seconds after the whistle to negate another. We shot the puck out of the ice surface on a penalty kill from one end to the other when we had all the time in the world to clear it. And we actually had seven guys on the ice at one point and got away with it. It's a formula for failure that has been proven here over the years, and we just proved it again tonight. It's kind of insanity, isn't it, when you keep hitting your head against the wall and you get the same result?"

McLellan's postgame synopsis ended swiftly, because he need not have said more. His remarks cut his team to the bone, even though they weren't aimed at any one player. And that, in a lot of ways, was one of the problems. At least on this night, there were too many to point fingers at.

With frustration etched across his face, McDavid spoke softly about the Oilers' sloppy performance.

"It's very frustrating," he said. "We're trying to get on a little bit of a roll here at the end of the season. I know we're putting together some decent games, but we have to find some consistency. We've gotten off to some bad starts, and tonight we had some uncharacteristic odd-man rushes against us. We have to clean that up."

There were eleven games left in the season, and seven were at Rexall Place, that venerable old arena that had seen better days. The same could be said for the Oilers, and their chances to reclaim their season were quickly evaporating.

ELEVEN

THE OILERS PLAYED INCONSISTENTLY OVER THE FINAL STRETCH, BUT CONNOR McDAVID remained extraordinary. Beginning on March 14, he put together his second seven-game scoring streak, with two points each against St. Louis on March 16, Arizona on March 22 and Los Angeles on March 26. At times, the Oilers looked good—beating the playoff-bound Blues and Sharks—and other times, awful, as in a 5–0 defeat by Calgary on April 2 in their next-to-last home game at Rexall Place. The final meeting of the season in the Battle of Alberta series wasn't much of one at all and McLellan was particularly miffed by his team's uninspired outing.

"We've been together for two hundred days and have talked a lot about competing and working hard and showing up, and we get that," McLellan said. "That's the exact crap we're trying to eradicate from this group. You work hard and you climb and you climb and you get some foundation in and you give it all back in one night? I don't think there is a number big enough to describe how disappointing that effort is."

Over the last three weeks, the Oilers were locked in a struggle with the Maple Leafs to see who would end up with the league's worst record. Toronto barely won the race for last place, and later won the draft lottery and the right to pick American centre Auston Matthews in Buffalo on June 24 at the NHL draft. As he had been in the two other months that he played, McDavid was again chosen the NHL's top rookie, this time for March. He ended up with five goals and sixteen points in fifteen games, to go along with twelve points in twelve games in October and seventeen points in fourteen games in February.

As play wound down in the long season, conversation started to turn to who would win the Calder Trophy. Had he not been injured, McDavid would have likely been the runaway favourite to collect the award handed out to the NHL's top rookie. Over the course of the season, he was the only player to win the rookie of the month honours more than once, and the first to win it three times since Alexander Ovechkin in 2005–06. By capturing the honour in each month he played, McDavid really left little doubt who the league's top rookie was. But it was still no sure thing that the Professional Hockey Writers Association would pick him after he had missed three months.

The Oilers' young centre had started spectacularly, and he was rounding it out in fine form. In between, however, he had missed nearly half the season while recuperating from surgery. That cracked the door open for other candidates, and other first-year players squeezed their way into contention.

The wild card in the running was Chicago's Artemi Panarin. Playing on a line with NHL scoring leader Patrick Kane, the slightly built winger racked up far more points than any other rookie: thirty goals and forty-seven assists. He seemed to be the most logical and deserving choice apart from McDavid, but there were several factors that could derail his candidacy, foremost among them the fact that, at twenty-four, Panarin was older than the other contenders and had already played three seasons in the KHL.

For its own reasons, the NHL refuses to recognize the rival Russian circuit as a professional organization. Due to that, Panarin met the standard for rookie status, even though he had already played in the elite European league. None of those things were Panarin's fault, of course, but it was unclear whether voters would look favourably upon him.

Buffalo's Jack Eichel, the nineteen-year-old selected immediately after McDavid in the NHL draft, was in the process of finishing an exceptional rookie campaign. He was second to Panarin in points and goals among newcomers, and he had missed only one game all season.

In their only head-to-head matchup, however, Connor had outshone Eichel. The two rookies met for the first time in early March. McDavid set the tone when he scored just twenty-two seconds into the contest. Buffalo answered, and the game eventually went to overtime. With time winding down, Eichel nearly ended it with a spinning backhand at the end of the rush. But the puck sailed past the net and around the boards, where McDavid picked it up. Connor streaked down the rink and buried the backhand past Robin Lehner to steal Eichel's thunder and win the game.

"I think they were the two best players on the ice," McLellan said outside the Oilers' dressing room. "They are both big-time players. They didn't disappoint."

Other than Panarin, Eichel and McDavid, the other most viable candidates were Philadelphia defenceman Shayne Gostisbehere and the Coyotes' Max Domi. A twenty-two year-old who grew up in South Florida, Gostisbehere had set a Flyers' record for rookies and an NHL record for first-year defenders by putting together a fifteen-game scoring streak. The son of the fiery tough guy Tie Domi, Max had a great inaugural season, but his numbers were similar to Connor's, who played in far fewer games.

Heading into the spring, then, it had looked like a race between Panarin, McDavid, Eichel and Gostisbehere, as long as voters didn't hold the Blackhawk winger's age and three years' experience in Russia against him. After a practice on April 1, McDavid acknowledged for the first time that winning the Calder Trophy would be thrilling.

"It's not something I've been too worried about or focused on," he said. "If I get some votes, that would be very nice. Winning would be a dream come true, but it's out of my hands. I've played some good hockey, but so have a lot of other guys."

That day also marked the first time that Connor's coaches and teammates began wading heavily into the rookie debate. McLellan said he believed McDavid warranted consideration despite missing those thirty-seven games.

"It's unfortunate he got hurt, and that's something voters will have to take into consideration," the coach said. "In the games he has played, he's been our go-to guy. In the three months that he's played, I think he's established what he can do."

Eberle, who benefitted greatly from playing on the rookie's line, believed the injury actually helped McDavid's argument for rookie honours. In the first twenty-nine games after his return, Connor amassed thirty-three points and put together one seven-game scoring streak.

"I don't think I can say much that hasn't already been said," Eberle said. "If his production is there, why not give him the Calder? He's had a great season. If anything, it has been amazing that's he's been able to come back from an injury like that and play the way he has."

Connor's housemate and friend, Hall, was turning into his most ardent supporter. He noted that McDavid had accumulated most of his points down the stretch, a period when teams were fighting for the playoffs, making defence that much tighter and scoring all the more difficult.

"Everyone knows who the best rookie is," Hall said. "I think it's a lot harder to put up points like Connor has. The pace is much higher than the start of the season. He has my vote."

In the preseason, the Oilers had tried to take the pressure off McDavid. When they talked about him, they lowered the bar in terms of expectations.

Some had expressed doubt, at least publicly, that he would have much of an impact in his first season. Now, months later, they were acknowledging his greatness.

"It's not like he came here as a project by any means," Hall said. "He was an exceptional player from the moment he stepped on the ice and put on our jersey. It has been fun to watch what he's done month after month and game after game. It's great to see for the future of our team."

If Connor failed to win the Calder, Hall said, it would leave him in good company. Wayne Gretzky, who won the rookie of the year in the WHA, wasn't eligible to win again the following year when he jumped to the NHL. And Crosby, who was edged out by Ovechkin, didn't win either. "It is a great honour," Hall said, "but I'm sure Connor is looking forward to bigger and better things."

That would be a fitting mentality, given the legacy that McDavid was establishing. But even with one eye on Connor's long-term impact, no one could deny that the young man's talent in the present still spoke for itself.

A prodigy who received his first pair of skates when he was two years old and could almost skate before he could walk, Dale Hawerchuk joined the Winnipeg Jets as an eighteen-year-old in 1980. The first player taken in that year's draft, he became the youngest in history at that time to reach one hundred points before going on to win the Calder Trophy. After scoring ninety-one points in his second year, Hawerchuk had one hundred or more points in each of the next five seasons, and retired in 1997 with 1,409 points in fewer than 1,200 games. Although the Jets ended up with forty-eight points more in his first season than the year before, Hawerchuk remembers it as a challenging time.

"At that age, you really just try to find your way along," Hawerchuk, who was inducted into the Hockey Hall of Fame, said. "You don't really know what to expect, and simply want to fit in on the team. For me, that was the big thing. I didn't try to overthink it too much."

The coach of the Barrie Colts since 2010, Hawerchuk watched McDavid in the three seasons he played for Erie. The Otters went from winning nine-teen games in Connor's first season as a sixteen-year-old to winning fifty-two the following year and fifty in 2014–15. Hawerchuk had no doubt that McDavid was going to be one of the NHL's elite players.

"He has good vision, a quick shot, great hands and skates so fast," Hawerchuk said. "Once he adds a little more strength to his game, who knows how far he'll go? He's still growing. People in Edmonton are going to get their money's worth."

Hawerchuk believed McDavid would benefit from the lessons he learned during his rookie season.

"It's a big transition," he said. "In the NHL, you're playing a demanding schedule in different buildings in different cities against different teams, and you're going up against men every night. It takes a while to get to know your opponents, and you have to get know your teammates as well.

"You learn on the fly, and that's not easy at the start. It's kind of sink or swim, and nobody else comes to the rescue to help you get out of the storm. But it gets easier once you realize you can play at that level. Suddenly you notice you aren't being pushed around, and you're doing things that you never had in your repertoire before."

On May 2, the finalists for the Calder award were announced, with McDavid, Panarin and Gostisbehere the candidates for the trophy pre-sented on June 22 in Las Vegas. One had to feel a bit sorry for Eichel, who finished second among all rookies in scoring with fifty-six points but was still overshadowed by his alter ego in Edmonton.

While making a case to become the first Oiler in history to be chosen rookie of the year, McDavid finished fourth among all first-year players with forty-eight points, had a dozen multipoint games and ended up third over-all in points-per-game-average behind only Kane and Jamie Benn of Dallas. Panarin finished ninth in scoring, led all rookies in goals, assists, power-play points and game-winning goals. The Flyers' first Calder finalist since forward Mikael Renberg in 1994, Gostisbehere made a strong play for the

"None of us had any idea that was going to happen," McDavid said. "It as a shock to everyone, really. There was an announcement, but it was in Russian first, so nobody knew what was going on. And then all of a sudden e saw him at the podium. Everyone was in awe."

Kept in hiding amid tight security during the gold-medal game, Putin addressed the crowd and players on both teams before hugging and shaking the hand of Canadian captain Corey Perry.

"I thank Canada for giving the world this brilliant, extraordinary sport," Putin said in a short speech. He also congratulated Finland, as well as Russia's entry, which won the bronze medal.

"I know that [our] fans hoped for a better outcome," Putin told the audience. "But sport is sport and hockey is hockey. Our men played with full commitment. They have shown themselves well and I congratulate them heartily."

As music blared and streamers fell onto the ice, a handful of Team Canada players approached the president for a polite handshake. In many ways, Putin is a polarizing figure politically, but he was completely apolitical, in keeping with the occasion.

Oilers executive Bob Nicholson, who serves as vice president of the International Ice Hockey Federation, shared the stage with Putin. He was initially told the Russian president might want him to step away, but Putin allowed him to stand beside him and even exchanged small talk.

"Only a few people knew he was coming into the building," Nicholson said. "When he came onto the ice, it was like the air was sucked out of the arena. The crowd went crazy."

As they waited to hand out medals, Putin and Nicholson discussed the importance of hockey, and afterwards, Putin made himself available for pictures with IIHF staff members and Team Canada officials. Nicholson was among those who stayed to have a few frames snapped with him.

"I was going to ask if he would sponsor a vodka bar in the Oilers' new arena," Nicholson joked.

award by scoring seventeen goals, the most by a rookie defenceman since Dion Phaneuf had twenty for Calgary in 2005–06. Gostisbehere also set a league record for first-year blue-liners with four overtime goals, a number that tied the most ever extra-frame goals by a defenceman in a season.

Leading up to the awards announcement at the Hard Rock Hotel, arguments were made by fans on behalf of all three of them, with Don Cherry wading in on McDavid's behalf on a segment of Coach's Corner.

"Folks, let's face it, he is the guy that should win it," Cherry said. "If you were starting a franchise tomorrow, who would you want to pick? The best rookie. So, who's the best rookie?"

According to the writers, it was Panarin, whose award was the first introduced that night. McDavid, as good as he had been, had to be satisfied with being a finalist.

In the month after the season, McDavid continued to impress at the International Ice Hockey Federation World Championship in Russia.

The Oilers' young centre scored the first goal in Team Canada's 2–0 victory in the gold-medal game against Finland on May 22 and finished the tournament with that lone goal and eight assists in ten games. The victory in Moscow avenged Team Canada's 4–0 loss to the Finns in the round robin and secured the Canadians' second consecutive world championship.

McDavid's goal in the first period stood up, backing a sixteen-save effort from Edmonton teammate Cam Talbot, who was outstanding while recording four shutouts and a 1.25 goals-against average in eight games. Two other Edmonton players were also on the team: Eberle and Hall, who tied for the lead among all forwards with six goals.

With the victory, McDavid became the youngest player ever to win three of hockey's most prestigious international events: the IIHF World championship, the world U18 tournament and the world junior championships.

As Team Canada players gathered for the postgame ceremony, they were stunned to see Russian President Vladimir Putin walk across the ice to oversee the festivities.

"None of us had any idea that was going to happen," McDavid said. "It was a shock to everyone, really. There was an announcement, but it was in Russian first, so nobody knew what was going on. And then all of a sudden we saw him at the podium. Everyone was in awe."

Kept in hiding amid tight security during the gold-medal game, Putin addressed the crowd and players on both teams before hugging and shaking the hand of Canadian captain Corey Perry.

"I thank Canada for giving the world this brilliant, extraordinary sport," Putin said in a short speech. He also congratulated Finland, as well as Russia's entry, which won the bronze medal.

"I know that [our] fans hoped for a better outcome," Putin told the audience. "But sport is sport and hockey is hockey. Our men played with full commitment. They have shown themselves well and I congratulate them heartily."

As music blared and streamers fell onto the ice, a handful of Team Canada players approached the president for a polite handshake. In many ways, Putin is a polarizing figure politically, but he was completely apolitical, in keeping with the occasion.

Oilers executive Bob Nicholson, who serves as vice president of the International Ice Hockey Federation, shared the stage with Putin. He was initially told the Russian president might want him to step away, but Putin allowed him to stand beside him and even exchanged small talk.

"Only a few people knew he was coming into the building," Nicholson said. "When he came onto the ice, it was like the air was sucked out of the arena. The crowd went crazy."

As they waited to hand out medals, Putin and Nicholson discussed the importance of hockey, and afterwards, Putin made himself available for pictures with IIHF staff members and Team Canada officials. Nicholson was among those who stayed to have a few frames snapped with him.

"I was going to ask if he would sponsor a vodka bar in the Oilers' new arena," Nicholson joked.

against the Maple Leafs. Two goals in the overtime triumph over Eichel in Buffalo. Three points in front of players from Edmonton's greatest players in the final game at Rexall Place.

As players filed out of the Oilers dressing room on the day following the end of the season, a pattern emerged. Each talked about how it had been a discouraging year, then gushed about how it had been exciting to play beside and watch the rookie wearing ninety-seven.

Hall, who led the team in scoring with sixty-five points, started out by launching a blistering critique.

"We finished in twenty-ninth place," he said. "There are a lot of guys that expect more of themselves, and I'm no different. I'm very disappointed right now. I'm not going to lie. It's hard to see the light at the end of the tunnel right now."

Then, he softened. The biggest bright spot, he said, had been McDavid. Hall watched as Connor shouldered enormous pressure early in the year, and comforted him in the days following his accident, then watched him come back and set the league on its ear.

"He was everything and more than he was cracked up to be," the left wing said. "By the end, he was our leader on the ice. With all of the expectations that were on him, and the way he conducted himself off the ice and the kind of kid he is, he was a lot of fun to be around."

For the first time in a number of years, the Oilers headed into summer feeling comfortable about their goalkeeper. After a shaky start, Talbot had become one of the most efficient in the league. As a bonus, he said that his position provided him with a splendid view from which to watch McDavid.

"He does everything the right way," Talbot said. "He doesn't take shortcuts, he is always the first one up the ice, and he is always the first guy back on the backcheck. There are different ways you can lead, and it doesn't always have to be vocal. Connor is one of those guys who leads by example. He's a guy you want to follow."

Acquired late in the season from the Anaheim Ducks for a fourth-round draft pick, Maroon flourished when playing on McDavid's left wing. A 230-pound grinder, Maroon added beef to the lineup and had eight goals and fourteen points in sixteen games. In fifty-six games before he joined the Oilers on February 29, he scored only thirteen points.

"There's no room for him to pass, and he finds a way to put the puck right on your stick," Maroon said. "To have his speed and vision and those hands, you can't teach that. He is going to put a lot of fans in that new stadium, and they are going to enjoy every second."

For Maroon, joining the Oilers was the start of a renaissance. It was short—barely more than a month's worth of work—but it was enough for him and the organization to look forward to trying it next year.

"There's an opportunity for me to grow as a leader, and playing with Connor is an opportunity for me to succeed in this league," Maroon said. "It gives me a chance to put up good numbers. If the opportunity is there and I'm on the left side with number ninety-seven, I'm going to run with it."

Having played in nearly five hundred regular-season games in his career, Hendricks appraised McDavid as captain material. As an eighteen-year-old, Crosby was named an alternate captain midway through his rookie season and then became the youngest captain in NHL history the following year.

"You couldn't ask more of Connor in the dressing room, and I don't know if you could ask more of him as a player, either," Hendricks said. "He came to a struggling group as a young guy with a lot of expectations, and he overwhelmed a lot of us. I feel real fortunate to play with him and enjoy his rookie season."

Hendricks said he had no doubt McDavid is up to wearing the C should the Oilers choose to give it to him in his second season.

"Connor has a lot of attributes in terms of playing ability, but I see him as a good leader as well," Hendricks said. "I absolutely believe he could be the captain. You've seen players his age do it after their first year. There's no doubt in my mind he would excel at it."

In his final news conference, McLellan said McDavid was in the running for the captaincy. If appointed, Connor would replace Gabriel Landeskog of Colorado as the youngest in NHL history; Landeskog was eleven days younger than Crosby when the Avalanche made him captain in 2011.

"Connor was a tremendous leader this year in his short time with us," McLellan said. "His presence when he walks into the room exudes confidence. I think leaders attract people, and people want to be around him.

"He's nineteen, but I think he's close to being ready to be the guy. We'll talk more about it this summer. He'll need a good supporting crew around him. We'll see what the team looks like in the fall to determine whether or not that's the right thing."

McDavid was grateful to hear that teammates were talking about him becoming the captain.

"That's a huge honour, and that means a lot to me," he said. "I think that's something I aim to do. I'm not the loudest guy in the room or on the bench, but I try to do whatever leading I do by example on the ice."

In a frank summarization of his first season as the Edmonton general manager, Chiarelli acknowledged disappointment. The Oilers finished 31–43–8 with seventy points, an eight-point improvement over the preceding season, but twelve shy of what Chiarelli expected.

"I didn't like losing all of those games," he said. "I am disappointed where we are, but in this business you have to expect everything. So it wasn't completely surprising, but I did expect better."

Chiarelli said major changes were coming.

"As a manager, you look at every option," he said. "I guess nobody is untouchable, except for a couple of guys. I have to look at everything. We did have improvement in areas, but the bar was pretty low, and I want to be better. What we have now isn't good enough."

Although he never mentioned Connor by name, it was clear Chiarelli would not consider trading him, just as he had refused to entertain offers for the first pick before the 2015 draft.

That summer Chiarelli predicted McDavid would finish his rookie season with forty points. After watching Connor skate circles around everyone during rookie camp and blaze through preseason, Chiarelli revised his estimate to sixty points. He wasn't far off, but only because the brilliant centre missed nearly half the season, which put Connor in elite company: Steven Stamkos had forty-six points in seventy-nine games during his rookie season in 2008–09, and John Tavares had fifty-four in eighty games in 2009–10.

"I think Connor had a very good year," Chiarelli said. "I think we saw a lot of special games out of him. His competitive spirit flourished during the time he wasn't playing, and I thought that made him a better player. Heavy-handedly or clumsily, I tried to temper expectations for him. He is a heck of a player."

ALTHOUGH THE OILERS' SEASON OFFICIALLY ENDED AFTER THEIR FINAL GAME AGAINST the Canucks, in a sense, it was over before the team plane even took off for Vancouver. On April 6, 2016, Edmonton said goodbye to the giant concrete house in which generations of hockey fans had grown up. The day was packed full of celebrations that included as many alumni, fans and players as possible.

Raised on the outskirts of Edmonton, Messier had taken a bus to the Edmonton Gardens as a kid to watch Bobby Hull. He saw the coliseum being built, and then had the good fortune to play in it for a dozen seasons starting in 1979.

"As a kid, I had a dream to play in the NHL," he said. "Who would have thought I would get a chance to not only do that, but at the Northlands? It was the building that put Edmonton on the map, and galvanized the city in so many ways."

In the morning, as he drove to the arena for a reception, Messier was flooded with memories.

"I was here from the start," the fifty-five-year-old said. "It's incredible how a building can take on a personality. If I described it as a hockey player, I'd say it had a lot of heart, a lot of passion, it was tough for opposing teams to play against and had a lot of grit and dedication."

Jari Kurri, the Hall of Famer who excelled on Gretzky's right wing, recalled arriving in Edmonton from Finland in 1980.

"I was a young guy and didn't know what to expect," Kurri said. "There was so much going on in my mind. Was I going to make it? Would I only be here for one year? I'm sure tonight, when I look around the building, there will be a lot of flashbacks."

In the early afternoon, thousands of fans gathered in a square outside city hall in downtown Edmonton to pay tribute to the team in a rally presided over by Edmonton Mayor Don Iveson.

"It's a bittersweet day, in a sense," Iveson said. "I remember my first Oilers game in 1988. We sat in the second row in one corner, and I watched Wayne Gretzky skate past. I get emotional thinking about it. It was magical for a little boy."

With the wind whipping around them, players spanning five decades stood on the steps in orange-and-blue jerseys. Fans lined the streets, patiently enduring the cool spring weather as they honoured heroes from their past.

"This is similar to 1984, when people came here to celebrate the Stanley Cup," Messier said, addressing the throng. As he spoke, construction continued a few blocks away on the team's new rink. "We used to say, if we win, the stage is big enough for everybody. Well, all of you deserve to be up here with us. We look forward to turning the page into Rogers Place, making more memories, winning more Stanley Cups and restoring the pride we all had."

The Great One was also in town to mark the end of the era of the 16,839-seat house he built. Early in the afternoon, Gretzky rode to the arena in a limousine and posed for photos with his wife and kids beside the statue of him that stood in front of the arena since 1989. When he arrived for the game a few hours later, he stopped for a picture beside the bronze bust with his dad, Walter, and then had a few more photos taken with fans.

"Glen Sather would tell us, 'These are memories you'll have the rest of your life,'" Gretzky said. "Until now, I didn't realize how right on he was. It was a very special time and a very special place."

Spectators streamed into the arena as soon as the doors opened at three thirty that afternoon. The start of the game—a sell-out for which tickets were sold online at prices ranging from $300 to $3,000—was moved to five o'clock to accommodate closing festivities. A few fans tailgated in the parking lot, determined to celebrate every last moment of the venerated rink to its fullest.

Before the game, fans sang "O Canada" louder than ever before. They stood and cheered during a ceremonial puck drop that brought together representatives ranging from long-time arena employees to team executives and players from long in the past. The group included Mark Lewis, the arena's retiring announcer of thirty-five years, Miles Poliak, an usher since 1974, and Fonteyne, the first player chosen by the Alberta Oilers in the 1972 WHA draft.

In the four decades since the Northlands Coliseum opened its doors, Canada had ten prime ministers and Edmonton's population doubled to nine hundred thousand. There had been more than ten thousand goals scored, ten thousand penalties served and four Stanley Cups won on home ice. Ron Buchanan scored the first goal for the Oilers on November 10, 1974, and on that April night, Leon Draisaitl scored the last in a 6–2 thumping of the Canucks.

As the final seconds wound down, the din was deafening as fans serenaded the old arena. Tears flowed as the standing-room crowd watched the Oilers play the last of more than eighteen hundred games at the only rink they had known since 1974. After the final buzzer, few spectators went home. One hundred and forty-seven Oilers alumni were on hand to participate in farewell ceremonies, and the fans wanted to be a part of those final moments with them.

"It's like when I got married," Kevin Lowe said. "My mom asked who was invited and I said, 'Anyone who wants to come.'"

With great fanfare, players from the four decades were introduced and walked along a carpet to stools set up for them on the rink. At the other end, the Edmonton Symphony Orchestra played. Gretzky, who registered 933 points at the arena, was last, but hardly least, in the long line of players. As Gretzky joined the other alumni around the Oilers logo at centre ice, the arena lights bathed the heroes and legends in bright white light.

"I don't think there's another city where people would still be sitting here two hours after a game," Gretzky said to the thousands cheering him. "I wish we could go out and play for you again."

After forty-two years, no one was in a hurry to leave. The former Oilers players and staff stayed for a reception and celebrated late into the night.

"Last week, I went and sat on the bench where I used to stand and I looked around the building," Barrie Stafford, who served as the head equipment manager from 1982 through 2010, said. "I had the best seat in the house for twenty-five years. I stood there watching the clock tick down when we won our first Stanley Cup. Standing there thinking about it, I was surprised at how emotional I was."

Like so many others that night, Stafford looked nostalgically upon the past but still had an eye on the future. Alberta's northern landscape was ravaged by massive fires and its economy was still fighting to recover. It might not happen as quickly as everyone wants, but trees will rise again in the lush green forest, and the price of oil will climb. The Oilers will continue to build around Connor McDavid, who will thrill huge crowds in a sparkling new arena in a revitalized downtown.

Sometimes hope is dashed in the cruelest way, but never is it lost.

EPILOGUE

SUSAN DARRINGTON WAS RUNNING A SOCCER STADIUM IN BRAZIL WHEN A headhunting firm called in the summer of 2015. A spectacular new home was being built for the Oilers in downtown Edmonton, and the recruiter wondered if she would interview for the position of general manager at Rogers Place.

"Of all the towns in all of the world, Edmonton was the one that came knocking," Darrington said, smiling at the irony.

What neither the recruiter nor the team's parent company knew was this: Darrington had grown up in Edmonton and worked as an usherette at the Northlands Coliseum, a building where her stepfather, Neil Campbell, had served as events manager and general manager.

"Nobody would have known I had a connection to the city because my last name was different from my stepdad's," Darrington said. "I grew up eating, sleeping and breathing *Hockey Night in Canada* and the Oilers. I had six Oilers T-shirts in storage that dated back to 1985."

award by scoring seventeen goals, the most by a rookie d
Dion Phaneuf had twenty for Calgary in 2005–06. Gostisb
league record for first-year blue-liners with four overtime g
that tied the most ever extra-frame goals by a defenceman in a

Leading up to the awards announcement at the Hard Rock
ments were made by fans on behalf of all three of them, with L
wading in on McDavid's behalf on a segment of Coach's Corner.

"Folks, let's face it, he is the guy that should win it," Cherry sai
were starting a franchise tomorrow, who would you want to pick?
rookie. So, who's the best rookie?"

According to the writers, it was Panarin, whose award was the f.
troduced that night. McDavid, as good as he had been, had to be sat
with being a finalist.

In the month after the season, McDavid continued to impress at
International Ice Hockey Federation World Championship in Russia.

The Oilers' young centre scored the first goal in Team Canada's 2–
victory in the gold-medal game against Finland on May 22 and finished th
tournament with that lone goal and eight assists in ten games. The victory
in Moscow avenged Team Canada's 4–0 loss to the Finns in the round robin
and secured the Canadians' second consecutive world championship.

McDavid's goal in the first period stood up, backing a sixteen-save effort from Edmonton teammate Cam Talbot, who was outstanding while recording four shutouts and a 1.25 goals-against average in eight games. Two
other Edmonton players were also on the team: Eberle and Hall, who tied
for the lead among all forwards with six goals.

With the victory, McDavid became the youngest player ever to win three
of hockey's most prestigious international events: the IIHF World championship, the world U18 tournament and the world junior championships.

As Team Canada players gathered for the postgame ceremony, they
were stunned to see Russian President Vladimir Putin walk across the ice to
oversee the festivities.

The next morning, McDavid boarded a plane for a seven-hour flight to Beijing, where he made appearances on behalf of BioSteel, the pink drink that ranks among his major sponsors. Then he returned to Toronto to take in a Blue Jays game and hang out in the clubhouse with pitcher Marcus Stroman, resumed training with Gary Roberts and began to prepare for September's World Cup of Hockey. One season was over, but it seemed like he was transitioning to another with barely a breath in between.

TWELVE

THE OILERS' FINAL GAME OF THE 2015–16 SEASON WAS ON APRIL 9 AGAINST THE Vancouver Canucks. The team was on the road, and they lost in a shootout, the 4–3 defeat marking their twenty-fourth loss by one goal since the campaign had started six months earlier on a hot, muggy day in St. Louis. The loss meant that the Oilers finished last in the Pacific Division and twenty-ninth among thirty teams, ahead of only the rebuilding Maple Leafs. It had been a long, frustrating year, to say the least.

"[Losing] eats me alive," McDavid said on the morning after. "I think if it doesn't, you shouldn't really be here. It gets to a point where you just have to say you can't do it anymore. I am someone who definitely doesn't handle losing very well, so this year has been hard on me. I hope it's something we can change next year."

Ah, next year. The rallying cry for the Oilers for too long. In missing the playoffs, Edmonton extended the league's longest postseason drought to ten years.

There were positives; just not enough. The Oilers found the goalie they had been sorely lacking in Talbot. But that didn't stop them from finishing one spot lower than they had the year before. Still, there was always McDavid.

On the day after his last game of his rookie season, Connor stood outside the Oilers dressing room and talked about his first year.

"Hockey is a funny game," he said. "Some games you play great and have no points, and some games you don't have it and end up with two or three. The NHL is the best league in the world, and it is tough to get points in it, but for whatever reason I felt fairly comfortable right away."

There were adjustments that needed to be made, but he didn't find them overly onerous.

"I think the biggest thing for me was learning how to be a pro," he said. "When you are playing in Junior, on the road, it is very normal to come down for a two o'clock bus at 1:59 and a half, and you are dressed sloppy. That is just something that doesn't go on in the NHL.

"It's a different experience. In Junior, you live away from home but you're not really on your own. You have billets to look after you, and I was fortunate to have some of the best. And for me, living with Taylor Hall and Luke Gazdic helped. Luke kind of took care of the house, and we had a good time as well. It was a great experience."

McDavid's fondest memories were similar to the ones that fans hold up and admire: returning from his injury and threading his way through three Blue Jackets to score a remarkable goal; torching the Maple Leafs for five points in his first game against his hometown team; playing in his first NHL game in the Oilers' season opener on October 15 in St. Louis.

"There are a lot of different moments for everyone," McDavid said. "For me, it was taking in the warm-up before my first game. You're looking around and the crowd is already packed and you're seeing guys you grew up watching. I think that's when it really hit me that I was in the big leagues.

"Everything is so fresh. Soon, I'll have a chance to reflect for a little bit.

There will be some memories, like the game I came back from my injury. They'll mostly be very good."

Injuries could not be blamed for the Oilers' disappointing season, but they didn't help. The team's run of bad luck included losing defencemen Oscar Klefbom and Brandon Davidson for fifty-two and thirty-one games, respectively. They also lost Nugent-Hopkins and Pouliot for twenty-seven games apiece, as well as Yakupov for twenty-two. Ference, one of the alternate captains, suffered a hip injury and played in only six. Gryba was doing a good job on defence when he suffered a knee injury on February 16 and never came back.

"I think it kind of gets lost that we're putting our bodies on the line and stuff does happen," Connor said. "It was unfortunate for me that it happened in my first year in the NHL, but I've moved on from it. How could you not? In the grand scheme, everything kind of happens for a reason, and for me I think it was a good chance to learn a little more about the game and watch from a different angle.

"I don't think my return could have gone any better. I was talking with a couple of guys that had to come back from injuries this year, and they all kind of said the same thing: That first you just go on adrenaline without really thinking. It's those second and third games where the adrenaline starts to wear off and you start to feel the effects of sitting out three months."

McDavid missed thirty-seven games and still finished fourth among rookies in scoring. He never went more than two games without a point and had five winning goals, two seven-game scoring streaks and two four-game scoring streaks. After returning from injury, he had twelve points in the first half-dozen games. In short, he had what could be described as a great season, despite the fact that he only played little more than half of one.

"The way Connor came back and responded, he didn't use the injury as an excuse," his agent, Jeff Jackson, said. "He used it as motivation."

There were a number of magical moments that showed the impact Connor had for the team. Three points in his return against Columbus. Five

After graduating high school in Edmonton, Darrington moved to Seattle to attend college, then landed a job as an event coordinator with the Washington State Convention Bureau. Later, she was hired to oversee CenturyLink Field, the home of the NFL's Seattle Seahawks. At the same time, her stepfather was running the Kingdome, the baseball stadium across the street.

In 2013, she moved to Brazil to supervise the construction and opening of the forty-five-thousand-seat Allianz Parque in São Paolo. Two years later, when the headhunter called, Darrington was just beginning to mull her next career move. Living in a city of more than twenty million people in South America made returning to northern Alberta a hard sell.

"My initial reaction was, 'There is no way I am going back to Edmonton,'" Darrington said. "But once I talked to the recruiter and she told me it was going to be an Oilers-run stadium and part of a bigger downtown development, I was very interested. It's a game changer for the city."

Darrington flew seven thousand miles to meet Oilers officials on August 2, 2015, and was given a tour of the building the team would move into at the start of the 2016–17 season.

"The steel was in place, the roof was becoming completed and you could see the form of the arena taking shape," she recalled. "It was the most beautiful building I had ever seen."

Less than three weeks later, Darrington was introduced as vice-president and GM of Rogers Place. She invited her stepfather, now retired and living in Arizona, to be there for the occasion.

"It's the best job I could ever ask for," she said. "The arena is an amazing facility to be part of, but the vision for a downtown entertainment corridor is truly spectacular. It's an opportunity to be a part of redefining this city and being able to tell the world how great a place Edmonton is. I grew up here. I understand the people, the weather . . . I still have a tremendous sense of hometown pride."

In May, more than two thousand hopeful applicants handed in résumés at a job fair in hopes of claiming one of the five hundred positions under Darrington. A second corporation, Aramark, hired another nine hundred people to staff the arena's concession stands and restaurants.

"My job is to make sure people who have held season tickets for thirty years feel this venue is their home, that it fits in Edmonton and that they have a great time," Darrington said. "At the end of the day, you have to connect with fans. I tell my staff to act as if they are throwing a party for twenty thousand guests. I ask them how would you treat them if they were in their own house."

Rogers Place opened in September with a series of concerts including Drake, Keith Urban, Dolly Parton and the Dixie Chicks. The Oilers season would start in October, their first home games outside of the old coliseum.

For fans that had grown weary of the since-retired building, Rogers Place was something to behold. It boasts wide corridors, bigger seats and the largest high-definition scoreboard in the National Hockey League.

All fifteen thousand season tickets that were made available at the new arena were immediately snapped up, leaving a waiting list of more than three thousand people. Despite their lack of success, the Oilers had sold out four hundred home games dating back to 2005, and a fresh new season was generating even more interest. Not only would Edmonton have the league's most beautiful new rink, it would also field a decidedly different-looking team built around number ninety-seven. Near the end of June, Chiarelli dismayed many fans by trading Taylor Hall to the New Jersey Devils, receiving in return a promising young defenceman in Adam Larsson. A few days later, on Canada Day, the general manager announced that tough guy Milan Lucic had agreed to a seven-year deal in one of the biggest free-agent signings of the summer.

"It's a great opportunity to play with one of the best players of this time," Lucic said at a news conference atop a parking garage across from Rogers Place. "Connor McDavid played only half the season last year and has already showed he's up there with the Sidney Crosbys of the world in his ability. An opportunity to play with a guy like that doesn't happen very often."

A gritty forward who plays with chips on both shoulders, Lucic relishes the chance to toss his 235 pounds around. After wearing number seventeen for eight years in Boston and one year in Los Angeles, Lucic was going to switch jerseys to number twenty-seven in Edmonton, the same numeral Dave Semenko wore while protecting Wayne Gretzky. It was no coincidence, with Lucic's duties expected to include protecting McDavid.

"You need a guy with a couple of screws loose on your team to be successful," Lucic said about himself. "It's about time that this team plays with a little swagger and a little confidence. I truly believe in a couple of years we'll be contending for the Stanley Cup. This is an exciting time for me, and it's exciting for Oilers fans."

As many as a dozen teams had shown interest in Lucic, and some had even offered him more than the $42 million he would get from the Oilers. But there was something else at play in Edmonton, something other teams couldn't offer.

"It was the McDavid factor," Lucic said.

If the Northlands was hailed as the House That Wayne Gretzky Built, Rogers Place will soon be known as Connor McDavid's cathedral. The arena was built as a bold step into the future with a nod to the past. The Oilers uprooted the bronze bust of the Great One that sat outside Rexall Place and had it refurbished and moved to the new venue. The statue of Gretzky hoisting the Stanley Cup was placed in an honoured space. Adjacent to it is an exhibit room full of Oilers' memorabilia that was created in conjunction with the Hockey Hall of Fame. The artifacts include a selection of trophies and gear and souvenirs from the franchise's Golden Era, as well as all other periods of the team.

"In 1987, when I was seventeen, the Oilers won the Stanley Cup,"

Darrington remembered. "I was an usherette, and we were called down to stand on the ice as security so fans wouldn't climb over the boards. I remember it as a time the entire city was passionately invested in a hockey club."

A majority of spectators would pour into the arena through the Winter Garden, an expansive space that features a magnificent rendering by Alex Janvier, one of Canada's most acclaimed contemporary painters and preeminent aboriginal artists. A circular mosaic made up of colourful tiles, Janvier's abstract installation is forty-five feet in diameter and depicts the landscape in Alberta. An elder of Dene and Ojibway descent who grew up on a reserve a few hours east of Edmonton, Janvier has pieces in the National Gallery of Canada and the Canadian Museum of Civilization, and he was asked to do the work because the arena sits on land that's subject to a treaty signed in 1876.

The exterior of Rogers Place is decorated with a graphic wall that stretches the length of a football field along the building's south facade. Raised above the streets of Edmonton, the display is a celebration of the Oilers' place in the history of hockey, their reign as the last true dynasty in the NHL and the iconic players on those teams that made it all happen: the Messiers and Gretzkys and all. There is hope that the franchise will soon revisit that magical place that still lives in the hearts and minds of its fans. And that hope comes in the form of Connor McDavid.

EDMONTON OILERS TIME LINE

NOVEMBER 1, 1971: Oilers become one of the twelve founding members of the upstart World Hockey Association, a league created to rival the NHL. The original team is owned by Bill Hunter, owner of the Oil Kings, a junior hockey franchise.

OCTOBER 11, 1972: Oilers play in the first game in WHA history, defeating the Nationals, 7–4, before 5,065 fans at the Ottawa Civic Centre. Ron Anderson, a right wing for Edmonton, scores the first goal in league history at 6:19 of the first period. "I whacked at a bouncing puck near the Ottawa blue line and it kind of floated and knuckle-balled all the way into the net," he said. "If the goalie had seen it, he could've stopped it with a fly swatter."

OCTOBER 17, 1972: Oilers play their first home game at the Edmonton Gardens, beating the Winnipeg Jets, 3–2, in overtime.

1976: Entrepreneur Peter Pocklington buys a half-interest in the WHA Oilers from Vancouver real estate tycoon Nelson Skalbania, for $700,000 and assumption of the Oilers' $1.6 million in debt.

NOVEMBER 2, 1978: Peter Pocklington announces that he has acquired seventeen-year-old Wayne Gretzky from the Indianapolis Racers of the World Hockey Association.

JANUARY 26, 1979: Gretzky celebrates his eighteenth birthday by cutting two cakes shaped like nines during a ceremony before a game between the Oilers and the visiting Cincinnati Stingers. As part of the festivities, Pocklington announces he has signed Gretzky to a twenty-one-year contract that will keep him in Edmonton for the rest of his hockey career.

OCTOBER 10, 1979: Oilers lose their first NHL regular-season game, 4–2, to the Blackhawks at Chicago Stadium. Kevin Lowe, the franchise's first draft pick, scores Edmonton's first goal with 10:11 left in the first period, with assists from Brett Callighen and Gretzky.

APRIL 20, 1982: Pocklington, his wife and two staff members are taken hostage inside his home by a Yugoslavian immigrant demanding $1 million in ransom. Hours later, Pocklington and the gunman, Mirko Petrovic, are shot by a police officer rushing to the rescue. Pocklington, with superficial wounds to his arms and chest, growls at police: "Do you know who you just shot, assholes?"

OCTOBER 5, 1983: Gretzky scores a goal and has an assist as the Oilers open the 1983–84 season with a 5–4 victory over the Maple Leafs. It is the first game in a fifty-one-game point-scoring streak for Gretzky.

JANUARY 28, 1984: Kings goalie Markus Mattsson holds Gretzky pointless for the first time in the season in a 4–2 Los Angeles victory. In the first fifty-one games of the season, Gretzky scored sixty-one goals and had 153 points.

MAY 19, 1984: Gretzky scores two first-period goals and Ken "the Rat" Linseman gets the winner as the Oilers win their first Stanley Cup with a 5–2 victory over the defending champion Islanders in Game 5 in Edmonton. The Edmonton victory ends the Islanders' four-year reign as NHL champions.

MAY 30, 1985: Oilers repeat as Stanley Cup champs by beating the Flyers in five games.

MAY 31, 1987: Jari Kurri scores the go-ahead goal 14:59 into the second period as the Oilers capture their third Stanley Cup over the Flyers in Game 7 at Northlands Coliseum.

MAY 26, 1988: Gretzky breaks a scoreless tie 9:44 into the second period as the Oilers win their fourth Stanley Cup in five years with a 4–0 sweep of the Bruins. An oddity: Five games were played, but Game 4 was abandoned with the score tied at 3 due to a power failure at Boston Garden.

JULY 16, 1988: Gretzky marries actress Janet Jones at St. Joseph's Basilica in Edmonton in a lavish ceremony televised across Canada. The couple met in 1984 when Gretzky was a celebrity host on Dance Fever.

AUGUST 9, 1988: Pocklington shocks fans by trading Gretzky to the Los Angeles Kings for Jimmy Carson, Martin Gelinas, $15 million and the Kings' first-round draft picks in 1989, 1991 and 1993. In the House of Commons, Nelson Riis, an NDP MP from Kamloops, demands the government block the trade. Stunned, Edmonton's mayor, Laurence Decore, says, "It's like ripping the heart out of a city."

MAY 25, 1990: Oilers win their only Stanley Cup without Gretzky by beating the Bruins in five games. Edmonton wins Game 1 at Boston Garden in triple overtime on a goal by Petr Klima with assists from Kurri and Craig MacTavish. At 115 minutes, 13 seconds, it is the longest game in Stanley Cup finals history.

JUNE 19, 2006: The eighth-seeded Oilers reach the Stanley Cup finals for the first time in sixteen years before losing to the Carolina Hurricanes in seven games.

JUNE 18, 2008: After making a $200 million offer to investors, billionaire businessman Daryl Katz receives permission from the NHL to purchase the Oilers. He is formally introduced as the team's owner at a news conference at Rexall Place on July 2.

APRIL 15, 2009: General manager Steve Tambellini fires MacTavish as head coach after the Oilers fail to make the playoffs for the third year in a row and fifth time in seven seasons. After coming on as head coach in 2001, MacTavish had a 301–252–47 record.

MAY 26, 2009: Pat Quinn, a two-time Jack Adams award winner, accepts a position as head coach of the Oilers.

JUNE 22, 2010: Tom Renney, an associate under Quinn, is promoted to Oilers' head coach. After a 27–47–8 record in one season behind the bench, Quinn takes on a role of senior hockey adviser.

JUNE 25, 2010: At the Staples Center in Los Angeles, Oilers use the first selection of the NHL draft to take left-winger Taylor Hall of the Windsor Spitfires.

JUNE 24, 2011: Oilers choose centre Ryan Nugent-Hopkins of the Red Deer Rebels with the first pick of the NHL draft at the Xcel Energy Center in St. Paul, Minnesota.

OCTOBER 31, 2011: Edmonton's city council acquires approximately fifteen acres in the city's downtown core for $25 million and begins planning for a downtown hockey rink and commercial redevelopment.

FEBRUARY 2, 2012: Sam Gagner collects eight points—four goals and four assists—in a victory over the Chicago Blackhawks.

MAY 17, 2012: Oilers announce Renney's coaching contract will not be re-newed. In two seasons under his direction, the club has a 57–85–22 record.

JUNE 23, 2012: Right-winger Nail Yakupov of the Sarnia Sting becomes the newest Oiler, chosen with the draft's first selection at the Consol Energy Center in Pittsburgh.

JUNE 27, 2012: Oilers name associate coach Ralph Krueger head coach, re-placing Renney.

APRIL 15, 2013: Four years to the day after he fired MacTavish, Tambellini is fired as Oilers general manager, and is then replaced by MacTavish.

MAY 15, 2013: Edmonton city council approves the final piece of funding for the downtown arena, paving the way for a $600 million project.

JUNE 8, 2013: Krueger is fired after leading Oilers to a 19–22–7 record in the lockout-shortened 2012–13 season.

JUNE 10, 2013: Dallas Eakins is named head coach, replacing Krueger.

DECEMBER 23, 2013: Eakins unloads about a fan who tosses a jersey onto the ice at the end of a 6–0 loss to the St. Louis Blues, the club's sixth in a row. "Whoever threw that jersey, he quit on the team," Eakins says. "We don't want that here. That's a bunch of bullcrap."

JANUARY 4, 2014: Group calling for the firing of the Oilers' director of hockey operations starts a Facebook page called Kevin Lowe Must Go.

JANUARY 20, 2014: In an apology letter on the team's website, owner Daryl Katz acknowledges the Oilers are likely to miss the playoffs for an eighth straight year, asks fans for continued patience and tries to defuse anger against Lowe.

JANUARY 22, 2014: Police respond to a call from the Oilers' administrative offices after disgruntled fan Bill Day hauls a "Kevin Lowe Must Go" sign

behind his vehicle and drops anchor in the parking lot. A police spokes-
woman says staff was concerned the situation might turn violent. Police in-
vestigate but don't ticket Day or force him to leave after determining he is
not a threat.

MARCH 3, 2014: Construction begins on the arena in downtown Edmonton.

MARCH 22, 2014: A frustrated fan pitches a jersey onto the ice during an
8–1 loss to the Flames at Rexall Place. Ben Scrivens skates over, hooks the
sweater with his goalie stick and tosses it back into the stands.

JUNE 20, 2014: Bob Nicholson, who retired in April after twenty-five years
with Hockey Canada, joins the Oilers as Vice-Chairman of the new Oilers
Entertainment Group. Nicholson's first directive from Katz is to review the
organization from the top on down.

OCTOBER 9, 2014: Forgetting he has his phone in the pocket, an annoyed fan
throws his hoodie onto the ice during a 5–2 loss to the Flames in the Oilers'
first game of the 2014–15 season.

OCTOBER 10, 2014: More than 17,000 fans turn out at Rexall Place for a
thirtieth anniversary celebration of the Oilers' first Stanley Cup. All seven
members of the Hall of Fame from the 1983–1984 team attend: Gretzky,
Mark Messier, Coffey, Kurri, Grant Fuhr, Glenn Anderson and Glen Sather.
"We were just kids and we thought we knew everything," Gretzky tells the
crowd. "We didn't. But we knew how to play hockey." Tears roll down Pocklington's cheeks as the audience gives him a standing ovation.

DECEMBER 1, 2014: Oilers captain Andrew Ference blasts teammates after a
5–2 loss at home to Arizona in which Edmonton allowed two short-handed
goals in less than a minute. "It shouldn't be much of a chore to come here
and pay attention to what you are supposed to do and work hard and have
pride in being in the NHL," Ference says. "To come here and have to eke

pride out of guys to get out there and pay attention to details . . . it's one hundred percent unacceptable."

DECEMBER 15, 2014: Eakins is fired as head coach with the Oilers last in the Western Conference with a 7–19–5 record and having lost fifteen of the last sixteen games. Todd Nelson, coach of the Oilers' American Hockey League affiliate in Oklahoma City, is appointed interim replacement.

DECEMBER 19, 2014: Kevin Lowe Must Go Facebook Group pays $5,680 to take out a full-page newspaper ad begging Katz to fire him.

DECEMBER 23, 2014: Jacob Hamel is given a $172 ticket by Edmonton police after heaving a Ryan Smyth sweater on the ice at Rexall Place during a stoppage in a 5–1 loss to the Coyotes. Hammel also receives a six-month ban from the arena under provisions of the Alberta Gaming & Liquor Act for doing something "detrimental to the orderly operation of the premises."

FEBRUARY 20, 2015: Scuffle breaks out at Rexall Place between fans after one tosses his jersey onto the ice during a 4–0 loss to Minnesota. Scrivens tosses it back, again. "Throwing a jersey on the ice may be warranted and is your prerogative," one fan says on Twitter. "However, I will fully support someone's choice to punch you."

APRIL 11, 2015: Oilers end the season with a 6–5 overtime loss to the Canucks in Vancouver. They finish with a 24–44–14 record and miss the playoffs for the ninth straight year.

APRIL 18, 2015: Despite having only an 11.5 percent chance, the Oilers leap over the Sabres and Coyotes to win the NHL lottery and the right to select Connor McDavid with the first selection in the 2015 draft.

APRIL 20, 2015: Nicholson is announced as CEO of the Oilers Entertainment Group, putting him in charge of all hockey operations and the Katz Group's sports and entertainment businesses.

APRIL 24, 2015: Oilers name former Bruins general manager Peter Chiarelli president and GM and announce that Lowe has been repositioned as Nicholson's vice-chairman of the Oilers Entertainment Group.

MAY 19, 2015: Todd McLellan is introduced as the fourteenth coach in team history and sixth in nine years. McLellan coached in San Jose for seven years, taking the Sharks to the playoffs in all but the 2014–15 season.

JUNE 26–27, 2015: Oilers select Connor McDavid with the first pick in the NHL Entry Draft in Sunrise, Florida. In other moves, they acquire defencemen Griffin Reinhart (Islanders), Eric Gryba (Senators) and goalie Cam Talbot (Rangers).

JULY 3, 2015: 3,000 fans show up at Rexall Place to watch McDavid in his first public workout during rookie orientation camp.

JULY 4, 2015: Oilers prospects are given a tour of the then-under-construction Rogers Place.

JULY 6, 2015: 7,000 fans turn out for an intrasquad rookie scrimmage at Rexall Place, in which McDavid scores five goals to lead his team to an 8–6 victory.

JULY 28, 2015: The Oilers Entertainment Group announces that Edmonton's new $2.5 billion downtown development, with Rogers Place as the centrepiece, will be called the Ice District.

SEPTEMBER 16, 2015: Oilers move their annual preseason game against the University of Alberta Golden Bears from a 2,700-seat on-campus arena to Rexall Place to accommodate interest in McDavid. More than fourteen thousand spectators see McDavid set up three goals as the Oilers' rookies win, 6–3.

SEPTEMBER 21, 2015: McDavid logs twenty minutes and fifty-nine seconds and records two assists in his first NHL game at Rexall, a 4–2 exhibition victory over the Calgary Flames.

OCTOBER 13, 2015: McDavid scores his first NHL goal by tipping in a shot by Andrej Sekera past Dallas goalie Kari Lehtonen. The goal comes in his third NHL game, as it did for Wayne Gretzky and Sidney Crosby.

NOVEMBER 2, 2015: The NHL names McDavid the Rookie Player of the Month for October after putting up five goals and seven assists in his first twelve games.

NOVEMBER 3, 2015: McDavid suffers a broken left clavicle after falling awkwardly during the second period of a game against the Philadelphia Flyers at Rexall Place. The Oilers announce he is likely out for months, and he undergoes surgery the following day.

JANUARY 16, 2016: More than five thousand fans brave minus-20-degree temperatures and wait outside in long lines for the first public sneak peek of Rogers Place. "This building is a cathedral," Jacob Golka, a lifelong Oilers devotee, says. "It looks incredible."

FEBRUARY 2, 2016: Showing a dramatic flare, McDavid returns to the lineup against the Columbus Blue Jackets, scoring a highlight reel goal in the first period and also notching two assists.

FEBRUARY 11, 2016: A week after electrifying the hockey world with a stunning goal in his first game in three months, McDavid records his first five-point game as a professional while leading Edmonton to a 5–2 victory over the Maple Leafs, the team he rooted for as a kid while growing up in the suburbs of Toronto. The rookie has two goals and stops to sign autographs after the game as he heads down the tunnel. "What can you say about

Connor?" Todd McLellan, the Oilers' coach, says. "You watch him and turn into a fan as coaches and players."

APRIL 6, 2016: The Oilers rough up the Vancouver Canucks, 6–2, in the final game at Rexall Place. McDavid scores one goal and has two assists, and poses in the dressing room afterward with Wayne Gretzky and Mark Messier.

MAY 2, 2016: McDavid is named one of three finalists for the Calder Trophy, awarded to the NHL's rookie of the year, despite playing in only forty-five games in his injury-abbreviated first season.

JUNE 22, 2016: Artemi Panarin of the Chicago Blackhawks wins the Calder Trophy in Las Vegas.

JUNE 29, 2016: The Oilers trade Taylor Hall to the New Jersey Devils for defenceman Adam Larsson. "It's disappointing," Hall says. "I feel like I've been a good soldier for six years, and I prepared the best I could. It's tough. It's pretty hard not to feel slighted."

JULY 1, 2016: The Oilers announce the signing of free agent Milan Lucic to a seven-year contract to help protect Connor McDavid.

AUGUST 2, 2016: The Oilers announce the hiring of Keith Gretzky as assistant general manager. The younger brother of Wayne Gretzky had most recently served as director of amateur scouting for the Boston Bruins.

ACKNOWLEDGMENTS

I GREW UP IN THE 1960S IN MIAMI, A GLORIOUS TIME AND PLACE TO BE A KID. MY brother and I played baseball and football and fished at every opportunity. I never tried on skates in my youth. Hockey was played in snowy, northern cities seemingly a million miles away. As best I remember, there was only one ice rink, a place called the Polar Palace.

The first live NHL games I attended were in 1993 at the old Miami Arena. I became a fan of the Florida Panthers right away. They played the Jets and the Nordiques, Canadian teams that eventually moved south, the first two times I watched. I remember arriving a few minutes late for the first one—by the time I got in, Teemu Selanne had already scored.

My interest in hockey grew exponentially when I came to Canada in the 1990s. We lived in an old sea captain's house overlooking the Bay of Fundy, and in winter, icy winds whistled through walls that had been insulated with newspaper a century earlier. My first month's heating bill was more than my mortgage, and I questioned the sanity of moving north.

ACKNOWLEDGMENTS

The longer I lived in Canada, the more hockey captured my imagination. More than baseball or football in the United States, it is engrained in Canada's culture, and it reeled me in like so many others. On Saturday nights, I gathered with friends to watch *Hockey Night in Canada.* They were mostly Toronto fans who dreamed of a Stanley Cup. They're still waiting, and life's unpredictable journey has since brought me to Edmonton. I have a son who began skating at three years old, played his first organized hockey at five, and is still playing a dozen years later.

It was Matthew who first mentioned Connor McDavid to me, touting him as the next great superstar in hockey. So many young players of repute come and go that I paid scant attention at the time. In the spring of 2015, I was hired by the *Globe and Mail,* and everything changed. I was handed the remarkable assignment of covering McDavid, whose arrival in the NHL was the most heralded of any player's since Sidney Crosby. The idea was the inspiration of *Globe* sports editor Shawna Richer, who in 2005 shadowed Crosby and penned a book about his rookie season.

I was in Edmonton, working as a senior writer at the *Journal,* when Shawna and proposed adding me to her staff. A little more than two months later, I was in Sunrise, Florida, when McDavid became an Oiler, and the greatest adventure of my life began. The stories generated prompted a query from my publisher, Simon & Schuster. I can't thank Shawna enough, and I'm grateful to *Globe* editor in chief David Walmsley and deputy editor Sinclair Stewart for allowing her to hire me. In Toronto, I'm blessed to work with some of the greatest journalists and editors in the world.

McDavid's arrival in Edmonton provided a vehicle to tell a broader and more meaningful story than one that is simply about hockey. The team he joined and the city he came to needed him for reasons beyond the game. He had the ability to change a franchise and the community around it.

How the rookie performed was important, but the Oilers hockey club and the city of Edmonton were critical characters. The hubbub around him at the draft came and went, and he looked more capable on and off the ice

...an any teenager should. He quickly adapted to the speed of the game, and his playmaking genius became more apparent by the night. He was a point-a-game player through his first dozen games and did not wilt under oppressive scrutiny. A spectacular season seemed inevitable.

Then, on November 2, McDavid got hurt. Shawna was visiting Edmonton and was sitting in the press box with Tim Shipton, vice-president of communications for the Oilers Entertainment Group, when the young centre crashed shoulder-first into the boards. In the moment, none of us realized the worst had happened. A half hour later McDavid's left arm was in a sling.

I was disappointed for Connor and for his parents, Brian and Kelly. I'd gotten to know them through the process of reporting and writing, and as a parent I knew how devastating this must have felt. I was also worried about where it left the story. What if Connor's injury kept him out for the remainder of the season? What if he returned to the lineup and got hurt again? Shawna was stoic. "The story is going to get more interesting," she said. I'm not sure I believed her at the time.

Injuries are so common in sports that we had considered the possibility but made a superstitious pact never to speak of it. After Connor was injured, many people said to me: "There goes your season-long project." But Connor's injury merely changed the narrative arc. How would he deal with the first serious setback of his career? How would the Oilers react to losing their young star? What would happen to his profile as the emerging face of the NHL?

In his absence, the Oilers rallied briefly before settling into a sad slide. McDavid eventually returned and went on a scoring tear—thirty-six points in his last thirty-two games. He scored the winning goal for Canada at the Ice Hockey World Championship and was named a finalist for rookie of the year despite missing nearly half the season's games. Like Crosby, McDavid came as advertised; maybe even better.

The Oilers move into a $480 million arena at the start of the 2016

season. Around it, a new and revitalized downtown is taking shape. Hoc
gods willing, Connor McDavid will be a sensational player for a long time
Should his career follow those of Crosby and Gretzky—and there's no reason to believe it won't—he will leave an enduring mark on the sport.

There's an interconnectedness between hockey and Edmonton that is
impossible to break apart. In a year that saw the city and province battle
falling oil prices, economic hardship and a wildfire that threatened to swal-
low Fort McMurray, hockey became a more meaningful and much-needed
distraction.

I am grateful to have been able to document it. Thanks has to be given to
Connor himself, who accommodated my many requests. The same is true
of his family; his agent, Jeff Jackson; Connor's teammates; and the Oilers'
hard-working staff. None of this would have been possible without them.

This story is, of course, far from over. My sense is that it will keep getting better for years to come.